Praise for *Angel Investing*

"As an angel investor and a longtime fan of David S. Rose, I was delighted to hear that he finally captured his wit and wisdom in the pages of a book. David is a born teacher—clear-minded, witty, and provocative, with amazing stories to illustrate every key idea and insight. Those gifts—as well as his unsurpassed knowledge of his field—are teaching me so much more about investing than I've learned over the years doing it! Read *every* page of *Angel Investing*."

—**Barbara Corcoran**
Real estate mogul, *Shark Tank* star, angel investor

"From the secret economics of angel investing and the best methods for finding and picking tomorrow's big winners to proven techniques for adding value to any business you invest in, *Angel Investing* provides readers with everything they need to know to get started in this fascinating, fun, and lucrative business arena."

—**David Bach**
#1 *New York Times* best-selling author of *The Automatic Millionaire*
and *Start Late, Finish Rich*; angel investor

"This is the most comprehensive and readable guide to angel investing ever written. The chapter on valuation and expectations lays out a clear framework for understanding one of the least-known pitfalls in the angel world. And its emphasis on creating a win-win relationship with the entrepreneur is at the heart of being a long-term successful angel—and continuing to see the best deal flow. I recommend this book to anyone even *thinking* about making or receiving angel investments."

—**Howard L. Morgan**
Founding Partner, First Round Capital

"The world of entrepreneurial start-ups is where the most exciting and creative action is happening in today's business world, which is why I was a strong supporter of the JOBS Act of 2012. No wonder millions of people are wondering how they can get involved as investors. There's no better place to start than by reading David S. Rose's *Angel Investing*."

—**U.S. Senator Charles E. Schumer**
Senate Finance Committee

"David S. Rose's *Angel Investing* is the best book on early stage investing ever written. His method of step-by-step explanation is better than any I have read in 20-plus years of professional angel investing. I will recommend this to every serious entrepreneur seeking investment as required reading before the effort."

—**Dave Berkus**
Chairman Emeritus, Tech Coast Angels;
author of *Berkonomics*

"Only an angel who has backed more than 90 start-ups could possess the mastery to provide such illumination into our craft. David's candor and insights will attract more investors to this entertaining and lucrative activity so essential to economic growth."

—**John Huston**
Founder and Manager, The OhioTechAngel Funds

"*Angel Investing* is an engaging, easy read, full of real stories, hard numbers, actual cases, and a whole lot of good advice. David S. Rose brings tons of real-world knowledge to the subject that makes this required reading for every new angel."

—**Tim Berry**
Author of *Business Plan Pro*;
entrepreneur and angel investor

"David S. Rose is one of the most insightful thinkers about the angel and venture investment markets. It's rare that an investment leader with so much experience and success takes the time to share (systematically!) his knowledge so openly. Whether you are new to angel investing or someone with lots of experience, you will learn a ton from reading this book."

—**Marc Bodnick**
Cofounder, Elevation Partners

"David S. Rose has distilled his vast knowledge into an easy-to-read yet comprehensive guide to angel investing. It is a must-read for all angel investors as well as for entrepreneurs seeking angel financing."

—**Jeffrey Seltzer**
Managing Partner, Pierce Yates Ventures;
Former Deputy Chairman, CIBC World Markets;
angel investor

"Anyone with a checkbook can be an angel investor, but it takes insight to do it well. David S. Rose has written a terrific new book that will help would-be angels make money, rather than lose it. From explaining the value of diversification, to tips on evaluating deals, to offering up plans to attract good deals, Dave's book will help you move from a money-losing amateur to a money-making professional angel. And if you're an entrepreneur looking for angel money, you should read this book, too. It will help you understand what knowledgeable angels are seeking and how they will evaluate you."

—**Scott Shane**
Author of *Fool's Gold? The Truth Behind Angel Investing in America*

"Angel investing is a new global asset class, with cross-border investments in early stage companies fueling worldwide innovation. David S. Rose's *Angel Investing* should be mandatory reading for every current and prospective business angel. It brings into one readable volume everything you need to know to join the start-up revolution, and clearly takes its place as the new standard textbook for our industry. I always recommend David's classic TED talk on 'How to Pitch a VC' to every entrepreneur. Now I will recommend this book to all existing and potential angel investors!"

—**Paulo Andrez**
President, EBAN, the European Business Angel
and Early Stage Investors Network

"Lots of books explain fundamental theories of investing. David S. Rose's *Angel Investing* does, too—but he also describes the on-the-ground reality of its frustrations and exhilarations, and he does it with candor, intelligence, and flair. This book is a must-read for anyone interested in this rapidly growing asset class."

—**Joan Finsilver**
Former Managing Director, Brean Murray & Co.;
angel investor

"I only wish I'd had a translated edition of David's observations when training overseas angels about the art of mentor capital. David tells it like it is, shares real-life stories, and packages the entire process in one book. I will encourage all my emerging angels to read it before writing their first check!"

—**John May**
Chair Emeritus, Angel Capital Association;
coauthor, *Every Business Needs an Angel*

"*Angel Investing* by David S. Rose is a how-to-invest book that is not merely informative and authoritative, but practical and enjoyable to read. Based on his many years running a reputable, leading angel group and his own portfolio of over 90 angel investments, David tells it like is. He covers a great many things that other books don't discuss, like 'building your reputation' and 'the financial life of a start-up.' I especially valued reading Chapter 6 and the 'signs of a weak founder': the long list of 'unrealistics' was spot on! Reading this book is like sitting across from David and listening to him share his lessons from his storied career as an angel."

—**Catherine Mott**
CEO/Founder, Blue Tree Allied Angels;
Past Chairman of the Board, Angel Capital Association

"David S. Rose explains the mysteries of angel investing in a clearly written, comprehensive guide full of great insights and stories. He has packed this book with everything you could possibly want to know about angel investing, gathered from his years of hands-on experience and research as one of the most active angel investors and angel evangelists in the country. I can attest that this book is what David has been practicing and preaching since I met him in 2002."

—**Thomas Blum**
Partner, GC Andersen Partners; angel investor

"Superb! *Angel Investing* by David S. Rose is without a doubt one of the best books I have read on the subject of angel investing, venture capital, and entrepreneurship. It is easy to read and completely captivating—David's real-world experience is compelling. He shows firsthand how to take the casual sport of angel investing to a whole new level, and make a real business out of it. There is a world of difference between managing a single investment and managing a whole angel portfolio. This unique book addresses everything, from the step-by-step process of due diligence, to negotiating win-win deals, to managing the most intangible—but most important—part of angel investing: your reputation. From every perspective, this is *the* book that every prospective angel should read before writing his or her first check."

—**David Freschman**
Managing Principal, Innovation Ventures;
CEO, Early Stage East; Founding Member,
ARC Angel Fund

"David S. Rose's book is great fun and a must-read for angels and would-be angels. For newbies it gives a very clear and simple explanation of the dynamics of angel investing, with a number of real-life anecdotes that drive the points home and make them unforgettable. For all investors, it gives a good sense of whether this asset class is something worth pursuing and whether one has the right skills and attitude for making angel investments. Whether you are already an investor or are looking to become one, this book covers in detail—and in a nonintimidating fashion—all you need to know to start putting money to work. Read it and start investing!"

—**Alessandro Piol**
Cofounder and Partner,
AlphaPrime Ventures and Vendanta Capital;
President, TiE New York

"Whether you are an angel investor or an impact investor, this riot of information and story will elevate your game. David takes us on a sometimes scary—but often hilarious—romp through the ins and outs of angel investing. Read it with caution, as this book is addictive!"

—Lisa Kleissner
Cofounder, Toniic, and Cofounder, Social-Impact International
President, KL Felicitas Foundation

"As David S. Rose points out, angel investing can be 'as much fun as it is possible to have with your clothes on.' But it isn't for the faint of heart. Rose's terrific book provides a sweeping guide for anyone interested in mastering the art of funding start-ups."

—Jeffrey Bussgang
Author of *Mastering the VC Game*

"David S. Rose's *Angel Investing* is a must-read for successful businesspeople on why they should be angels: you get to use your experiences and capital for maximum effect and have a blast doing it. It is also a must-read for entrepreneurs on why angels are important and what to look for from angel investors that goes well beyond the funding."

—Brad Higgins
Managing Partner, SOS Ventures
Former CFO, U.S. Department of State

"Early stage investing involves both art and science, and David S. Rose's *Angel Investing* brings together the best of both worlds. I've known and coinvested with David for many years, and he's one of the most knowledgeable and straight-shooting people I've met in the business of early stage financing. His book is the ultimate how-to for this rapidly expanding field, written by someone who really knows what he's talking about."

—Chris Fralic
Partner, First Round Capital

"David S. Rose has written a comprehensive, practical guide to angel investing. It is an excellent resource for anyone interested in the world of start-up finance. *Angel Investing* distills the tumultuous, esoteric world of start-up investing into a clear, paint-by-numbers guide for would-be participants and interested observers."

—Thatcher Bell
Managing Director, Draper Fisher Jurvetson Gotham Ventures

"For newly minted angels, *Angel Investing* is a must-read; for existing angels, a great refresher; for those in need of information and entertainment, David S. Rose packages the arcane into accessible language—and with a sense of humor that will have you read the entire book in one sitting. Thanks a lot, David—now existing angels will have more competition sourcing great deals. Where were you seven years ago when I needed to read this!?"

—**Joseph Ferrara**
Founder, Apparel Group International, angel investor

"David S. Rose has long been a staple in the angel world with a reputation for the highest integrity. While many will conclude this to be a must-read book for those considering angel investing, I'd also recommend this book to every entrepreneur before going out looking for capital. For the entrepreneur, David will bring you into the mind of potential investors and help you fashion the content of your pitch and the best ways to be persuasive."

—**Andrew Weinreich**
Serial entrepreneur, inventor of social networking,
Founder of SixDegrees, Joltage, I Stand For, MeetMoi, Xtify

"David S. Rose is one part iconic investor, one part eccentric entrepreneur, and one part stand-up comic. *Angel Investing* is required reading for anyone who is thinking about becoming an angel or raising money with them. David answers all the questions about investing that everyone is afraid to admit that they don't really get ... in simple, straightforward, and downright delightful prose. The result is an oxymoron: an entertaining textbook that is actually understandable and jam-packed with information you can really use."

—**Patty Meagher**
Founder, Stamford Innovation Center

"As an entrepreneur in whom David S. Rose has invested, I have seen him live by the rules he shares in the pages of *Angel Investing*. From a seed idea to a profitable company, he has provided invaluable counsel and thoughtful support during the often choppy waters of a startup journey, bringing his unique passion and enthusiasm, informed by integrity and experience. In this book he lays out the rules of the road for making smart early-stage investments and gives would-be investors the tools to define their goals in this emerging asset class. Whether you are an investor or an entrepreneur, David is unquestionably the guide you want to have at your side throughout your journey."

—**Steven Rosenbaum**
Founder and CEO, Magnify Networks;
Entrepreneur-at-Large of the City of New York;
Author of *Curation Nation* and *Curate This!*

ANGEL INVESTING

THE GUST GUIDE TO MAKING MONEY AND HAVING FUN INVESTING IN STARTUPS

DAVID S. ROSE

WILEY

For general information about our other products and services, please contact our Customer Care Department within the United States at (800) 762-2974, outside the United States at (317) 572-3993 or fax (317) 572-4002.

Wiley publishes in a variety of print and electronic formats and by print-on-demand. Some material included with standard print versions of this book may not be included in e-books or in print-on-demand. If this book refers to media such as a CD or DVD that is not included in the version you purchased, you may download this material at http://booksupport.wiley.com. For more information about Wiley products, visit www.wiley.com.

ISBN 978-1-118-85825-7 (cloth); ISBN 978-1-118-90121-2 (ebk);
ISBN 978-1-118-90113-7 (ebk)

Printed in the United States of America

10 9 8 7 6 5 4 3 2 1

Dedicated to the memory of David Rose (1892–1986)
Entrepreneur, Innovation Catalyst, Philanthropist, Angel Investor

Contents

Appendixes

Foreword

A LITTLE MORE than a decade ago, in the Fall of 2002, the company I worked for, PayPal, had just been acquired by eBay. In the wake of this deal, I was considering a long vacation. PayPal had been successful, but countless dot-coms had recently failed; many people felt that the consumer Internet boom was over.

But I began sensing opportunity. The entire online ecosystem was evolving. The Internet was becoming ubiquitous, increasingly integrated into everyday life. And real identity was beginning to play a more prominent role in the online world.

As real identity became a more important aspect of the Internet, so too did the connections between people. In the early days of the web, content was primary. But as we started shifting from the Information Age into a new era—the Network Age—relationships were taking precedence. Information was still critical, but people were starting to rely more and more on other people to make sense of the vast amounts of content available to them. Networks were starting to frame everything.

Once I began to fully see the import of this shift, I decided to lean all the way into Web 2.0 and the beginnings of the Network Age. To capitalize on how the Network Age would transform the world of work, I founded LinkedIn. But I didn't focus my attentions on only the professional side. I also became an angel investor to invest in the social aspects of the Network Age, backing such companies as Digg,

Facebook, Flickr, Last.fm, Ning, Six Apart, and Zynga. Over the course of a decade, I made angel investments in more than 100 companies.

Several of these companies generated significant returns. But I hadn't invested in Flickr or Facebook hoping to make a quick score. As David S. Rose will tell you in the book you are about to read, successful angel investors are usually the ones who take a long-term view of things. I felt as strongly as I did about the companies I invested in because I sensed that we were in the midst of a technological and cultural shift that was going to play out not just over months, or even years, but rather over decades. And these companies were creating platforms, products, and services that promised to be increasingly relevant as hundreds of millions of people started integrating the Internet more fully into their lives.

Picking winners on the stock market, where companies have established track records and there is a large body of information about them at hand, is hard. Picking winners when a company is little more than a few hundred lines of code is orders of magnitude more difficult. If you want to be a successful angel, you have to have an appetite for risk and the ability to accept failure. More importantly, though, you have to be curious. And studious. You have to want to know everything you can possibly know about an emerging technology and the entrepreneur who wants to bring that technology to market. If you're a new angel, identify mentors, develop allies, and start building the networks of trust that will ultimately inform your deal-making.

Picking up this book is a good start. David is an experienced angel himself, with investments in more than 90 companies. He's lectured at top schools, taught TED attendees how to pitch a VC, and created Gust.com, a platform for connecting angel investors with entrepreneurs. Let your education begin!

—Reid Hoffman

Introduction
How I Became An Angel Investor

ONE DAY DURING my junior year in college, I received a letter from my great-uncle, Dave, inviting me to join him for lunch in New York the following month. It seemed that a few of his close friends would be joining us, which was a bit disappointing, because I enjoyed talking one on one with Uncle Dave. But imagine my surprise when the other three guests arrived and it turned out that every one of them was a Nobel Laureate! How did an immigrant, who grew up in poverty on the Lower East Side of New York City and ended his formal schooling after the ninth grade, end up with friends like this? He was an extraordinary man, an entrepreneur ... and an angel investor.

As an industrious entrepreneur, he founded several companies with his older brother Sam (my grandfather), including one that is still going strong nearly a century later. As a generous philanthropist, he contributed time and money to a host of worthwhile causes.

But the most interesting thing to me about Uncle Dave was his propensity for finding and supporting a wide range of technological innovation. It turns out that this boy from the streets, with little technical education but boundless energy and curiosity, had met with Albert Einstein, and was the closest of friends with Vladimir Zworykin (inventor of the television tube) and Nobel winners like Rosalyn Yalow and I. I. Rabi. He described himself as an innovation catalyst decades before the term *angel investor* was coined. He would learn of a potentially exciting new technical development, bring it to the attention of an appropriate scientist or university, and provide the seed funding that would enable them to research and commercialize it.

He was the primary supporter behind the development of the portable artificial kidney developed by Dr. Willem Kolff (who invented the artificial heart); the hyperbaric operating unit at Mt. Sinai Hospital; vascular stapling for rapid surgery; and the Foundation for Medical Technology, one of the leading funders of new medical instrumentation. Did I mention that he also personally invented through-the-wall air conditioning for high-rise residential construction? Or that the graduate student intern working on one of his projects was Yossi Vardi … who went on to become the youngest ever Israeli Minister of Development, and today is one of the world's leading angel investors?

The inspiration that David Rose provided for me was carried on in turn by my father, Daniel Rose, who won Ernst & Young's Entrepreneur of the Year award when he was in his seventies, and who to this day is developing new projects and investing in new ventures well into his eighties. Their legacy has given me a unique perspective on the financing and development of entrepreneurship. While I am not alone in being a third-generation entrepreneur, I do believe that I may well be the world's only third-generation angel investor!

With these role models in front of me, after finishing my MBA in the early 1980s, I cofounded my first technology-related business with Dr. Peter Garrity, one of my business-school professors. By that time I was fully engaged in my day job of real estate development, but continued to start tech companies on the side. One of them developed enough traction in the nascent wireless communications space that I finally transitioned into the tech world full-time.

Thanks to an amazing amount of luck, my first business managed to get funding from a top-tier venture capital fund in the early 1990s, and eventually grew into a multinational, Internet-based communications company with 120 people on staff. But when the dot-com crash came along with the new millennium and wiped out a decade's worth of effort, my long-suffering spouse suggested that I take a vacation from entrepreneurship and get a real job.

So I became an angel investor.

The result is that over the past 15 years I have had just about as much fun as it is possible to have with your clothes on. Ten years ago I founded New York Angels, which today is the most active angel group in the world. I've invested in over 90 innovative companies, and had exits—making millions of dollars—from acquisitions by companies like Google, Facebook, Amazon, Intel, CBS, Kodak, and others. Along the way I've met some of the most extraordinary entrepreneurs and investors in the business (many of whom I will introduce to you later in these pages) and had the opportunity to teach and mentor hundreds of others through my lectures at Yale, Harvard, Columbia, and other business schools, as well as my TED talks on pitching to investors, which have been viewed over a million times. I founded the Finance, Entrepreneurship & Economics program at Singularity University, was named Mentor of the Year by NYU's Stern School of Business, Patriarch of Silicon Alley by *Red Herring* magazine, New York's Archangel by *Forbes*, and received an honorary doctorate from Stevens Institute of Technology.

After all this, my wonderful spouse finally relented and let me get back into the entrepreneurial business, which allowed me to found Gust.com, the online platform that today powers the global angel investing industry and has been used to track over $2 billion in early-stage angel and seed funding.

These experiences on both sides of the entrepreneurial finance table have provided me with a unique, birds' eye view of the world of early-stage investing, and made it clear that angel investing has moved from being a casual sport of the super rich to a legitimate asset class for everyone with a level of assets or income that would qualify them as an accredited investor.

Why Angel Investing Is About to Take Off

There is a major change sweeping through the world of business that began in the twentieth century and took off in the twenty-first, but whose full import has yet to sink in. Advances in technology are accelerating at an extraordinary rate, and the effect will be to turn upside down virtually everything that we think we know about business and finance. Every year, the power of technology is doubling at the same time its cost is being halved, and every year technology is being applied to an ever-increasing number of new industries. As a result, it is not an exaggeration to state that any company designed for success in the twentieth century is doomed to failure in the twenty-first. This is a great opportunity for people who have a sizeable amount of capital to invest (usually north of $100,000) and are willing and able to take prudent risks with a portion of it—angel investors!

Consider just a few examples: commercial airlines, retail booksellers, higher education, agriculture, music and entertainment, consumer electronics, even the urban taxi business. In every case, an existing industry is being completely upended by changes in technology, regulations, and/or marketplaces; 443 of today's *Fortune 500* companies were not even on the list when it was first compiled in 1955. The result is that the biggest, most valuable companies of tomorrow are just being formed today, but there is no way for public-stock-market investors to participate during the explosive growth phase of their value creation.

There is, however, a way for *private* investors to take part, by investing in—and supporting—a company from its very beginnings. And this form of investment can be extraordinarily lucrative. When Ben Silberman approached New York Angels in April 2009, seeking a small investment in his interactive mobile catalog idea, he valued his company at $2.5 million. Today, just over four years later, Pinterest is valued at $3.8 billion—an increase of 152,000 percent. As you can imagine, angel investors such as my friends Brian Cohen and Bill Lohse, who had the foresight (and faith) to participate in that initial-funding round, have done very, very well. Compare that to public-market investors who bought Facebook at the IPO price of $38. As of this writing, they would have seen a value increase of 76 percent. That's a difference of 2,000 times between seed and IPO investors.

The combination of advancing technology, changing federal regulations, rapidly dropping startup costs, and new online investment platforms means that it is now possible for any serious investor to undertake angel investing the right way ... and that is what this book is all about. I start at the very beginning and walk you through the market, the theory, and the practice of investing directly into early-stage companies. While there's no doubt that the flip side of a high-return asset class such as startups is a high risk of losing money, by taking a careful, professional approach over the long term, statistics show that you are likely to generate higher returns than virtually any other traditional asset class. And if you're at all like me, you may well have a great deal of fun along the way!

PART

The Basics of
Angel Investing

1

The 25 Percent Annual Return

Why Everyone with Six Figures to Invest Should Consider Angel Investing

ANGEL INVESTING IN the past few years has moved from an arcane backwater of the financial world to a business arena that receives coverage in mainstream newspapers and hit television shows such as ABC's *Shark Tank*. Today, any sophisticated investor with a portfolio of alternate assets should consider direct, early-stage investments in private companies as one potential component of that portfolio. Why? Because multiple studies* have shown that over the long run, carefully

---

*Robert Wiltbank and Warren Boeker, "Returns to Angel Investors in Groups," Ewing Marion Kauffman Foundation and Angel Capital Education Foundation, November 1, 2007; Ramon DeGennaro and Gerald Dwyer, "Expected Returns to Angel Investors," Federal Reserve Bank of Atlanta, March 2009; Luis Villalobos and William Payne, "Startup Pre-Money Valuation: The Keystone to Return on Investment," Ewing Marion Kauffman Foundation, 2007; Jeffrey Sohl, "The Angel Investor Market in 2007: Mixed Signs of Growth," Center for Venture Research, University of New Hampshire, 2008; Jeffrey Sohl, "The Angel Investor Market in 2008: A Down Year in Investment Dollars But Not in Deals," Center for Venture Research, University of New Hampshire, 2009; Colin Mason and Richard Harrison, "Is It Worth It? The Rates of Return From Informal Venture Capital Investments," *Journal of Business Venturing* 17 (2002): 211–236; Robert Wiltbank, "Siding with the Angels: Business Angel Investing—Promising Outcomes and Effective Strategies," British Business Angels Association and NESTA, May 2009.

3

selected and managed portfolios of personal angel investments—even those without a giant hit such as Pinterest—produce an average annual return of over 25 percent. Compared to average annual returns of 1 percent from bank accounts, 3 percent from bonds, 7 percent from stocks, 10 percent from hedge funds, and even 15 percent from top-tier venture capital funds, that is an impressive number. See Figure 1.1.

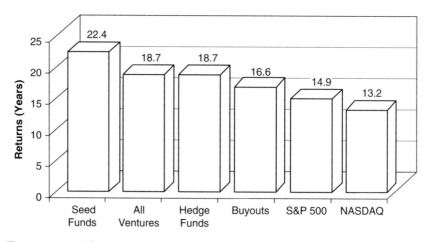

Figure 1.1   Alternative Asset Returns

Wiltbank study (Rob Wiltbank, Willamette University): Angel IRR = 27 percent or 2.6x in 3.5 years.

Sources: Venture Economics; HFRI Equity Hedge Index.

What is even more interesting about angel investing is that, unlike sitting back and clipping coupons, or reading the stock listings in the daily paper, being involved as a part owner of an exciting startup company can be a great deal of fun. You get a ringside seat at a venture that is out to change the world, direct access to company CEOs who may become the corporate magnates of tomorrow, and early access to the latest products and services before they become generally available. You may even have the opportunity to advise and mentor a company as it develops, pivots, and changes its business plan in response to real market experience.

By now, this must sound too good to be true: outsized returns and having fun—what's not to like? But here is the sobering reality: a large majority of self-proclaimed angel investors actually *lose* money, rather than make anything at all! How can these two facts be reconciled?

Simple: those 25 percent-plus returns are "over the long run, on carefully selected and managed portfolios of angel investments." In practice, however, most people who call themselves angel investors do not carefully select or manage their investments, do not take a long-term view, and do not have a clue about how to approach angel investing as a serious part of an alternative-asset portfolio. But you want to understand how to engage in angel investing as a serious part of your investment allocation. So let's begin with the basics.

What Exactly Is Angel Investing?

Angel investing is when individual people (as opposed to professionally-managed investment funds, corporations, governments, or other institutions) invest their personal capital in an early-stage company—often known as a startup. Angel investors are individuals who invest their own money, typically in small amounts, and typically very early in the life cycle of a company.

Angels find investment opportunities through referrals from people they know (such as CEOs of companies in which they've already invested), through attending regional or national events at which early stage companies launch their products, by being approached directly by ambitious entrepreneurs, through joining with other angel investors in organized angel groups, or, increasingly, by participating in reputable online early-stage investment platforms such as Gust. All of these techniques for identifying angel-investment opportunities, and many others, will be described in greater detail in Chapter 5.

The fact that angel investors use their money to back companies they hope will grow and bring them significant profit is not, in itself, unusual. Most mainstream investors do the same. They invest in blue-chip companies like Apple, Google, GE, and Coca-Cola, or in mutual funds that support an array of companies, hoping their money will grow as these businesses grow. The crucial difference between these mainstream investors and angel investors is that angels invest in startups—companies that are relatively new, small, and privately held (rather than publicly traded in a marketplace like the New York Stock Exchange or NASDAQ). Because these companies are like tiny plants, striving to become giant trees, the first investments in them by angels and others are often referred to as *seed investments*.

Unlike public companies, startups are often little known. They generally do not appear on the cover of *Forbes* or *Fortune*, and you won't hear them talked about by stock analysts on cable TV or even by your favorite broker. So understanding what these startup businesses are like, where to find them, and how to identify those with significant growth potential, is one of the keys to being a successful angel investor.

The world of startups and the ways in which angels and startups work together is a fascinating topic—and one in which change is constant. The stage at which an angel would typically begin supporting a startup with a cash investment has changed over the last few years as a direct result of the decreasing cost of starting up a scalable company using current technology. In the past, when the only way to get a company going was to spend cash, early investors would often have no alternative to "taking a flyer" and supporting an entrepreneur who had only a vision and a plan.

But today, with technology providing startup businesses with virtually free hosting, bandwidth, tools, and marketing (or at least free enough to get you started), the bar for a company to be considered fundable has been raised because it is so easy for anyone to get started. Since the large majority of opportunities with which angel investors are presented already have something going for them (a finished product, initial customers or users, perhaps even revenue), it is challenging for entrepreneurs with only an idea. Why should an angel take the added execution risk if he or she doesn't have to? Derek Sivers, an entrepreneur, writer, and frequent speaker at the TED conferences, summed up the idea versus execution relationship in a seminal blog post from which I've borrowed this eye-opening table for Figure 1.2.

Because of this, many companies in their earliest stages are unable to attract financing from angels and other professional investors. Consequently, so-called Friends and Family rounds of investment are the most common way (other than the founder's own capital) to fund a startup, and account for nearly a third of all financings. (A further explanation in more detail of the various stages of financing a startup is in Chapter 4.) Friends and Family investors do not base their investment on the merits of the business, but rather on their support for the entrepreneur. By contrast, the professional angel investor focuses on the long-term strengths and prospects of the business, in much the

---

Ideas Are Just a Multiplier of Execution

It's so funny when I hear people being so protective of ideas.
(People who want me to sign an NDA to tell me the simplest idea.)
To me, ideas are worth nothing unless executed.
They are just a multiplier. Execution is worth millions:

Awful idea =	−1	No execution = $1
Weak idea =	1	Weak execution = $1,000
So-so idea =	5	So-so execution = $10,000
Good idea =	10	Good execution = $100,000
Great idea =	15	Great execution = $1,000,000
Brilliant idea =	20	Brilliant execution = $10,000,000

To make a business, you need to multiply the two.
The most brilliant idea, with no execution, is worth $20.
The most brilliant idea takes great execution to be worth $20,000,000.
That's why I don't want to hear people's ideas.
I'm not interested until I see their execution.   **—Derek Sivers**

Figure 1.2   Ideas versus Execution

Source: Derek Sivers, http://sivers.org/multiply.

same way a mainstream investor picks stocks based on an evaluation of the strengths and prospects of the companies issuing those stocks.

As with investors in public company stocks, angels are part-owners of the companies in which they invest. The difference is that $10,000 invested in Google might buy you 10 shares of stock, representing one 33-millionth of the company. That same $10,000 invested in a promising startup might buy you 10,000 shares of stock, representing a full 1 percent of the company's ownership.

With that low a cost of entry, it is fair to ask if one angel ever becomes the majority owner of a startup. The short answer is virtually never. While there are, indeed, individuals who have put $1 million or more into one company, the vast majority of serious angel investors play with much smaller numbers. This is because investing at the seed and early stages of a company's life cycle is risky—the large majority of such investments fail completely. Angels therefore try to invest in at least 20 to 80 companies, thereby limiting the amount that will be lost on any one.

The average individual angel puts in about $25,000 per company, typically with 5 or 10 angels joining together to make up the investment round. (Many angels participate in angel groups or syndicates of various kinds. It's a very effective way to pool insights, ideas, connections, and other resources, and it enables angels to invest more powerfully than they could as individuals.) A 2009 survey* showed that the average total round size for an angel group is about $275,000 ... although increasingly groups are joining together to syndicate deals in order to raise larger rounds.

Outside of that context, the range is wide, with solo angels investing anywhere from $5,000 to $500,000 (or more) in a given company. "Super Angels," a misnomer usually applied to experienced investors who manage micro-venture funds, seem to average about $100,000 to $200,000 per investment. It is only when you get into the territory in which venture capital funds operate that you'll find early-stage investments getting close to $1 million from a single source.

So, in a nutshell, an angel investor is a private individual who invests significant, but modest sums, usually in five figures, in a variety of startup businesses. These investments collectively form a *portfolio* that, over time, will likely include both winners and losers. The key to being a successful angel is to have enough winners to more than offset the losers.

Can You Really Make 25 Percent a Year?

The essence of successful angel investing begins with recognizing and accepting one hard fact: your chance of making a profit by investing in startups is somewhere between very, very slim and almost negligible if you're talking about investing a very small amount in one company. Those odds increase significantly once you diversify your investments (even if they are relatively small) in dozens of companies.

Why is this the case? It is because a majority of all new, angel-backed companies fail completely, so if you invest in only one company, the odds are that you will *lose all your money*, not just "not make a profit." But when a company succeeds, it has the chance to *really* succeed, and return many times the initial investment. This is known as a "hits business."

So how much of a return does an average angel investor earn?

The data needed to answer this question doesn't really exist. because (1) there is no such thing as an *average* angel investor, and

---

*2009 ACA Angel Group Confidence Survey.

(2) there is currently no way to track the activities or record of individual investors.

That said, a rough summary of key statistics from Gust describing the activities of typical professional angel investors would be as follows:

- Individual angel investors receive anywhere from zero to 50 pitches a month, depending on how actively they promote their availability and how accessible they make themselves.
- Organized angel investment groups similarly might typically receive between 5 and 100 submissions monthly. All angel groups taken together probably receive about 10,000 submissions monthly. All individual angels taken together probably receive about 50,000 funding requests each month.
- Organized angel groups typically look at around 40 companies for each one in which they invest (compared to 400 for venture capital firms).

And of all requests for funding received by a typical angel group each year:

- 30 percent are invited for a preliminary screening review.
- 10 percent are invited to pitch to the full group.
- 2 percent receive funding from at least some members of the group.

On average, individual investors in U.S. angel groups invest about $35,000 per company, and members of a group taken together invest about $300,000 per company.

Once an investment is made, the rough outcomes (averaged from several independent studies of angel returns) are:

- 50 percent eventually fail completely.
- 20 percent eventually return the original investment.
- 20 percent return a profit of 2 to 3 times the investment.
- 9 percent return a profit of 10 times the investment.
- 1 percent return a profit of more than 20 times the investment.

Where do these numbers—assuming they are approximately accurate—leave our mythical average angel investor?

The reality is that results in angel investing tend to bifurcate.

The large majority of self-described angel investors, both domestically in the United States and internationally, are either new to the field, not taking it seriously as a financial business, not in it for the long haul, or are not willing to continue investing until they have a fully diversified investment portfolio. For those people, returns tend to be flat to negative.

By contrast, professional angel investors, who follow the approach described in this book, invest calmly, steadily, relatively rationally, over a long period of time, with a strong knowledge of both investment math and early-stage realities. They tend not only to make money, but do quite well: in fact, *the average return for a comprehensive, well-managed angel portfolio is between 25 and 30 percent internal rate of return (IRR)*.

Who Can Be an Angel?

Because angel investing is very risky (unless you take the approach described in this book, and invest rationally and consistently in at least 20 to 80 companies over a long period of time), until 2014 only a limited group of people were allowed access to this asset class. According to regulations of the U.S. Securities and Exchange Commission (SEC), in order to protect small investors from unrealistic, high-powered sales pitches, angel investments in the United States were historically available only to those people who qualify under the SEC's definitions of an Accredited Investor or Qualified Purchaser.* Similar rules exist in many other countries that have active financial markets.

In the United States, the definition of both an Accredited Investor and a Qualified Purchaser is specifically set out by the SEC. While there is legalese surrounding both definitions, for all practical purposes you can think of it this way:

- An *Accredited Investor* is a person who has a steady annual income of at least $200,000 (or $300,000 together with a spouse), or net assets (*not* including the value of one's primary residence) of at least $1,000,000.

---

*Actually, as I'll explain later, the restriction is not on the activity of the investor, but rather on that of the company selling the ownership shares … but the impact is much the same.

- A *Qualified Purchaser* is a person who has at least $5,000,000 in investable assets, or else manages at least $25,000,000 for other people.

Throughout this book I will refer back to this definition of Accredited Investors, the class into which practically all angel investors traditionally fall.

... And Who *Should* Be an Angel?

Because angel investing should be only one part of a well-balanced portfolio, most angels do not (and should not) invest more than 10 percent of their assets into such ventures. In fact, John Huston, the former Chairman of the Angel Capital Association, suggests that angels limit their annual early-stage investments to 10 percent of their free cash flow from other sources. Therefore, in the United States, it is probably fair to say that a typical serious angel investor has invested in between 5 and 10 companies, in amounts ranging from $25,000 to $50,000 each. There are individuals who regularly make much larger investments, and there are many more who invest smaller amounts. There are, however, few angel investors who regard this as a full-time occupation as opposed to venture capitalists, who are, by definition, professionals.

Who are these angels and what drives them?

Angel investors have always been financially motivated (investment by definition implies the expectation of economic returns), although there is often a healthy overlay of social giveback in their calculations. Many active angel investors are, or were, entrepreneurs, which is where they made the money they can now invest. Thus, they are often strong believers in the ethos of entrepreneurship, excited by the prospect of supporting small companies that they believe may one day transform some segment of the business world, spurring economic growth for the benefit of millions. Angels like Reid Hoffman of LinkedIn, Peter Thiel of PayPal, Yossi Vardi of ICQ, or Esther Dyson of EDventure are quite literally changing the world around them. Perhaps the purest case is Tony Hsieh, who has taken the money he made when Amazon acquired Zappos and invested the bulk of it in redeveloping the physical and economic infrastructure of downtown Las Vegas.

However, angel investors by definition are *not* philanthropists or do-gooders in this area of their lives. Instead, most angels I know are increasingly professional and serious about the economic aspects of the business, driven primarily by the prospect of strong financial returns over the long term.

Angel investing is an area in which the so-called Law of Large Numbers applies. This is a theorem that describes the result of performing the same experiment many times. According to the law, the average of the results obtained from a large number of trials should be close to the expected value, and will tend to become closer as more trials are performed.

The implication of the Law of Large Numbers for angel investing is that any one specific investment is almost by definition going to be unpredictable and, according to statistics, likely to be an economic disappointment … but if you invest consistently, intelligently, and over a long period of time, the results are demonstrably repeatable and quite lucrative.

This means that in order to be a successful angel (and, more important, to *enjoy* being an angel), it is imperative that you have the following personal characteristics:

- Long-term view (measured in years, if not decades)
- Strong economic base and the ability to tolerate losses
- High tolerance for risk
- High tolerance for failure
- Even temperament
- Strong people skills (to deal with Type-A entrepreneurs)
- Self-discipline
- Willingness to learn
- General love and respect for entrepreneurs and startups

There are other characteristics that come into play if you are considering being an active angel, one who spends time working with the company on its operations or strategy, and/or helping the company raise its financing. These include teaching/mentoring ability, domain expertise, business experience, financial savvy, personal networks, and the ability to suffer fools gladly. But the bullet list above generally applies to any prospective angel investor, whether active or passive.

As you may sense, being an angel investor has a lot in common with being an entrepreneur—and entrepreneurship is an inherently crazy business. By making a personal angel investment in one of these by-definition-crazy people, you, as the angel, have voluntarily entered into their Alice-in-Wonderland world of rollercoaster ups and downs, with all of the appurtenant "thrill of victory and agony of defeat."

From all the angel investments I have made myself, I can just about guarantee that you are going to experience every disaster, disappointment, and insane improbability you can imagine—and more. Because as crazy as each entrepreneur is, you're simultaneously doing this a dozen or more times! And the nature of the business is that the crazy, disappointing, aggravating, unpleasant, and economically disastrous outcome is likely going to be the default case for 50 to 90 percent of your investments!

So if you are the kind of person who is going to get upset when you lose 100 percent of your $50,000 investment in a promising startup, or can't deal with the fact that the day after your founder launches a breakthrough product, Google unveils a better, free version that soaks up the entire market, then angel investing *is not* the business for you to be in … just as you clearly *should not* be an entrepreneur yourself.

Don't for a moment assume that the warning I've just offered is pro forma, or that anything I'm saying does not apply to me. Yes, I have been successful as an angel. And yes, I have experienced my share of failures, mistakes, and heartaches. It comes with the territory. Like every experienced angel, I have many stories to tell about sure-fire winners that went down in flames, as well as my anti-portfolio—opportunities I passed on that turned into major hits.

For example, at an industry conference in 2004 I saw the first demonstration of a device that would take live broadcasts from your home TV and deliver them to you on your smartphone or computer through the Internet, anywhere in the world. I thought it was amazingly cool, and I quickly accosted the startup's founder, Blake Krikorian, as he walked off the stage. I told him how impressed I was with the product, and asked if he would be willing to come to New York and make a presentation to my fellow investors at New York Angels. He agreed, came to visit us, and demonstrated the system in the Starbucks downstairs from our angel group meeting. We all thought it was amazingly cool, and offered to invest several hundred thousand dollars at a valuation for this pre-shipping, pre-revenue company of something like $5 million.

As I was preparing the term sheet, Blake called us to say that two major Silicon Valley venture capital funds were prepared to invest $10 million at a $20 million valuation for his company—four times the value we'd assigned it! He invited us to participate in that round, and even pleaded with us to invest. But no, we were smart, experienced investors, and we knew full well that a $20 million valuation was simply out of the question for a company whose product hadn't even shipped, let alone generated any sales. So, despite the fact that we loved the product, that Blake and his co-founder/brother Jason literally begged us to participate, and that some really smart VCs thought it was well worth the high valuation ... we regretfully passed.

Less than three years later, Sling Media was acquired by EchoStar for $380 million. Ouch!

On the other hand, last year I came across an intriguing startup with an iPad application that was truly state of the art. It brought a novel approach to an existing, large, and lucrative market, and it had a killer founding team. The CEO had been one of the first executives at a major, high-powered public company in the industry, and the CTO had been a mobile engineering leader at Apple, who had brought with him a team of Apple engineers. Both co-founders had personally invested hundreds of thousands of dollars of their own cash already and the prototype they showed us was a combination of sexy and functional. I led the investment round in the company together with a dozen other sophisticated angels, joined the company's board of directors, and started working to introduce them to potential partners, investors, and customers.

Things seemed to be going well, as the company expanded with our new investment and got ready to launch its initial release. When it did, it was featured in the Apple App Store and got a great many downloads. Unfortunately, very few of them converted into sales that generated revenue. This was disappointing, but not necessarily unexpected. What *was* unexpected, however, was that less than 90 days after our $350,000 investment went into the company, the CTO/co-founder abruptly gave notice that he was leaving, walking away from $200,000 that he had personally put into the company! Then the whole engineering team quickly followed him out the door. The poor CEO was just as blindsided by his partner's desertion as we were, and is still struggling valiantly to save some value in the company, but it is now unquestionably an uphill battle. Ouch again!

The funny (or, to be accurate, not so funny) thing is that experiences like this are more the rule than the exception when you enter the wacky and wonderful world of angel investing. Although I didn't invest when I had the opportunity in companies like Sling Media, Quirky, and Pinterest, I *did* invest in quite a few companies that went belly-up, taking all my investment with them. In fact, since I've made well over 90 personal angel investments, and have been doing this for well over a decade, I've had more than 30 companies fail completely. But failure is part of the game, and if you are serious about becoming an angel investor, you need to understand this right up front. The flip side, however, is that I have also had more than a dozen exits so far that have returned millions of dollars, and still have many dozens of promising companies remaining in my portfolio. Some of them have recently raised additional capital at valuations well over $100 million, so the overall future value of the portfolio is looking quite good.

If you do have most or all of the angelic characteristics I listed above, and are the kind of person who enjoys uncertainty, competition, mentoring, taking risks, new ideas and technologies, then angel investing can be one of the most enjoyable, fulfilling, and exciting endeavors in which you can engage.

As the statistics suggest, successful angel investing is a numbers game. The odds of any single investment paying off with an enormous return are very small. But if you invest intelligently in enough companies, you have a good chance of having at least a few of those companies become profitable. If they are profitable enough, they will not only pay for the losers, but they will end up giving you a handsome overall rate of return. If done thoughtfully and correctly with a large enough portfolio over a long enough period, the Law of Large Numbers suggests that you will make a much better return than from any mainstream investment class.

Watching the long-term growth of some of my portfolio CEOs has been almost as fulfilling as watching my children grow up ... and the fact that these heartwarming stories come with a 25 percent-plus portfolio IRR over a decade makes it all the more delicious.

If you are the kind of person who should be an angel investor, you will find it an enormously fulfilling, exciting, mentally stimulating, and economically rewarding activity.

Getting Started in Angel Investing

The SEC regulations governing angel investing have recently begun to shift, opening up new opportunities for startup investing even among Americans who are not at the Accredited level ($1 million in investable assets, or $200,000 annual income). If you fall into this non-Accredited category, then all of your angel investing will be through what the SEC calls online funding portals, as described under Title III of the JOBS Act of 2012. (I will discuss these new platforms and the emerging world of *equity crowdfunding* at greater length in Chapter 20.) However, as of the date of publication of this book, none of these portals has actually begun operations, because the SEC has not yet finalized the rules that will regulate them. (Of course, you can still buy emerging *public* companies on the stock market like everyone else.) The general theories about startups and investing presented throughout this book, however, still apply to this new method of investing, although you will find yourself operating in a more constrained (and therefore simpler) environment.

On the other hand, if you already qualify as an Accredited Investor, you can legally invest in startups today, and this book will walk you step by step through the specific steps you can take to make your first investment.

One of the best options for a new angel investor today is to join a local angel investor group, where you work collegially with 25 to 250 other serious investors to hear presentations from companies, do your due-diligence homework, and then—if you are interested—pool your money with the others to make meaningful investments. While most of these groups meet in person and invest primarily in companies based in their region, there are an increasing number of virtual groups, meeting and investing online across geographies. (I discuss the advantages and disadvantages of angel groups—and their investment process—in Chapter 17.)

If you want to strike out on your own, however, this book will walk you through everything you need to know to find opportunities

(Chapter 5), do your due-diligence homework on the opportunity (Chapter 8), negotiate the terms of an investment (Chapter 11), and continue to add value during the term of your investment and beyond (Chapter 13).

This a great time to become an angel investor because the past few years have seen the establishment of a number of online platforms that aim to make the process more streamlined. The largest and most comprehensive of these is Gust, which I founded to provide an online infrastructure for the whole angel community. Most angel groups today, in the United States and internationally, use Gust to manage all of their investment operations, and the platform allows group members to easily collaborate both internally and externally on finding and executing investments.

Other websites specialize in specific industries such as real estate (Realty Mogul), films (Slated), consumer products (CircleUp), and the like; specific deal sources such as accelerator programs (Funders Club) or university alumni (Harvard Business School Alumni Angels); specific regions (Seedrs in Europe); or even specific types of investments such as so-called Main Street companies (Bolstr). There are also a host of general platforms that cover a range of industries (such as AngelList, EarlyShares, and MicroVentures). As the world of angel investing continues to expand and diversify, more and more online opportunities are sure to arise, either as independent platforms or by functioning as curated groups or collections on top of an existing platform such as Gust.

So getting started as an angel is becoming easier than ever. But what must you do to get started *successfully?* What kind of strategies do successful angel investors employ to make the numbers work in their favor?

There is no one answer to that question. Trying to generalize about angel investors is like trying to generalize about clouds: they share some fundamental characteristics, but after that, things differ.

One characteristic of most successful angels is a tendency to specialize in industries they know well. While I know some opportunistic angels who will take a flyer on a social networking site one day, a urological catheter the next day, and a sushi/steak restaurant at the end of the week, they are the exception rather than the rule. They tend to be rich people who have lots of money that they play with on a whim, rather than make a considered attempt to generate financial returns.

Most professional angels (that is, people who would self-identify with the term *angel investor* and are ultimately planning to do ten or more investments) invest in business arenas they already know well. That is why most serious angel groups tend to cluster around particular industries. For example, in New York we have, among others, New York Angels (tech-ish), Tevel Angels (Israeli-related), Golden Seeds (women-led), and New York Life Science Angels (self-explanatory). Other groups specialize in business sectors like space, entertainment, pharmaceuticals, consumer products, big data … the list goes on.

Experience, backed up by a number of studies, has shown that if you invest in an area to which you bring background and expertise, you do better over the long run than you would by putting money into a deal which sounds sexy on the surface but would not pass the "sniff test" for someone knowledgeable in the field. Keep in mind, though, that these are not hard-and-fast rules. Businesses in my own portfolio range from animal-lover social networking through zero-gravity space tourism, but they are all areas that I understand. On the other hand, that's also why I haven't invested in any drug discovery, restaurant, or film deals.

Another characteristic that virtually all successful angels share is a constant search for the "big vision" investment. Look at the numbers I presented a few pages back. You can see from this breakdown that, to be successful, an angel needs at least one or two really big winners to make up for the many losers a portfolio is almost certain to include. This is why angels aren't shy about looking for businesses whose equity value they expect to grow ten times or twenty times during the next several years.

As a novice investor, you want to avoid the common mistakes made by many first-time angels:

- Investing in one of the first deals they see.
- Not doing thorough due diligence.
- Investing outside their domain of experience.
- Investing at too high a valuation.
- Investing on an un-capped convertible note.

- Signing the company's documents without having a lawyer review them.
- Not reserving additional capital for the inevitable follow-on round.
- Investing in fewer than 20 deals.
- Becoming an angel without a long-term (10 years or more) commitment.
- Dragging out the investment process unnecessarily.

Some of the terms I use in this list (convertible note, follow-on round, and so on) may be unfamiliar. Don't worry—after you read a bit further you'll understand what you need to know about them (they're also listed with explanations in the glossary at the end of the book). Then you'll be prepared to return to this list, something you may want to do several times before you actually write your first check for an angel investment.

The bottom line is that this is a great time to start thinking about investing in high-growth, startup companies. Whether you're an Accredited angel investor or a non-Accredited crowdfunder; whether you want to invest with a group or on your own; whether you want to meet founders in person or do everything online; whether you want to invest $1,000 or $1,000,000; whether you want to lead an investment syndicate or participate along with other investors; there are—or shortly will be—groups, platforms, and services that will be delighted to help you get into the game.

Risks in Angel Investing

Because angel investing is still outside the mainstream (as compared with investing in blue-chip stocks or a well-known mutual fund), the idea may make you or your spouse a bit nervous. Frankly, if it doesn't, you may actually be too much of a risk-seeker to exert the discipline needed to make money in this asset class! The anxiety of unfamiliarity may be compounded by the uncertainty of investing in small companies with a modest (or no) track record that you may never have heard of before. So a realistic understanding of the risks in angel investing is critically important before you decide to take the plunge.

One worry you may have is that your money will be stolen by a con artist—that a company founder might simply abscond with your investment funds. In practice, this is exceedingly rare. Although there have been one or two cases where a portfolio CEO turned out to have a problematic past or proceeded to misappropriate funds, this is highly unlikely to happen to you. Keep in mind that angels or VCs fund only a few thousand early-stage companies each year, out of hundreds of thousands that seek such funding (and millions more that start up without seeking funding), which means that such investments are usually exhaustively vetted.

A venture capital firm typically engages in a process that lasts several months, familiarizing themselves with the company, its staff, operations, customers, and financials. (Remember, the funds are going to a company, not into someone's personal checking account.) The venture fund would typically have one or more seats on the company's board of directors and receive monthly or quarterly financial reports. Trying to abscond with a large amount of cash shortly after a financing event would be a major felony and the investors would, without question, spare no expense to track down the miscreant, who would likely end up in prison for a long time. I'm not aware of this *ever* having happened.

Angel investments, without a venture fund in the mix to provide a professional level of due diligence and background checks, can be somewhat riskier. But the underlying issues are the same, and after investing in more than 90 startups, and watching hundreds of others, I have never seen this happen. Not once.

Types of Angel Investors

There are almost as many different types of angel investors as there are public market investors. Many people who are angels are also concurrently entrepreneurs in their own right. I'm a serial entrepreneur as well as a serial angel investor, and I'd guess that at least a third to a half (perhaps more) of the members of New York Angels are also currently running their own startups. They range from an air-taxi service to a public relations platform, from a medical review website to advertising-technology services.

Many other angels are executives at Fortune 500 companies. Unless there are specific competitive or ethical issues with a particular investment, from their employer's viewpoint there is no difference between investing in a private company and a public one.

Some angels have retired from the legal or medical professions or from a corporate executive role. Others have inherited the capital they use to invest. They are young and old, male and female, of every race and ethnic background, and located in every state of the union and countless nations around the world. What they all have in common is a readiness to work hard, do their homework, and take calculated risks in pursuit of exciting business opportunities. If you are the right kind of person to take the plunge, I promise you that angel investing will be one of the most stimulating and personally rewarding activities you will ever enjoy.

Plus, It's Really Fun!

The Nonfinancial Rewards of Being an Angel

As I DISCUSSED in Chapter 1, early-stage angel investments—when approached professionally and over the long term as I outline in this book—can be a lucrative asset class, consistently outperforming most other forms of investment. But unlike putting money into the public stock market, or betting on soybean futures or investing in a real estate fund, becoming directly involved with high-growth startup companies can bring many additional benefits. It's a bit like growing fresh vegetables in your backyard instead of buying canned peas at the supermarket: both end up on your dinner plate, but the homegrown variety tastes better, is more nutritious, gives you a sense of accomplishment, and, if you like gardening, is fun to plant and nurture. So it is with startups.

The term angel originated around the turn of the twentieth century to describe well-heeled gentlemen who would seemingly appear from heaven to provide financing for theatrical productions—traditionally a high-risk proposition. In addition to the potential economic return from backing a Broadway hit, however, the theatrical angel would find himself credited as a producer, invited to opening night galas and cast rehearsals, and sometimes even invited backstage, where there might be an opportunity to meet one of the young chorines from the company. Such romantic side benefits, however, are not typically the case with high-tech startups.

Nevertheless, investing in startups has so many other dimensions that, for quite a few angels, the external rewards may be even more important than the financial ones. Here are some of the non-cash benefits that come with your angel wings.

Keeping Up with the World

Actively reviewing pitches and meeting young founders is one of the best ways to keep up with current developments in a familiar industry or to learn the latest about a new one.

Before I started my career as a technology entrepreneur, I spent over a decade in real estate development, construction, finance, and technology. I greatly enjoyed the field and could cheerfully have spent the rest of my working life developing new residential and commercial buildings … except that I liked creating new tech companies even more. I still retain a lot of knowledge about the real estate industry as well as contacts useful to an early-stage company in that space. That's why real estate tech startups are one area in which I invest. The neat thing, however, is that it's very much a two-way street, because in addition to the value that I can bring to the startup, the fact that the startup is breaking ground in innovative ways means that I learn as much from them as they do from me.

For example, FASTTAC: Technology Advancing Construction, is a company founded by veteran construction executive Ray Steeb, who had become frustrated with the way construction drawings and documents were handled on site. He found it time consuming and inefficient to keep current and up to date the multiple sets of drawings needed for a building project. It was even more challenging to update them remotely when a change was made to some or all of those drawings and nearly impossible to ensure that every document set was accurate and reflected all the latest notes and changes. So, working with a team from Carnegie Mellon University, he created a software platform to digitally share, distribute, and control construction drawings and documents, which is now in use across the country by clients including Turner Construction, Leggatt McCall, and Plaza Construction. As one of the company's earliest investors, I see first hand the exciting ways in which technology is changing the brick-and-mortar world of construction.

Similarly, my recent investment in Realty Mogul, the leading online real estate funding platform founded by Jilliene Helman and Justin Hughes, gives me fascinating insights into the intersecting worlds of real estate finance, angel investments, and crowdfunding that I would not be able to obtain from the outside.

While keeping abreast of the latest developments in my own industry is one benefit I get from my angel activities, I also have an insatiable curiosity about advancing technology, and that is another area in which seed investing turns out to be a lot of fun. Today, every industry is affected by developments in hardware, software, and connectivity. The result is that the world of today is a far cry from that of yesterday, and an unfathomable distance from that of tomorrow. If you are a person who wants to keep up with the latest developments, you can read *Scientific American* (which I love), or wait until your children show you why SnapChat will replace email ... or you can involve yourself directly at the cutting edge of the latest, coolest developments by becoming an angel.

Take, for example, the field of commercial space flight. Whereas Space 1.0 consisted of government programs creating expensive infrastructure and equipment for government projects such as moon landings and the Hubble Space Telescope, Space 2.0 consists of an explosion of small, private-sector startups taking advantage of space technology for commercial purposes. This is driven partly by a decision in 2009 by NASA, the U.S. space agency, to privatize space activities, and by the rapidly dropping cost of commercial technology.

Peter Diamandis, Chairman of the XPrize Foundation, the International Space University, and several other amazing ventures, pitched me a few years ago on what had to be the coolest idea of the year. NASA, he said, was retiring the old plane that had been used to train astronauts to work in zero gravity, and he and his colleagues (several of them formerly from NASA) had figured out an ingenious way to refit a commercial cargo aircraft to serve as a bigger and better zero-gravity platform. They had also managed to navigate the bureaucracy of the Federal Aviation Administration, getting authorization to take paying customers up in a cargo plane and then sending it into a steep dive (think about that one for a minute).

The idea was to set up a company that would combine servicing NASA's training program with support for tourist flights, enabling ordinary people to experience the same weightless flying which U.S. astronauts practice before their space missions. The way he projected the financials turned out to be a very feasible—and lucrative—plan. Oh, and did I mention which each of the company's angel investors would also get a free zero-gravity flight every year? Suffice it to say that I was one of the first people to sign up, along with fellow space-loving angels such as Esther Dyson and Howard L. Morgan.

Since investing, I've made several flights on G-Force One, each more fun than the previous one, and I celebrated my last big birthday with a party floating around in weightlessness and flying like Superman. All thanks to angel investing!

Cool as that may sound, however, there's always the one kid in the class who can top you. Esther and I were founding members of the national Space Angels Network, and Space 2.0 is one of her major investing interests. After a number of years of increasingly successful operations, ZeroG merged with another company called Space Adventures that specializes in working with the Russian space program to send tourists to the International Space Station (ISS). Since that little trip costs something like $30 million, you can be sure that they have a no-cancellation policy. So what happens if the officially booked space tourist comes down with a cold the day before blastoff? They need a backup, of course! Esther signed on as the backup crewmember for Charles Simonyi's rocket trip to the ISS in 2009, and spent several weeks alongside him in Star City, becoming certified as a fully trained cosmonaut.

At the announcement of her joining the crew, Esther said "As an investor in Space Adventures, I am thrilled to be training as a cosmonaut and learning about space travel firsthand. . . . My father helped design a rocket ship when I was a kid, and I have always assumed I will go into space myself." Me too!

Entrepreneurship without the Responsibility

While keeping up to date on the latest developments in a particular industry is a boon for those angels who are still working full-time on their own enterprises, angel investing can be just as much fun for those who have put the rigors of day-to-day operating roles behind them. The Angel Capital Association, which counts among its members the majority of North American angel groups (more about them in Chapter 17) conducted a demographic survey that showed their typical angel investor member had 15 years of entrepreneurial experience and had personally founded two or three companies. As every entrepreneur is aware, founding and running a company may appear simple ("Set your own schedule! Work your own hours! Don't have a boss!"), but it is one of the most toughest, psychologically grueling lifestyles one can choose. Paul DeJoe, founder of the technology startup Ecquire, summed this up eloquently in a contribution to the question-and-answer network Quora, about the life of a startup CEO:

> Very tough to sleep most nights of the week. Weekends don't mean anything to you anymore. Closing a round of financing is not a relief. It means more people are depending on you to turn their investment into 20 times what they gave you. It's very difficult to "turn it off".... You feel guilty when you're doing something you like doing outside of the company.... You start to respect the Duck. Paddle like hell under the water and be smooth and calm on top where everyone can see you.

Many entrepreneurs who have successfully navigated these shoals eventually face a dilemma once they come to an exit that gives them economic flexibility. They love the game of company creation and overcoming challenges, but after 20 or 30 years of paddling like a duck, they (or at least their spouses) would finally like to take a vacation. Or be able to get to their child's class play. Or have the flexibility to take a month hiking in the Alps. On the surface, it seems that there is no way to reconcile these two goals because true entrepreneurship is an all-in sport. But angel investing can come close. Being an active seed investor in a startup—especially if you also serve in an advisory, mentoring, or board of directors role—is the next best thing to doing it yourself. You get much of the thrill of the chase, while at the same time you can go home at night and put the company behind you, safe in the knowledge that your CEO is taking full responsibility. It's like being a grandparent (or so I'm told): all the fun of parenting, but someone else gets to change the diapers and suffer the sleepless nights.

In the summer of 2012, I attended a meeting of the NY Tech Meetup, the unofficial, offline heart of the New York City startup scene. Each month, a dozen or so startups get five minutes to demonstrate their new products or websites to a crowd of their peers. On that particular evening, one of the presenters was a young entrepreneur named Ryan Rzepecki who unveiled a new approach to urban bike sharing called Social Bicycles.

Over the past few years, cities such as Paris, London, New York, and Shanghai installed systems for sharing pools of public bicycles. In each case, subscribers to the service use a special electronic key card to unlock a bicycle from a large rack at one of several hubs, pedal it to another hub, and re-lock it into the rack at the destination. When enough of these smart hubs were installed in a city, the systems were actually quite usable, and ridership was slowly beginning to move from a novelty to part of the urban fabric.

The only problem was that having *enough* hubs began to be a bigger problem that grew worse as ridership increased. Paris, for example, had to install nearly 2,000 stations at enormous cost. Even in New York, where the initial deployment involved just 330 hubs in midtown and lower Manhattan, there was an immense outcry over the space taken up, and the inconveniences caused by these large stations.

What Ryan and his team were demonstrating that evening, however, was a new-generation bike-sharing system that took the computerization and electronics out of the stations and put it directly on the bicycle. With Social Bicycles' prototype system, there was no longer a need for bulky, expensive stations. Bikes were no longer limited to trips between Station A and Station B; they could go anywhere. And by incorporating wireless communications, GPS tracking, and computerized locks into the bikes themselves, the system could take full advantage of congestion pricing, real-time route tracking, automated incentives for riders to redeploy bikes into areas that needed them, and much more.

Given my personal experience with urban planning, online platforms, and real-time economics, I saw the potential of this concept to revolutionize the bicycle-sharing world. More than that, I saw a concept so elegant that it was breathtaking. I had to get involved!

I raced down from the balcony the minute the meeting ended and practically bowled into Ryan. I told him on the spot that I wanted to invest in the company, lead his next financing round, and see how I could be helpful. Although he appeared a bit taken aback, he succumbed to my charm (or maybe got tired of my perseverance) and agreed to accept me as an investor and chairman of the board. I then brought the company to New York Angels, where a number of my fellow members also invested, and helped Ryan bring on several early-stage investment funds as well, notably SOS Ventures, whose investment was led by Brad Higgins, a professional international investor with enormous experience.

Social Bicycles was not only the first company that Ryan founded; it was also the first company for which he had ever worked. His experience with bike-sharing systems came from his time at the New York City Department of Transportation, which he joined directly out of school. In fact, Ryan's lack of entrepreneurial or business experience had scared off some other potential investment funds, even though they were impressed with his vision and technology. But Brad and I saw true entrepreneurial determination in Ryan, and felt that we could help round out his passion and domain expertise with our business and strategic experience.

And that's exactly the way it has turned out. Our small board meets regularly in my office, Ryan keeps in close touch with us on a weekly basis, Brad and I have used our industry contacts to assist the company with contracts and recruiting, and helped Ryan strategize and negotiate the next steps for the company. In the short time since the company received its initial outside funding from us, Social Bicycles has become a significant player in the bike-sharing world. It has won contracts to install systems in Buffalo, Boise, Tampa, Phoenix, Orlando, Atlanta, and Las Vegas and is on track to become the leader in this rapidly growing industry.

As for me, I get to put my business, technical, strategic, and financing experience to use for a company that is using technology to re-invent urban transportation. But at the end of the day, it is Ryan who is doing the heavy lifting, while Brad and I get the pleasure of serving as his consiglieres and support team.

While my involvement with Social Bicycles is a good example of the enjoyment that can be had from deploying carefully honed business skills on behalf of something (and someone) in which one believes, it also illustrates another of the non-financial benefits that lead many people to devote more time to their angel pursuits than might otherwise make sense from a purely economic perspective: the opportunity to help create an enterprise that is socially beneficial.

In the context of angel investing, we often call this opportunity by the serious-sounding name of *impact investing*. I directly address this part of the angel world in Chapter 18, but it *is* possible both to do good for society and do well for yourself at the same time.

The Joy of Giving Back

Although over the years I have served—and continue to serve—on many charitable boards and contributed to many worthy organizations, my work as an investor, advisor, mentor, teacher, and trainer for young entrepreneurs has given me more pleasure, by far, than any other activity in which I have been involved. I once responded to a question on Quora by describing how I feel about giving back by mentoring young entrepreneurs and answering questions:

> It's roughly equivalent to a fat person being approached by the Mayo Clinic saying, "We have an experimental program that seems to result in healthy, rapid, weight loss, but unfortunately it requires you to be willing to eat gourmet French food interspersed with Japanese banquets, while being massaged by gorgeous physiotherapists. Would you be willing to sacrifice yourself for society to try this program if we paid you a few thousand dollars for your troubles?"

That's exactly the kind of pleasure I receive from watching the next generation of talent bloom in front of my eyes, and sharing a part, however small, in nurturing their development.

Take, for example, Mind's Eye Innovation. Adam Potash spent a summer working as an intern for me during college as he pursued a major in business. But when he graduated into the recession of 2008, the only job he could find was as a taxi dispatcher for a small suburban cab fleet. After a few years of increasing frustration with the antiquated technology and operations of taxis outside the major urban centers, it occurred to him that technology had advanced enough to be able to solve a whole industry's problems at a very achievable cost. So he worked up a proposal and business plan that was convincing enough for me and two fellow angels, John and Richard Katzman, to invest just enough cash for him to build a prototype.

Within a year, Adam had a working unit built around a generic Android tablet that combined a taxi meter, GPS, dispatch system, two-way radio, credit card terminal, and passenger hailing system. This was enough to get his boss at the taxi company to give him an order for 75 units for the entire fleet, and that order was what we needed to fund him enough to build and deliver the units. Six months later, with over 100 units installed in cars from four different fleets, Adam presented his pitch to New York Angels, which gave him a term sheet for enough money to hire a full-time sales and technical staff, and bring the company to profitability.

Or take Comixology. In 2007 David Steinberger was finishing up his MBA at NYU's Stern School of Business. The time had come for him to retrieve his large comic book collection from his parents' house, and he needed a way to catalog them. A few years earlier he had met John Roberts, a programmer then working for Marvel Comics. David had kept John's contact info as a fellow comic aficionado, so David called John and asked if he could perhaps develop a quick little comic book cataloging application. Together with Peter Jaffe, a statistically-minded fellow MBA student and also a comic fan, they entered NYU's annual Business Plan Competition, and ended up tying for first prize. As one of the judges of the competition, I was impressed with the Comixology team, and together with Kit McQuiston—another judge—and a group of my fellow New York Angels members, we put together the company's first financing round and started on a seven-year journey of funding the company without any venture capital investment.

As of the end of 2013, Comixology had over 100 employees, had delivered more than 200,000,000 digital downloads of comic books, has a 90 percent market share of its industry, powers the official mobile services of both Marvel and DC comics, and is beloved by its customers and comic creators alike. More important to me, however, has been watching the founding team grow, change, and deal with the stresses of running a startup.

Having the opportunity to observe this firsthand, and play some part in mentoring these next-generation rock stars, has been one of the most fulfilling aspects of my angel-investing career.

Brian Cohen, who followed me as chairman of New York Angels, wrote about the joy of mentoring entrepreneurs in his book with John Kador, *What Every Angel Investor Wants You to Know*:

> The founder and the angel need to stay close, and not just during the courtship phase of the relationship. The mentorship that founders so desire and the mentorship angels are willing to offer really defines a mutually beneficial relationship ... it means the angel really leans into the world that the team is in. The angel has to appreciate this world in a visceral way, not only for the benefit of the investment du jour, but to help sharpen the instincts of the angel for emerging opportunities.

As fulfilling as is the one-on-one mentoring of portfolio CEOs, there are other ways in which angel investing provides opportunities to get a warm feeling by paying forward all of the good things that we have been fortunate enough to receive ourselves. Entrepreneurship is rapidly emerging as a pillar of modern economic development, with cities, states, and countries coming to understand that their futures depend on new people creating new businesses that, in turn, create new jobs. With all the challenges that are inherent in starting a venture, there are new programs springing up every day that attempt to provide scalable mentoring and advising to ever-larger groups of would-be entrepreneurs.

For all of these, angel investors are eagerly sought after to serve as judges, advisors, mentors, reviewers, and in other roles. Whether it is helping with the Big Apps competition established by New York City to encourage the development of mobile applications that take advantage of newly public city databases, or serving as a speaker at programs inviting international entrepreneurs to establish headquarters in our city, I do my best to give back to the community. And I have found consistently that the more I give, the more I get back. You will, too.

The Social Side of Angel Investing

There is one more intangible aspect of angel investing that I have saved for last, and I almost hesitate to mention it. It is the social dimension of the activity, which has historically been one of the biggest motivating factors for affluent people to become angels in the first place. The reason I don't want you to focus on it is because the point of this book is to show you how to make money by approaching the investment process as a rational, serious investor with a long-term plan. It would be inappropriate for me to suggest that one reason you might consider becoming an angel is because it will improve your social standing.

However, angel investing these days *is* a cool thing to do. Just think about what it must be like for my friend Tim Ferriss, author of *The 4-Hour Workweek*, to hear someone in a conversation refer to Twitter. As a result of his angel investing, he can casually mention, "Yeah, I was one of their early investors. And Facebook's. And Stumbleupon's. And Uber's. And ... " But that, of course, would be incredibly shallow. So I'm sure that Tim wouldn't think of doing that, nor would you. Right?

In fact, the best social aspect of angel investing is *not* the cachet that comes from being seen as one of the cool kids. Rather, it is the chance to hang out with two groups of interesting people.

One set consists of other people like you, who are not only successful (remember, you're all Accredited Investors), but are also interested in entrepreneurship, mentorship, and new technologies. Over more than a decade of angel investing, I have developed deep and lasting friendships with some of the smartest, funniest, and most effective people I've ever had the pleasure to meet. Nicholas Negroponte, legendary founder of the MIT Media Lab, was my co-investor in the first angel investment I ever made. Esther Dyson and I have invested in over a dozen deals together. Scott Kurnit, Gideon Gartner, Alan Patricof, Yossi Vardi, Dave McClure, Mitch Kapor, Dennis Crowley, Gary Vaynerchuck, Stephen Messer, Jeff Pulver and I regularly cross paths in the early-stage space, and often end up investing in the same deals.

Even more interesting than the boldface names are the many other—more private—angel investors whom I have met through New York Angels, the group I founded more than 10 years ago that is currently the most active angel organization in the United States. These angels aren't high-profile entrepreneurs or business rock stars. They are financial professionals, lawyers, real estate developers, art collectors, retired corporate executives and, yes, even doctors. But the fact that they have decided to spend the time, mindshare, and money to become serious angel investors sets them apart.

We'll examine angel groups more fully in Chapter 17, but for some groups, socializing and fellowship are seen as an integral part of the group dynamic, leading to better collaboration among investors, more opportunities for social service, and more fun. In fact, Keiretsu Forum, an angel network with 27 chapters around the world, specifically differentiates itself by noting that "Fellowship is enhanced not only through our charitable activities but also through countless fun activities for and by the members, such as golf, tennis, hiking, educational field trips, to name a few."

The other group with whom you'll get to associate as an angel is that of the entrepreneurs who are building the high-growth companies of tomorrow. While there is certainly no age limit to entrepreneurship (as I write this, my entrepreneurial father, now 84 years young, is in Ghana negotiating to develop a new shopping center), the fact is that the founders of today's technology-powered startups are for the most part in their twenties and thirties. They grew up in a time of exponentially accelerating technology, and see the world through a different set of glasses than do most angels, who tend to be in their fifties and sixties.

They are also likely to be found all over the world. Because we are living in a world of change, working with startups means that you may be working anywhere, with anyone. Originally a solo pursuit of driven innovators, entrepreneurship and its financing have become a team sport, and the team can be any group with which one identifies. Examples of this include the Harvard Business School Alumni Angels, U.S.-based angels from the Portuguese diaspora, and Singularity Angels, made up of the ever-expanding family of faculty, friends, and fellows from Singularity University. Bringing together entrepreneurs and investors who are bound by common interests, backgrounds, or affiliations enhances trust and communication, lubricates the process of collaboration, and aids in the discovery of opportunities and partners that one might otherwise never meet.

I teach at business schools, attend startup community events, and host small gatherings of young entrepreneurs. By serving as a mentor at accelerators such as Columbia's Greenhouse, Yale's Entrepreneurial Institute, DreamIT Ventures, and Founders Institute, and as a speaker/participant at events organized by groups such as

Sandbox Network, StartupGrind, Astia and Singularity University, I have my assumptions challenged, my eyes opened, and my perspectives changed. The result is that my psychological age is probably half of my chronological one, and my worldview has increasingly more in common with the best and the brightest of the next generation than it does with the pundits of the past.

This, by itself, is enough to justify the time I spend as an angel.

The Portfolio Theory
of Angel Investing

Why Every Angel Needs to Invest in at Least 20 Companies

WHEN PEOPLE HEAR about the 25 percent annualized rate of return that active angel investors obtain, they assume that there must be some secret involved—perhaps an old-boy network of hidden links that connects angels to brilliant entrepreneurs and tech innovators, or a mathematical algorithm developed by some genius at MIT that helps angels identify and invest in the businesses that are guaranteed to be the Apples, Googles, and Facebooks of tomorrow.

In reality, there are few secrets about the investment world, including the world of startups. But there are some little-known truths that serious startup investors (both angels and venture capitalists) take for granted, and to which most people—including entrepreneurs themselves—are oblivious. These deal with the fundamental nature of the industry, and you need to completely internalize them if you are going to be successful at investing in startups.

Truth 1: Most Startups Fail

It's a message that most angels or venture investors could deliver to would-be entrepreneurs dozens of times a month—and that they *would* deliver were it not for the fact that they don't want to burn their bridges or ruin their reputations for being nice guys. The message runs something like this:

> I'm sorry, but your business idea simply doesn't make sense. It shows zero understanding of startups in general, your market in particular, and basic economics. Even if your plan made sense, you appear to have no ability at all to execute it. As a matter of fact, the best thing I could do for your own good is to tell you that this is a ridiculous, useless pitch, and you should really forget this whole entrepreneurial thing and go get a job somewhere.

I know, this sounds harsh. That's why this message is very rarely delivered in precisely this form.

But let's do the math. Forget the fact that, according to the U.S. Small Business Administration, venture capital funds invest in fewer than 1 in 400 companies who pitch them. Let's talk instead about angel investors, who are more prolific, less picky, and individually see fewer opportunities than large venture funds. Tracking data from Gust shows that angels invest in roughly one out of every 40, or about 2.5 percent, of the companies they see. So what about the *other* startups?

Going down the scale, figure that there is little, if any, difference between the top 2.5 percent and the second 2.5 percent, and that it is almost random as to who gets funded in that top 5 percent. Now, double that number, and figure that the top 10 percent *would* get funded if we could actually match the right investors to the right companies. And because we're living in a globalized world, with platforms like Gust now connecting many hundreds of thousands of startups and investors, double it again to account for all of the super-specialized tastes, interests, and investing theses that might *conceivably* get a startup funded. Then, because "all progress depends on the unreasonable man," to quote George Bernard Shaw, throw in the *next* 5 percent, because who knows if that wild and crazy idea really *is* the next big thing?

Add all that up and you'll see that, being 10 times as generous as the entire angel industry, and 100 times as generous as the venture capital industry—we would still have funded only the top 25 percent of hopeful startups. And since the world of business isn't Garrison Keillor's Lake Woebegon, "where every startup is above average," it means that at least *75 percent of startups really shouldn't be funded ... by anyone, under any circumstances.*

And that is the first truth that most angel investors won't tell you, because to do so would be to spit in the face of the brave, visionary entrepreneurs on whom the angel's livelihood rests.

Truth 2: No One Knows Which Startups Are *Not* Going to Fail

The biggest change in my investment approach over years as an angel investor is the one that all serious angels eventually arrive at. I've come to accept that, no matter how smart or experienced one is, there are too many exogenous factors affecting business outcomes for anyone to be able to pick only winners.

Having now invested in more than 90 startups, my angel investing has been extremely successful. Yet paradoxically, I find that there is little correlation between my home runs and failures—and my personal guesses as to which will be which.

One of my very early angel investments was in a company with the unwieldy name of Design2Launch. The company, founded by CEO Alison Malloy and her brother Ron, developed a digital-workflow solution for the collaboration needs of marketing, creative, and production professionals in the consumer-packaged goods marketplace. Alison was introduced to me in the early days of New York Angels by Stephanie Newby, one of our group's newer members. Stephanie later went on to found the Golden Seeds angel network, won the Hans Severeins Award from the Angel Capital Association, and is now a rock star of the angel-investing world. Back then, however, she and I were still in the getting-our-feet-wet stage of the business.

Alison's company at that point had been around for a few years, and was generating revenue from a useful, but rather unsexy product. Shortly before I met her, the company had gone through a rough period of a failed merger with another company, some internal turmoil with a former employee, and a slowdown in sales. Altogether this was not a strong candidate for an angel investment—only four of us out of some 50 members of New York Angels at the time decided to invest. But Alison was smart, passionate, and determined to pull the company back together, she and her brother made a strong team, and Stephanie and I, along with a few other angels, were willing to bet on her.

Because of the rough circumstances, and the likelihood that the company would have no choice but to close its doors if we couldn't pull an investment round together, we invested a total of a few hundred thousand dollars at a relatively modest company valuation of around a million dollars. For all of us, this was not a bet on the next Facebook or Twitter, but more of a show of faith and support for a deserving entrepreneur in a tough situation. If that year you had asked me to order all of the investments in my portfolio in terms of expected outcomes, Design2Launch would have ranked closer to the bottom of the list than the top.

But quality tells, and often a great entrepreneur can snatch victory from the jaws of defeat. So it was with Alison. Buoyed by our investment and support, she quickly got the company back on its feet, expanded its product line, and forged serious partnerships with some major industry players. Imagine our delight when in the summer of 2008, Kodak, their largest partner, made an all-cash offer to acquire the company for around $15 million!

And here is where things became interesting. For a big-name company that you might read about in the tech blogs, a $15 million acquisition would be tantamount to a disastrous failure. For a company that had made it through one or two rounds of VC financing before failing, an acquisition at that number would be considered a *soft landing* or an *acqui-hire*—where the amount received in the sale would reflect primarily the value to the acquiring firm of adding Alison to their leadership team. In any case, the purchase price might be enough to pay back some of the initial investment, but not enough to generate any meaningful return for the company's founders or investors.

In this case, because of the tight ship that Alison ran, and the modest valuation at which we had invested, the acquisition produced a roughly 10x return for the company's angels! When I cashed that check for nearly $1 million (the first real payout I had received from one of my angel investments) I realized (1) that it *was* possible to make money in this asset class, and (2) that it's possible for a seemingly unimpressive investment to turn into a home run.

A few years later, I invested in a company called CE Interactive, the brainchild of a highly successful serial entrepreneur with extensive experience in the consumer electronics space. He had recently stepped down as CEO of the previous company he had founded, which had become the largest online electronics parts supplier in the world, with customers including virtually every major consumer electronics retailer. His new idea was farsighted and brilliant: to create a database with detailed information about every single piece of consumer electronics equipment, and use it to generate a variety of products, such as instant, illustrated instructions about how to connect all the different electronics in one's home.

The company had a big vision, a great management team, a solid track record, and widespread support, including from the Consumer Electronics Industry Association itself (the first and only time in its history that the *industry* had made a commercial investment), and from a top tier, seed-stage VC firm. One of the company's signed customers was Circuit City, then the largest consumer electronics retailer in the country. It seemed that there was little chance of this being anything but a megahit.

But there is a saying: "Man proposes, but God disposes." Within a few years of our investment, (1) the company struggled to find an adaptable and scalable business model; (2) maintaining and improving the database platform proved to be more costly than anticipated; (3) Circuit City, the company's largest customer, went out of business; (4) the economic crisis of 2008 made it virtually impossible for the company to raise additional capital; and (5) the recession put pressure on all of its other retail customers, who cancelled their pilot programs. By the summer of 2011 CE Interactive was out of business, taking with it our entire investment.

Smart investors are aware of their inability to pick only winners, and this distinguishes professionals from amateurs. I always smile when I hear tourist angels boast about how they've only made two or three investments "and they are all home runs." Whenever you start thinking that the experts pick all the winners and *only* winners, stop by the anti-portfolio page on the website of top-tier venture fund Bessemer Venture Partners. Here you will see a list of companies in which the nation's oldest venture fund declined to make an early investment: Apple, eBay, FedEx (they passed seven times!), Google, Intel, Intuit, Compaq, PayPal, Cisco, and more.

Oh, but you're more astute than the folks at Bessemer, right? Think again!

Truth 3: Investing in Startups Is a Numbers Game

To recap: most startup businesses aren't worthy of investment, and no one, regardless of experience or expertise, is capable of routinely identifying which startups are worthy of investment and which are not. Despite these facts, angel investing—when done correctly—really *can* produce a consistent IRR in the 25 to 30 percent range. The way to achieve this is to invest intelligently in many companies, which has the Law of Large Numbers working on your behalf.

Several studies and mathematical simulations have shown that it takes investing the same amount of money consistently in at least 20 to 25 companies before your returns begin to approach the typical return

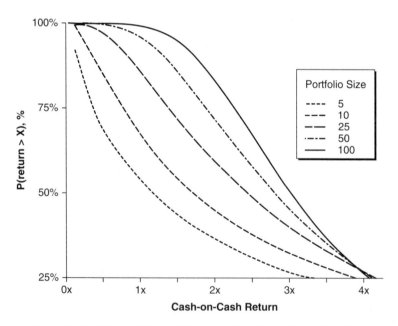

Figure 3.1   Probability of Angel Returns Based on Portfolio Size

Source: Data Driven Patterns of Successful Angel Investing by Sim Simeonov, www.slideshare.net/simeons/patterns-of-successful-angel-investing-8306787

of over 20 percent for professional, active angel investors. This means the greater the number of companies into which an angel invests, the greater the likelihood of an overall positive return. Sim Simeonov, a veteran software-industry entrepreneur and angel investor, has produced a detailed proof of this thesis, see Fig. 3.1.

It shows that because of the hits-oriented nature of angel investing, even though any one particular company has roughly similar odds of succeeding or failing, the lopsided nature of the returns means that, on balance, the more companies in which you invest, the more likely your *whole portfolio* is to generate higher returns.

Truth 4: What Ends Up, Usually Went Down First

Angel investing (like venture capital) follows the classic J-curve. Because unsuccessful companies tend to fail early, and big exits from the successful ones tend to take a long time to develop, when you graph it on a timeline the overall value of an angel portfolio makes a shape like the letter "J." It begins dropping for several years as soon as you start investing, and only after a fair amount of time does it change direction and begin to be worth more than the original investment (see Figure 3.2).

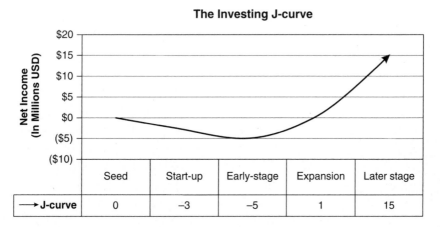

	Seed	Start-up	Early-stage	Expansion	Later stage
⟶ **J-curve**	0	–3	–5	1	15

Figure 3.2   The J-Curve Graph for a Startup Investment Portfolio

Source: David M. Townsend and Lowell W. Busenitz, "Resource Complementarities, Trade-Offs, and Undercapitalization in Technology-Based Ventures: An Empirical Analysis (Summary)," *Frontiers of Entrepreneurship Research* 29, no. 1, issue 5 (2009), http://digitalknowledge.babson.edu/fer/vol29/iss1/5

Since the average holding period for an angel investment in the United States is nine years, after only five years it is likely that the value of your angel portfolio will still be underwater, unless it happens to include one unusual, quick, *Black Swan*, home run. The fact that early profitability is so rare is personally frustrating and likely to cause strain on your marriage. But just as parents survive the terrible twos by remembering that their contrary toddler will eventually morph into an adorable, parent-worshiping three-year-old, you can help yourself through the early dark years by keeping in mind the right-hand side of the chart.

This also means that in addition to investing in a large number of companies, it is a good idea to spread those investments evenly over a long period of time. Venture capital funds typically operate on a five-years-in/five-years-out philosophy. That is, once a VC firm raises a fund, they will spend the first five years putting the money out as investments, and then begin to harvest the returns from those companies that have exits. They will also, around that time, start raising their next fund, so that they always have fresh money to invest.

Similarly, you should decide up-front how much money you are comfortable with investing each year in angel opportunities—**such as 10% of your free cash flow**—and mentally commit to maintaining that level for 5 to 10 years. That should be long enough to get you through the bottom of the J-Curve and up to the right, where you have a chance of funding future investments from past successes.

Truth 5: All Companies Always Need More Money

Companies always need more money. It doesn't matter what the founders' projections are, or how fast they believe they will turn profitable. They will need more money. Although there is the rare case where the company becomes an overnight smash hit and needs more capital than expected to meet overwhelming customer demand, that is true in perhaps 1 out of 10 cases. For the rest, the odds are that the entrepreneur was too optimistic, and/or exogenous factors negatively affected the path to profitability. In either case, however, early investors aren't usually beating down the doors to throw in more money.

Therefore, the company will typically provide incentives for its investors to participate in these follow-on rounds. These incentives invariably come at the expense of the early investors who choose *not* to participate ... which is why venture capitalists always reserve the same amount as their initial investment to put in later into the same company. Unless, as a serious angel, you are planning to reserve a certain amount of your angel-investing capital for follow-ons, your interest in the company is likely to be significantly reduced over time (a phenomenon referred to as equity *dilution*).

Truth 6: If You Understand and Follow Truths 1 to 5, Angel Investing Can Be Very Lucrative

I realize that much of the foregoing sounds daunting, not to mention taking a lot of time, effort, and commitment to deploy capital over a long period. But there is a light at the end of this particular tunnel:

- If you are an Accredited Investor, *and*
- If you are prepared to invest at least $50K to $100K per year, *and*
- If you make sure to reserve quite a bit for follow-on financings, *and*
- If you develop a strong deal flow of good companies, *and*
- If you invest consistently so that you have at least 20 companies (ideally quite a few more) in your portfolio, *and*
- If you are professional in both your due-diligence investigation and your deal-term negotiation, *and*
- If you go in with the knowledge that you are going to be in it for at least a decade, holding completely illiquid assets, *and*
- If you can help add value to your portfolio companies above and beyond simply money, *and*
- If you follow the advice on all of the above that I'm going give to you in the following chapters ...

then the odds will be in your favor to join the rarified band of successful, professional angel investors who show average IRRs over their investing years of over 25 percent per year.

4

The Financial Life of a Startup

Where Angels Fit in the Big Financing Picture

THE WORLD OF startup businesses is enormous. How enormous? That depends on how you define "startup." Take a college student who advertises her dog-walking services. She might consider herself a startup. So would a two-person team accepted into a tech accelerator to create a new social network. A 10-person, venture-backed, digital media company is still a startup. How about a 23-month-old iPhone app company with 13 people and no revenue? They're a startup too. But what if that 13-person company is named Instagram and has just been acquired for a billion dollars? Umm ...

Each year in the United States there are millions of people starting up something (like a dog-walking service or an iPhone app) on their own. Of these, approximately 3 million actually incorporate their businesses. Of those, approximately 600,000 both incorporate and hire at least one person other than the founder.

How does one of those 600,000 employer businesses go from being a gleam in an entrepreneur's eye to a billion-dollar corporation? It's a process with many steps that the would-be entrepreneur needs to understand and master. But a potential angel investor needs to understand the process as well, since the angel plays a critical part in that process in an intelligent, productive, and effective way. So let's examine what happens at each step along the path of a startup as it grows from a speck of an idea into a living, breathing organism with the potential to build meaningful wealth and to change the world—or at least a part of it.

Financial Stages of a Startup

Stage 1: The entrepreneur's own money is the first cash in the business. Entrepreneurs should not even think about trying to raise money from anyone else until they have reached deep into their own pockets, for two reasons: First, the bald fact is that investors no longer fund ideas. In an era of increasing technology and decreasing costs, the expectation is that the entrepreneur will be bringing an operating company with at least some traction. After all, as an investor, given two teams equal in entrepreneur, market, business model, and potential, why should you invest in one that exists on paper, when the other has reduced its risk and improved its viability by actually getting started?

The second reason is that investors want to know that the entrepreneur believes in his own startup … and the best proof of this is to show that he has put his own money in. Any cash invested by the entrepreneur will remain in the company as *founders' equity*, and will come back to him only at the time of a successful exit in which the other investors make money.

I'm often asked by entrepreneurs, "How much do I need to invest of my own money before an investor will step up?" The answer is there is no set amount. Rather, it is relative to the resources of each specific founder. If a 16-year-old high school student who has saved up $5,000 from a decade of running a newspaper delivery route and invested $4,000 of it into the new venture gives me a pitch, I would be completely satisfied. On the other hand, if Elon Musk came looking for seed financing for his latest startup, I'd be delighted at the opportunity, but I'd expect that Elon would have first invested a few dollars of his own—or more likely a few hundred million. As investors, we want our entrepreneurs to have what is known as skin in the game; that is, an amount of their own capital serious enough for them to pay close attention to, ... but not so much that they will be distracted by having to worry about where their next meal is coming from.

In practice this means that, other than the outlier case of the kid with the paper route, it is likely that the first money into a company, up to $25,000 or $50,000, will come from the entrepreneur directly.

Stage 2: The first outside capital is usually raised from friends and family. Although this stage is not required, most startups do raise money from friends and family in the form of equity or loans, to help get the company to a stage at which it is legitimately investable by third parties. The amount raised here can vary significantly based on family resources, but we typically see investments at this stage of $25,000 to $150,000. I've seen a number of cases, however, where well-heeled entrepreneurs and their families start off with $1 million or more.

The important thing is that the money should probably go into the company directly as a *convertible note* (an investment form discussed in detail in Chapter 10) that will convert into the same security as the next professional round, but with a discounted conversion price. However, depending on the personal relationships involved (and on whether or not the family member is an Accredited Investor), the money might actually go in as a personal loan to the entrepreneur. The loaned money would then be invested by the founder as equity in the company, but must be repaid even if the company fails.

Stage 3: The entrepreneur begins fundraising. This phase is a combination of weapons of mass destruction and sniper fire. In the same way that you, as an angel, are looking under every rock for a great entrepreneur, so is the founder of a startup looking in every nook and cranny for a great investor. The entrepreneur, if he is smart, will start by letting everyone know that he has a great startup looking for early investors. And I mean *everyone*. I have been led to deals by my barber, my interns, my cousin, my high school classmates ... even my mother. So keep your eyes and ears open for leads to interesting investment opportunities, even from the most unexpected sources.

At the same time, the entrepreneur must research which specific investors would be productive to approach. Some angels only invest in their home city, others only invest $5,000 at a time, others only invest in biotech opportunities. Blindly sending a business plan or PowerPoint deck to every angel and VC in the world will have zero effect, and simply clogs the system while annoying everyone—the smart entrepreneur knows this and behaves accordingly.

Stage 4: The entrepreneur should consider applying to one of the new breed of accelerators. A relatively recent development in the startup world, these organizations typically provide several months of intensive mentoring—together with small but meaningful stipends for company founders—at the end of which they host a Demo Day to introduce their graduating companies to a number of local angel investors. While Y Combinator (based in Silicon Valley) and TechStars (with several locations and affiliates around the world) are two of the best known, there are dozens of others: local, national, and international, many specializing in specific areas (including fashion, food, finance, gaming, and more). We'll examine the world of accelerators and incubators in Chapter 15.

Accelerators are an interesting sidestep when it comes to the usual trajectory of fundraising, valuations, and amounts raised. Rather than negotiate with each company and set valuations based on the company's traction to date, accelerators tend to be extremely selective in the participants they accept into their programs, and thus come from a position of strength. While there is some variation, most accelerators provide investments of $25,000 to $50,000 to cover the team's expenses during the three months of the program in exchange for 5 to 6 percent of the company's equity (which works out to roughly a $500K valuation: low for a typical high-growth startup, but made up for—at least in theory—by the mentoring, contacts, and support from the accelerator).

Stage 5: Enter the angels, either independently or in groups. As a very rough range, from $150,000 to $1.5 million in invested capital, the entrepreneur enters angel territory, either by lucking into one rich and generous angel, or (more likely) by pulling together either a group of individuals (at $10,000 to $100,000 each), or one or more organized angel groups, or one or more micro-VCs (colloquially known as "*super angels*"). Depending on the circumstances, these more-or-less professional, arms-length investors will fund their money either in the form of a convertible note (with a cap on valuation), or in a Series Seed or Series A convertible preferred stock round, using similar documentation to that used by venture capitalists. (These terms will be explained in some detail in Chapter 10.)

The angel stage is the heart of this book, and the following chapters deal in detail with the specifics of how angels source and make investments, and the intricacies surrounding discovery, diligence, term sheet negotiation, valuation, investment forms, and more.

During this period and each of the subsequent fundraising episodes in a company's life, the most important goal for the entrepreneur is to identify a lead investor or champion. For many reasons—most notably limited experience/skill in the case of a novice angel, and limited bandwidth/capital in the case of an experienced angel—this is often a challenge. The *deal lead* will be critical in rounding up other investors, drafting a term sheet, and getting the deal done. He or she will be the entrepreneur's primary champion and often mentor. The lead investor can vouch for the entrepreneur other investors in their circle or who follow them on online financing platforms. Finding a lead is one of the most frustrating challenges for a startup entrepreneur—but it is also one of the most important.

Angel groups are an interesting and useful way for new angels to get their wings wet. There are hundreds of these groups across the United States and around the world, and the majority of them accept applications from entrepreneurs over the transom through Gust (although, of course, a personal connection is always valuable). An invitation to come in for a preliminary screening by an angel group provides the entrepreneur with an opportunity to present her business to experienced investors, yielding pitching experience and solid feedback on the business plan. (A discussion of these groups from the perspective of an angel-investor member is in Chapter 17.)

Stage 6: Venture capital and the Series A crunch. After angels have been tapped for whatever funds they can supply (generally no more than $1 to $2 million), the company has to deliver on its rosy projections. Just as the majority of companies that raise money from friends and family never make it to the angel stage, the vast majority of companies—90 to 95 percent or more—that are funded by angels never see venture financing. It is this tough winnowing process that periodically has entrepreneurs bemoaning the apparent crunch in funding once they begin to need large amounts of cash.

For the successful/lucky ones that do make it, they will raise amounts from roughly $1.5 million (perhaps from one or two seed-stage funds joining together) up to $5 million to $10 million (likely from one or two traditional venture funds). In either case, these professional investors will almost certainly be investing in the form of convertible preferred stock (discussed in Chapter 10) using something like the National Venture Capital Association's Model Series A documents. They will likely make their first investment about half of what they're prepared to put in, with the rest coming in one or more follow-on rounds if the entrepreneur successfully executes the business plan.

Stage 7: Growth capital and the letters beyond B. Finally, north of $10 million to $20 million in total capital raised, the entrepreneur will be getting money from a later-stage VC growth fund, whose paperwork will be similar to the earlier venture capitalists. They will put in much larger amounts of cash in successive rounds of convertible preferred stock investments (known as Series B, Series C, Series D, and so on) but the business valuation will be much higher, so they may end up with a smaller stake than the earlier investors (who likely would have continued to invest in each round in order to maintain their percentage ownership).

At this point, the role of the early angel investor will change dramatically. In the early days of the company's life, angels are perceived as heavenly beings bringing cash, validation, advice, connections, and other good things. They may have a seat on the board of directors, and may get used to speaking with the entrepreneurial CEO every few months, or even weeks. This close relationship begins to weaken when the venture fund comes along, at which point the angel will probably step down from the board. By the time the later-stage fund enters the picture, to the entrepreneur the angel is typically only a fond memory of days gone by. But like children leaving the nest after college, this is generally a good and natural thing, freeing the angel to get involved with the next generation of startups, and letting the company play in the big leagues. Provided the initial investors haven't been overly diluted by this point, this is normal and not something that should be resisted.

Stage 8: The public or private exit. Once the later stage funds have provided the company with the cash it needs to generate value, the focus shifts to the long-term future of the venture, and, more important, how to provide liquidity for the company's founders and investors. The choices here are typically an acquisition by a larger company, or entering the public markets through an initial public offering (IPO).

The former path is much more common than the latter, but in both cases the company's investors are able to see the fruits of their prescience and bold actions. While the bulk of acquisitions happen in the $30 million to $50 million range after a Series A or Series B round, if the original investments were priced correctly, those exits can often return 10 to 20 times to the company's early investors. And, in the unlikely case of an IPO (which would typically happen only after several later stage investment rounds), the returns can be 100x or more.

Although the foregoing steps comprise the canonical progression of startup financing, keep in mind that the number of companies that go all the way through it is very, *very* small. A majority of companies started in the United States begin and end with the first stage: the founders' own money. The number of companies able to get outside funding then begins to drop by orders of magnitude: the percentages (again, very rough) are that 25 percent of startups will get friends-and-family money; 2.5 percent will get angel money; 0.25 percent will get early-stage VC money; and probably 0.025 percent will make it to later-stage VC funds, with only one or two dozen startups (out of the 600,000 that started) making it to an IPO.

But the great thing about approaching angel funding in a professional manner is that you can actually make money at *any* of these stages, provided the company stays alive. How to do that will be what I discuss in the next part of this book.

PART

II

The Nuts and Bolts

Develop Your Deal Flow

Sourcing and Identifying
High-Potential Opportunities

In Chapter 3, I talked about angel investing as a numbers game, and that to make the Law of Large Numbers work in your favor you need to invest in many different startups. Just as critical, however, is that the startups in which you invest must have a decent chance of being successful. Since most startups will *not* be successful, the trick to making this work is the Law of Large Numbers—Part II.

The way that the world's finest universities turn out the brightest, most successful graduates is that they start by enrolling the brightest and most successful applicants. Yale, Harvard, Stanford, and their ilk do their best to get a large number of the country's top students to apply for entrance. They send admissions representatives to every major high school; they use the SAT mailing list to recruit top scorers; they prevail on their alumni to host regional parties to attract local student leaders. In 2013, those three schools alone had 75,000 applicants. Having welcomed all those applications with open arms, the schools then proceed to winnow their applicant pool to the 6 to 7 percent they eventually accept.

As an angel investor you will do the same thing, but you must be even *more* ruthless than the Ivy-est of the Ivies. For every investment I make this year, there had better be 40 serious, passionate entrepreneurs sitting on my doorstep, of whom I will only invest in one. That means I need to be three times pickier than Yale, Harvard, and Stanford when it comes to the decision process. It also means that I must develop extensive top-of-the-funnel opportunities from which I will choose the ones on which I place my bets.

Thanks to the recent development of online platforms that have fundamentally changed the nature of the discovery process (thousands of new startups every month post their investor-focused profiles on Gust), it is easier than at any time in history to seek out innovative, exciting opportunities.

The best and most successful angels spend much of their time proactively looking for hidden startup gems, an advantage described by venture capitalists as *proprietary deal flow*. What follows are some of the routes that you can use to develop your own opportunities, so that your investments will ultimately be selected from a pool containing the entrepreneurial equivalents of only 800 SAT, 4.0 GPA, class valedictorians who are curing cancer while conducting symphony orchestras and tutoring underprivileged children.

Personal Connections

To broaden the range of opportunities they see, and to insure that those they do see are the kinds of companies they're looking for, many angels prefer to have opportunities referred to them from people they know. That is not because they're elitist, but because experience has shown that the odds favor ventures where a known, trusted entity has done the preliminary vetting.

This is actually easier than it sounds. In today's hyper-connected world, it is practically impossible not to know someone who knows someone who knows the entrepreneur who would be a perfect match for your portfolio. In my case, there are over 16,000,000 people who can reach out to me through a first-, second-, or third-degree connection on LinkedIn, the business networking website. Do the math and you will probably find that the numbers in your case are comparable. Personal connections are also important in the context of online funding platforms like Gust, where you can specify that the only opportunities you want to see are ones that have been referred by someone you know.

While there will always be cases where early-stage investors cold-call cool companies whose sites they have happened across, and thereby discover the great success story of the next decade, such instances of serendipity are rare. Many investors will tell you that the majority of their investments are sourced from personal networks they have cultivated over the course of their careers. These include companies referred by CEOs whom the investor has already backed; other investors with whom the investor co-invests; and people with whom the investor worked at other points in his career.

Personal connections are also a good way to find companies that match your personal interests, talents, background, and other nonfinancial resources. In the real world, money is fungible, so given two potential investments with an equal shot at success, the decision will come down to externalities such as connections, wisdom, integrity, interpersonal relationships, and other intangibles.

For precisely these reasons, angels appreciate it when an entrepreneur with an interesting deal can explain why that particular angel is someone they want as an investor. After all, would you want someone to marry you just for your money? Or would you prefer to hear that they are dating you because they feel you would be a great life partner?

Beyond personal connections, a major source of opportunities (particularly for early stage and seed deals looking for initial rounds of funding) is direct approaches from entrepreneurs who have seen, heard, or read about the investor, and believe that the investor would be a strong addition to their team. That's why some of the best angels have the best deal flow: they go out of their way to contribute to the community through writing blogs, speaking at conferences, and tweeting out interesting industry-related items. In Chapter 15 I'll talk more about how you can contribute to the ecosystem of angel investing in such a way that you can benefit from a great flow of potential deals.

Angel Groups

If you are just getting started in angel investing and don't have many personal startup contacts yet, an excellent strategy is to join a local group of established angel investors that actively welcomes new members at the level at which you're planning to invest. I'll discuss angel groups in depth in Chapter 17, but let me note that when angel investors band together and put out the welcome mat for submissions, they typically receive dozens or more applications each month and have a multistep process through which they review opportunities. This is a great way to get ready-made, prefiltered deal flow and a lot of collegial handholding as you learn the ins and outs of angel investing.

Meetups

In 2001, soon after the dot-com crash, New York entrepreneurs Scott Heiferman and Matt Meeker founded a website with an unusual premise: to persuade people to turn off their computers and meet off-line. Meetup.com was born, and today it is used by over 15 million people in over 150,000 groups to organize nearly half a million local, in-person, get-togethers each month. Thousands of these meetups relate directly to new ventures, startup entrepreneurs, and innovative companies. In most cases, the program for the meetup will include demonstrations—often the first public showing—of products or services from one or more intriguing startups seeking seed funding.

Our local startup group in New York is the NY Tech Meetup founded by Scott himself with Dawn Barber, which now has over 38,000 members (the single largest group on the Meetup platform). Of course we can't fit all our members into a lecture hall at the same time, so competition is tough for the 800 inexpensive tickets available each month. During the two-hour meeting, a dozen companies will demonstrate their new products. It was at one of these events that I first saw Social Bicycles and chased the CEO down the hall pleading to be allowed to invest.

Even if none of the demonstrating companies catches your fancy, the odds are good that many other attendees may have a cool startup themselves. Regularly attending one or more of your local tech/startup meetups is a great way to discover new deal flow and to integrate your-self into the fabric of your local entrepreneurship ecosystem. You can find a schedule of all local meetups at www.meetup.com.

Business Plan Competitions

With entrepreneurship having become mainstream, most busi-ness schools and many universities have integrated business plan competitions into their academic programs and extracurricular activ-ities. In the old days, these were just what the name implied: events at which students would present theoretical plans for new businesses. Over the past few years, however, they have evolved into pitch events for real companies that have already been started, and in many cases are already generating revenue. Participants may include students, professors, and alumni, and the companies that present are usually at the perfect stage for angels to become involved. It was at the NYU Business Plan Competition that I first saw Pinterest, Comixology, CourseHorse, Social Bomb, and other exciting ventures.

Startup Conferences and Launch Events

The big brothers of business plan competitions are major industry events where new companies apply to be selected for introduction to investors, the press, and potential corporate partners. Some of these events are specifically focused on new company introductions, and the audience sees every presentation. Others are general industry con-ferences that include a startup competition or launch segment as one part of the scheduled program. Among the annual industry events that have competitive launch venues for new startups are the following:

DEMO. This is the matriarch of launch conferences, at which I introduced my first tech company, Ex Machina, in 1991, and Gust, 20 years later. Produced by the computer industry media giant IDG, DEMO has high production values and is a good way to see 50 to 75 companies launch at the same time. The primary requirement for pre-senters is that they launch a new product or company at the event. The audience tends to be corporate-, investor-, and press-focused, and launches include a mix of new startups and new products from major companies.

TechCrunch Disrupt. Disrupt, when it was first held in 2008 under the name of TechCrunch40, was the brash newcomer, taking on DEMO head to head. In the years since AOL acquired the TechCrunch website and conference, Disrupt has grown in size and spread to other cities, becoming an expected stop on the launch path of many startups. With companies exhibiting in Disrupt's Startup Alley, presenting on stage, or competing in its Disrupt Battlefield, these conferences can showcase over 200 startups competing for investors' attention.

South by Southwest. SXSW, as it is universally known, began as a spring Music Festival in Austin, Texas. It soon added a Film Festival before the music events and then layered on an interactive conference, showcasing panels, sessions, and exhibits from tech and media companies. The Interactive Festival includes a multiday startup competition known as the Accelerator (for which I have served as a judge on several occasions), and hundreds of lectures, panels, launches, and other activities throughout Austin for an entire week. SXSW is a rapidly growing powerhouse on the startup scene.

CES. The International Consumer Electronics Show, held every January in Las Vegas, is a good place to do tech-investing homework. The value to an investor of attending this mammoth, week-long show (aside from the general fun and parties) is to get an immersive, instant overview into the current state of consumer electronics technology. While it is too noisy and crowded for a small company to launch a product effectively (with the possible exception of smaller, CES-based launch venues like ShowStoppers, or the CES Startup Pavilion), if you want to stay up to speed with the pace of technological advancement, CES can be a good experience.

Other conferences and events that showcase new and exciting startups include the Launch Festival in San Francisco, produced by Jason Calacanis; VatorSplash, from the team at Vator.tv; SoCap, presenting social ventures "at the intersection of money and meaning"; Early Stage East, produced by David Freschman; Ingenuity from the New York Venture Capital Assocation; FashInvest, showcasing fashiontech startups; and many events produced annually by SIIA, the Software & Information Industry Association. There are specialized conferences in every industry segment, from financial services to clean technology, publishing to fashion, education to enterprise software.

At such conferences, startups introduce their product or service to the public for the first time, often by demonstrating on stage, exhibiting at a booth, putting out press releases, and opening the doors to their initial public users. You will usually have the opportunity to see a short demonstration of the product or site, and then be able to speak directly with the company's founders.

Accelerator Demo Days

There has been an explosion of startup incubators and seed accelerator programs in recent years, most modeled after the successful Y

Combinator accelerator in Silicon Valley founded by Paul Graham. These programs, such as TechStars, Wayra, DreamIt! Ventures, Launchpad, Astia, Founder Institute, and others, do an amazing job of raising the level of entrepreneurial startups. I will discuss the role of accelerators at greater length in Chapter 15, but now just note that each accelerator program, which typically lasts three months, ends with a Demo Day, to which a number of local angel investors and venture capitalists are invited. These are something like a debutante's coming out party, and the onstage presentations by the companies are such exquisite productions that you may be tempted to write checks immediately to all 15 to 20 companies.

Online Deal Sources

Finally, the fastest growing sources of opportunities—in terms of sheer numbers—are online equity funding platforms for Accredited Investors. Although Gust is the largest of these platforms, there are many smaller ones already in operation, and more being established every month.

Many of these websites curate a limited number of startup companies seeking funding, list them online, and then let individual investors put in small amounts of money that is combined with that of other investors to fund the company. With estimates of as many as 300 funding platforms launched or in the works following the passage of the JOBS Act of 2012, it is important that prospective investors do their due diligence on the platform before they look at specific companies. Among the reputable online funding sites already in operation are Seedrs, SecondMarket, and AngelList. As noted previously, there are also specialized sites that deal in film funding (Slated), consumer brands (Circle Up), real estate (Realty Mogul), accelerator graduates (Funders Club), and other industries.

Deal Brokers

What if you are approached by a startup that is using a paid advisor to find investors? This person is called a broker, *finder*, or intermediary, although they may sometimes style themselves as investment bankers. Most angels, and virtually all organized angel groups, tend to be averse to participating in brokered funding rounds.

There are many reasons for this, but in essence early-stage investors want all their cash going into the company, not out the door to an intermediary. They also have personal networks for deal sourcing that make them pro-active investors, rather than re-active. Finally, anyone receiving money in exchange for helping in the sale or purchase of stock must be registered as a broker/dealer under the rules of the U.S. Securities Exchange Commission. In my experience, the majority of intermediaries who approach me about funding a company are *not* broker/dealers, and thus operate outside the SEC rules, which is never a good thing.

The situation is different, however, in private equity, even at the low end, where brokers are the norm, not the exception. And there are certain groups of investors, such as family offices or casual angels, who may be more likely to consider brokered opportunities.

What to Expect When You Meet a Founder

There is a huge imbalance between the number of would-be business founders (millions) and the number of serious investors looking for startups in which to put their money (thousands). If you are a serious investor, you can expect to be courted by company founders—if not besieged by them. You will need to exercise patience, discipline, tolerance, and a willingness to say a polite but firm "No" when necessary to retain some semblance of sanity when deluged by startup pitches— many are likely to be unattractive or inappropriate for your personal investment preferences and goals.

I spend a lot of time counseling entrepreneurs on the ways they interact with investors, with the goal of making the conversations between these two mutually dependent parties as interesting and productive as possible. I urge company founders to be respectful of the limited time and energy of investors. That means, among other things, holding back on setting up meetings until the founder is ready to pitch. And "ready to pitch" means having a product in the market (or at least a prototype done), a team assembled (or at least the key people), a well-crafted financial plan, and a clear and detailed investor pitch refined and rehearsed, with all the necessary backup materials in one place (such as a company profile on Gust).

The bottom line is that you need to avoid wasting time scrutinizing startups that are not ready for prime time. But once you've begun to have a flow of possible investment ideas cross your desk, the next challenge—an even bigger one—is to identify opportunities worthy of your time, attention, energy, and (ultimately) money. Which companies deserve your in-depth scrutiny? I'll tackle that question in the next chapter.

6

Bet the Jockey, Not the Horse

Evaluating the Entrepreneur and Picking the Right One to Back

TECHNIQUES OF EVALUATING companies for their potential as investments have been studied and practiced by some of the business world's most brilliant minds, from Graham and Dodd (authors of the classic book on investment analysis) to Warren Buffett. Still, investment analysis remains more art than science—and nowhere is this more true than in the field of startup investing, where clues to identifying tomorrow's superstars are particularly elusive.

The number one thing I look at when making a startup investment is the quality of the entrepreneur. In this, I—and a majority of professional angel investors—follow the old adage: "Bet the jockey, not the horse." There are countless examples in which a great entrepreneur has taken a moderately good idea and ridden it to outstanding success—but very few in which a mediocre entrepreneur has turned a great idea into a smash hit. A great entrepreneur—especially one backed by an outstanding team—can tweak, improve, and refocus a business idea as needed, while a mediocre entrepreneur is likely to ruin the promise of a brilliant business concept.

If I have to choose between a great business idea and a great entrepreneur, I'll take the entrepreneur every time.

Some early-stage investors consider technology the key to all web-based businesses, and set their store by hacker culture which places primary importance on the founder's technical skill. Others, particularly those specializing in retail-oriented startups, would bet the farm on a founder with amazing sales skills. For me, the calculus is somewhat different.

Entrepreneurship is at the core of starting a company, whether tech-based or otherwise. It is not to be confused with the functional skills of coding or selling or business operations. Instead, it consists of a combination of character, skills, knowledge, experience, and willingness to take risks that brings together all of these pieces and creates an enterprise that fills a value-producing role in our economy. The entrepreneurial function can be combined in the same package as a technical expert (Bill Gates), a salesman (Richard Branson), a user-experience maven (Steve Jobs), or a financial wizard (Mike Bloomberg). But no matter how the skills are packaged, the most important person in a startup is the entrepreneur.

What Makes a Great Entrepreneur?

Integrity. The *sine qua non*. This is what I listen for first when I meet any company founder, and if I don't get an internal reading that the entrepreneur is completely forthright and square, I don't go further, no matter how much potential I see in the company. Period.

Passion. The entrepreneurial life is tough, and starting a business is as much a labor of the heart as of the mind. The entrepreneur needs to have something driving him or her through the sleepless nights and agonizing days of getting a company off the ground. Passion comes in many flavors: some loud, some internalized; some verbal, some shown by actions. It doesn't matter to me if the passion is the quiet passion of a James Earl Jones or the loud passion of a Jim Cramer—but it had better be there. Passion alone doesn't make a successful entrepreneur. But without it, all the talent, intelligence, and experience in the world is not likely to produce impressive results.

Startup experience. The old saying, "I'd prefer that you learned how to shave on someone else's whiskers," certainly applies to startups. This is so important that I will be devoting a whole section to it.

Domain expertise. I am regularly amazed to hear pitches from people who have no background in the industry they are attempting to enter. While newcomers can often bring a valuable outside-the-box perspective to an industry, my experience has shown me, again and again, the importance of understanding the market in which you hope to operate. If an entrepreneur approaches me with an online payment-related venture and the founder has no background in banking, finance, debit cards, billing, accounting, or related fields, I would likely pass without digging into any other element of his proposal.

Operating skills. A startup requires the same major job functions as a large company. The only difference is that the founder often has to fill every one of them personally. So it's helpful if the entrepreneurial package includes skills in product development, sales and marketing, finance, operations, business development, fundraising, and so on. The more of these skills the founder has, the better the company's chance of succeeding.

Leadership ability. If the entrepreneur is not a ninja-coder-saleswoman-finance wizard, then he or she needs to recruit other people to fill those roles. For a risky startup on a small budget, finding A+ players and then inspiring them to greatness is difficult, and much of the success or failure of the venture will come down to the leadership qualities of the CEO. I look for these both on paper (Has this person ever led anything?) and in person (What kind of feeling do I get from talking with her? Would I follow her through fire in pursuit of our shared goals? Has she ever built a team before? Can she attract and manage talent?)

Commitment to the venture. There's an old saying that when it comes to a ham-and-egg breakfast, "the chicken is interested but the pig is committed." So it is with angels and entrepreneurs. I am interested in all of my portfolio companies … but I go home at the end of the day and get a good night's sleep. My CEOs don't have that luxury. The minute they take my money, they need to be committed to staying with the venture until I pry it from their cold, dead fingers. The last thing I want is a founder who will cut and run the first time the going gets tough.

Long-term vision. Because of the hits-oriented nature of startup investing, I want to see a light at the end of the tunnel. Entrepreneurs must be able to convince me of their vision to create something significant and meaningful—with the potential to change the world. Just as a great athlete is able to swing *through* the point of impact in golf or baseball toward a target hundreds of yards away, founders should be able to aim for the stars while carrying out the day-to-day operations of their business.

Realism and pragmatism. At the same time, a starry-eyed dreamer without feet on the ground does not make for a viable company. I need to see a hardheaded business person in total command of a startup's numbers, customers, channels, sales projections, production costs, and more. I have no problem with optimism as a trait, but it has to be optimism based on a realistic understanding of how things work. I don't want to hear vague, rosy promises like, "We'll attract 10 percent of our addressable market." Instead, I want to know who the first customer is. The second. The third. Through which channel they will each be recruited, and at what cost. And will they reorder?

Flexibility. If there has ever been a startup in which everything went off without a hitch, I haven't heard of it. In all cases, *something* is going to go not as planned, and the entrepreneur needs to be able to adapt and pivot if necessary to deal with problems and to take advantage of opportunities. That's how startup Tote turned into blockbuster Pinterest, and how the comic book cataloging site and blog Iconology turned into the digital-comics superstore, Comixology.

Even temperament. I confess that this last requirement is a personal bias of mine *not* universally shared by other investors. But for me, life is too short to deal with prima donnas or high-volume fights with temperamental founders. At the risk of losing out on some great economic possibilities, I will only invest in founders with whom I have a professional, mutually respectful relationship. I can do this because—like you—I am investing out of my own pocket, rather than bearing a fiduciary responsibility to others, thus I have the option of taking that risk.

Are Startups a Young Person's Game? How Young?

Many people assume that all entrepreneurs are young, especially in the high-tech world. This is often true, but there are countless exceptions. And the quality of an entrepreneur has nothing to do with age *per se*. I know world-class entrepreneurs who are 15, and others who are 90. I was once asked by a precocious young entrepreneur if I would consider investing in a 14-year-old. I replied that I would have no problem, subject to four caveats:

1. The deal needs to make sense. That means I would scrutinize and judge the 14-year-old founder the same way I would a 35-year-old. If youngsters want to play in the big leagues, fine—but they shouldn't expect to get cut any slack because of their age.
2. Minors—entrepreneurs or otherwise—are unable to sign legally binding contracts. That means I would require a responsible adult to structure and sign the paperwork on the young entrepreneur's behalf. I need to be able to enforce my contracts.
3. Typically, when we fund entrepreneurs, we expect them to work 24/7 and put in blood, sweat, and tears to make the company a success. Young founders need to show me (along with their parents) how they are able to put in the time and energy required to make a startup successful, while ...
4. Completing school. Unlike my colleague, Peter Thiel, who is paying young entrepreneurs to drop out, I swing the other way. I insist that the founder show me a plan (and a commitment in writing) to finish high school and college, regardless of whether the company is a success or a failure.

Given all of the above, I'm open to the idea of investing in a very young entrepreneur.

I haven't yet invested in any junior-high-school-aged founders. But I have invested in young entrepreneurs who were still in school. One of my portfolio companies (which received a Series A round from a top-tier VC) has two cofounders. While the business partner (and CEO) works full-time on the company, the tech partner (and CTO) works part-time while finishing his PhD at MIT.

I know of students (at Penn and Yale, respectively) who started their companies during their summer breaks, and received a limited amount of angel funding that allowed them to keep the company going while finishing their degrees. Some schools, including Yale and Columbia, actually have official programs that provide stipends or investments for student-founded companies conditioned on the student staying in school. First Round Capital, one of the country's leading early-stage venture capital funds, has established a network of Dorm Room Funds—special seed funds run *by* college students, to identify and invest *in* college students.

The issue here is the trade-off between full-time, single-minded, skin-in-the-game, live-or-die commitment to the entrepreneurial venture (*very* hard to pull off if the founder's primary focus is elsewhere), and the strong (although not unanimous) belief among leading investors that a college education is a good thing, and that the entrepreneur (and hence the company) will be better off in the long run if the founder shows the maturity to understand the value that comes from education.

Instead of age, I like to focus on personality traits. Whether I'm considering investing in a 25-year-old or a 55-year-old, I want to know the answers to questions such as:

- How much energy does the entrepreneur have?
- How technologically up to date is the entrepreneur?
- Can he put in the 24/7 work day I expect from my CEOs?
- How much of a meaningful cash commitment has been made?
- How much of a salary does she expect during startup time?
- How willing is the entrepreneur to take advice?
- How much optimism and enthusiasm do I see?
- What does the previous life/work/startup experience show?
- What do I learn when checking personal references?

I don't know any entrepreneur who works less than 60 hours a week, and many work much longer hours. Entrepreneurship is an all-in sport ... which means that real founders are working on—or at least thinking about—their ventures 168 hours a week (yes, that's 24/7). This is *not* conducive to having the same work/life balance as in a normal job. That's probably why another critical component of a successful entrepreneurial enterprise is spousal support.

Serial Entrepreneurs versus First Timers

Starting a company is not easy, and unfortunately there is no way to learn other than by doing. No book, school, mentoring, or apprenticeship can substitute for hands-on experience. When you consider that doctors spend a minimum of two years in premed, four years in medical school, one year in internship, and two years in residency before you put yourself in their hands, think how investors feel putting hundreds of thousands—or millions—of dollars into the hands of a startup team with no experience. Isn't creating a viable company at least as difficult as treating a patient?

Several studies have shown a positive correlation between past and future entrepreneurial success, but the same studies showed *no* correlation between past entrepreneurial *failure* and future success. Therefore, it is logical for investors to lean toward experienced entrepreneurs, because it increases the odds in their favor.

In addition, from a purely pragmatic perspective, first-time entrepreneurs require a great deal of support, mentoring, and handholding, which is an unspoken deal that both sides subscribe to going into the relationship. This takes time, and time is the scarcest commodity for successful people.

So, given all of the points above, why should we *ever* invest in first-time entrepreneurs? The answer is that every successful serial entrepreneur was once a first-timer. Investors would have missed out on Steve Jobs, Bill Gates, and Mark Zuckerberg if they hadn't taken the chance on a newbie.

What About Tech Savvy?

The current stereotype of an entrepreneur is a young computer geek who grew up writing programming code in a garage somewhere. And of course in the twenty-first century, even businesses that don't appear to be high-tech businesses are crucially dependent on technological tools. Does this mean that tech savvy should be on a list of crucial characteristics of a successful entrepreneur?

It depends on how one defines "tech savvy."

An analogy is to ask if you need to be "auto savvy" to drive around the United States today. If the question means, "Do I need to know how to operate a car, be comfortable fueling my vehicle at a gas station, and understand the difference between a sports car, an SUV, a panel van, and a semi-trailer?," the answer is an absolute yes.

On the other hand, if the question means, "Do I need to be able to take apart a carburetor, replace my timing belts, and rebore my cylinders?," the answer is a resounding no.

The tech translation would be: "Does an entrepreneur need to be able to code in Python, understand the technical differences between Postgres and MySQL, and architect a high-speed trading system ?" No.

But: "Does an entrepreneur need to understand the concepts of things such as cloud computing, APIs, and search engine optimization, be able to craft a basic query on Google and know the key differences between LinkedIn, Facebook, Yahoo!, and Quora?" Yes!

What About Education?

It is fashionable in this fast-paced era of exponentially accelerating technology to deride the value of a traditional MBA. Some people believe that even an undergraduate degree is not particularly useful for a would-be entrepreneur, and the most vocal adherents of this school of thought are encouraging ambitious young people to drop out of college and start their own businesses.

I could not disagree more.

As a personal rule, I do not invest in college dropouts. While there have certainly been amazingly successful dropouts, I believe that encouraging students to drop out before finishing their undergraduate degrees is a major mistake, and one that could have long-term repercussions for the student and the student's employer.

College is a four-year commitment, which is about the same time commitment one would be expected to put into a startup. If a founder shows by his actions that he doesn't have the self-discipline to finish what he started, and is unable to defer the instant gratification of working on his new business until after graduation, that signals to me that he may do the same thing if I fund him in a startup ... and the last thing I want is for him to run off to the next shiny opportunity without finishing the startup in which I've invested.

At the same time, for a student, taking the long view of life is a sign of maturity. Going for the quick hit of dropping out because she is not willing to put into her academic career the amount of work it takes to do it right is a sign of immaturity.

Finally, if students have discussed this decision with their parents, school advisors, or other mentors, the odds are high that they were strongly advised to stay in school and finish their degree. If that is the case, the fact that they are rejecting reasoned advice from mature, experienced people who know, trust, and support them would give me pause to consider whether they would turn out to be the kind of person who won't listen to advice from me, too ... and I consider my advice to be an even bigger investment in them than the cash I bring to the table.

As for graduate school, whether it is internalizing crucial concepts such as the time value of money or understanding the core values of agile project management, an MBA from a strong program is an indication (along with many other factors) of someone who can potentially make a positive contribution to a business team.

Warning Signs of a Weak Founder

At the end of the day, just as there are behaviors that mark a great entrepreneur, there are other traits that I've learned represent warning signs. Even if a startup business seems otherwise promising, I would think twice about investing in it if its founder exhibits one or more of the following characteristics:

- Perceived lack of integrity (an instant disqualifier)
- Unrealistic assessment of market size
- Unrealistic assessment of competitive offerings
- Unrealistic assessment of competitive advantages
- Unrealistic assessment of execution challenges
- Unrealistic assessment of execution costs
- Unrealistic assessment of timing
- Unrealistic financial projections
- Unrealistic valuation expectations
- Unrealistic declarative statements
- Unrealistic fundamental business idea
- Lack of execution track record
- Lack of domain expertise
- Lack of technical expertise
- Lack of long-term vision
- Lack of historical knowledge of the market space
- Lack of perceived leadership capability
- Lack of perceived communication skills
- Lack of necessary operational skills on the management team
- Lack of perceived ability to grow with the company

- Lack of perceived willingness to accept advice or mentorship
- Lack of carefully considered go-to-market strategy

It takes time to learn to recognize the traits that distinguish a winning entrepreneur from a likely loser. That is another reason why finding ways to generate a flow of potential deals is so important: the more experience you have in meeting, talking with, and evaluating company founders, the better you will become at spotting potential champions.

7

Here Comes the Pitch

Listening to the Story
Does It Make Sense for *Your* Portfolio?

ONCE YOU HAVE identified a potential opportunity it is time to get down to brass tacks and meet with the company. Your first goal is to make an initial determination of whether the entrepreneur has the characteristics listed in Chapter 6, and is the kind of person in whom you'd want to invest. You are also going to run through a basic checklist to see if there are any warning signs that would cause you to pass on the opportunity.

The point here is not to make an investment decision; instead, it's the opposite: you are doing a negative screen to see if there are any issues that would stop you from investing. This is the beginning of a series of rituals that will either result in your deciding not to put money into a particular company (which is what happens in the vast majority of instances) or in your deciding to take the plunge and become a part owner of a fledgling new business.

At the first meeting, for which you should expect to allocate about an hour, the entrepreneur will typically pitch his or her company. There are several ways the entrepreneur may choose to do this, including jumping right into a demonstration of the product or service or simply talking conversationally. However, the most typical approach is for the founder to give a comprehensive overview of the company, 15 to 20 minutes long, supported by a computer-based, on-screen slide presentation usually created with Microsoft's PowerPoint program. In entrepreneur/angel circles you may hear this presentation referred to as a slide deck, a pitch deck, or a PowerPoint.

In 99 percent of cases, the founder/CEO of the startup will be the one to deliver the fundraising pitch. This is as it should be: you are investing in the entrepreneur. If for some reason the company wants someone else to give the pitch, I'd suggest that you ask to reschedule the meeting at a time when the founder/CEO can be with you.

After you've attended more than two or three pitches, you will discover that there are a number of statements that should be taken with a large grain of salt. Some examples:

- "This is absolutely going to be a 100x!"
- "Our financials are conservative."
- "We have no competition."
- "We're unique in that we're social/mobile/local."
- "I know that investors are just waiting to steal my idea."
- "We're Facebook for X."
- "All we need is a 2 percent market share."
- "BigNameVC is really interested in us."
- "We'll do a Series A six months after our seed round."
- "Our competitive advantage is that we're first to market."
- "We're closing next week, and want to squeeze you in."
- "I know you don't invest in Z, but we're the exception."
- "All those investors who turned us down just don't get it."
- "Scott Kurnit got a $100 million valuation for his startup before he had any traction, so obviously we should too."

While I've never laughed outright during a pitch, I've had quite a few occasions where I had to work hard not to wince. But assuming that everything is going along smoothly, now is the time to put on your objective analysis hat, set aside for the moment how sexy and wonderful the opportunity sounds (they all do!), and look closely at the fundamentals of the business.

There are many ways for a business to fail, but for it to succeed, it needs to do just about everything right. That's why successful angels try to look objectively at as many factors as they can, and place their money on companies that can check all (or nearly all) the boxes. Each situation is different, but let me walk you through what we look for during New York Angels' screening sessions when we listen to initial pitches to select the companies that will advance to the next step in our process and present to the whole group. To help structure our analysis, we use a Screening and Valuation Worksheet similar to that used by many other angel groups in the United States. I've included the full rubric in Appendix A, but what follows are the major points.

Strength of the Management Team

Founder's business experience, founder's domain experience, founder's skill set. Suffice to say the entrepreneur/founder is the key to any new venture.

Founder's flexibility. This is not just a willingness to pivot when necessary, but the personal characteristics that will make the entrepreneur easy to work with. One key issue is to figure out up front whether the founder would be willing to step away from the CEO role if it becomes apparent that this would be best for the company.

Completeness of the management team. If the CEO is Superwoman and able to do everything in all areas, this might be something you could overlook, but in the case of mere mortals, it's important to get a good idea of which skills the company has in-house and which need to be hired. Depending on the industry and business model, different roles are more or less critical to a company's success. For a big-data company, a Chief Technology Officer (CTO) with a PhD might be key, whereas for an e-commerce platform you might be legitimately wary if the company were missing a talented and knowledgeable Chief Revenue Officer (CRO).

Size of the Opportunity

Market size for the company's product or service. This is to give you a sense of the scope of the overall industry market. You need to consider the specific amount of money that customers are already spending each year on substitute products for the one that the company you're considering will offer. If all the possible customers in the world are today spending only $20 million or $30 million for similar products or services, it is hard for the entrepreneur to claim that his company is likely to achieve a monster hit. Smart investors look for market segments where people are already spending many hundreds of millions—or, ideally, billions—of dollars, with a growing field of potential customers.

Potential for revenue within five years. There is nothing inherently wrong with a long-payoff venture, such as building a nuclear power plant. However, angel investors (as opposed to venture capital or private equity funds) do not usually have deep pockets. Large-scale, capital intensive ventures that will take a decade or more to generate profits are typically not appropriate for angel funding. The question then becomes how quickly the company will be able to start and increase its revenues, and how likely they are to be within a reasonable time frame (say, five years, beyond which time frame no one can project). You are looking for the answers to two questions:

1. Are the projected revenues enough to make this an interesting and profitable investment? (Hint: A projection of $1 million in sales after five years is not.)
2. Is the entrepreneur realistic about how the world works? (Hint: A projection of $100 million in Year 1 revenues is not.)

Strength of competition. Here, you are looking for the Goldilocks answer: not too much, not too little, but just the right amount. In an ideal world, the company will be entering a space not already overcrowded with entrenched, well-funded competitors. On the other hand, if it truly has no competitors, that should be a warning sign to a savvy angel investor. *Why* are there no competitors? It often means that no one currently thinks that what the company is doing is worth paying for.

Product or Service

Product/market definition. If the product or service is something generic that everybody will want, because it can do everything—the company may be doomed to failure. You should be looking for a clear, focused, definition of the specific need for it, and who the market will be.

Product/market fit. How well does this specific product fit the market need that has been identified? Even more important, why? As investors, we much prefer to invest in "painkillers" that solve an existing problem, rather than "vitamins" that are simply better/faster/cheaper than an existing solution.

Path to product acceptance. Do people immediately know what it is, why it is of value to them, and how they can use it today? With one of my first major tech products, the AirMedia Live Internet Broadcast Network, we had a technically amazing, patented, award-winning, brilliant solution. Unfortunately, few people at the time were comfortable with the idea of the Internet, fewer still understood the concept of streaming digital broadcast information, and no one had heard of our company or the actual product we were trying to sell. The result, unfortunately, was not pretty. (As Benjamin Franklin wrote, "Experience is a hard school, but some will learn through no other.")

Barriers to entry. How hard is this product or service to copy, and who is likely to copy it? Sure, Google or Apple probably *could* knock it off, but is this something that is likely to face stiff competition in the near term? If so, how would this company emerge as the winner?

Other Issues

Sales channels. How will the product actually get into the hands of customers? Have methods for selling, marketing, and promoting the product been tested and implemented, or do they exist purely in theory?

Stage of business. Is this just an idea? A runaway smash hit with happy, paying, repeat customers? Or is it something in the middle?

Size of this investment round. The size of the whole round and the amount you are being asked to invest. Can you afford the minimum investment level being proposed by the company? Will you end up with a meaningful enough percentage interest to benefit significantly if and when the company is eventually acquired?

Needs for future financing. How far will the current round of seed investment take the company? (Anything less than a year is probably wishful optimism on everyone's part.) What happens if the company can't raise a follow-on round? Will they go out of business? Or could they slash costs and live to fight another day?

Quality of business plan and presentation. While the correlation between the quality of the plan and presentation and prospects for the business isn't perfect, it is more accurate than most entrepreneurs would like to think. If the founder has a clean, comprehensive business plan, presented in a cohesive, persuasive way, the odds are good that the business itself has a better than average chance of succeeding. Conversely, a confusing, sketchy plan presented in a way that is sloppy and unappealing suggests a business that is likely to struggle.

Location. Many angels prefer to invest close to home, so this can be an important filter. A business that is geographically close will be easier for you to monitor and support.

Type of industry. If the industry is based on rapidly advancing and highly cost-effective information technology, that is a plus, because a small angel investment can help such a company go a long distance. So is a business-to-business venture, or even a consumer-facing startup that is highly scalable (that is, susceptible to easy and rapid growth). A traditional business that demands a lot of cash upfront but doesn't provide investors with much leverage can be problematic.

Where Is My Money Going?

In the pitch, the entrepreneur will generally discuss how he plans to use the investment funds raised to help grow the business. How detailed and specific should you expect these plans to be? It depends on the amount of capital to be raised and the context of the projections. The smaller the raise, the more specific and detailed the plans for the use of funds should be, and for a shorter presentation, the projections should be more general.

For example, if a company is raising only $50K, it would likely know—down to a few thousand dollars—what the money would be used for. But if it were raising $5 million, then it would likely round to the hundreds of thousands.

Similarly, in the context of a five-minute elevator pitch or even a 15-minute angel/venture pitch, the projected use of funds would probably be broken down into no more than five to ten chunks. But in the context of a printed business plan, investors should expect to see detailed projections by category.

The pitch should contain clear, specific answers to the most important basic questions about the business and the entrepreneur's plans for the business:

- How will you attract customers and make money? (and no, "advertising" is not the answer)
- Who, specifically, is your first customer? Second? Third?
- What is your contingency plan for when this seed round is exhausted, and you are unable to raise any more?
- What is your interface/platform/partnership strategy?
- How are you going to sell the company, and to whom, within six years?

The answers to these questions need to satisfy you—better yet, *excite* you—before you go any further down the path to signing a deal and handing over a check. Furthermore, the answers need to be backed up with specific information, including a significant amount of quantitative data. Remember, as the investor, you are in the driver's seat. Don't even think about being parted from your cash until you've become convinced that this opportunity represents the best and highest use of a portion of your hard-earned investment money.

Materials You Should Expect to See During the Pitch Process

Since angel investing in most countries is effectively limited to Accredited Investors, these investments are exempt from the registration requirements for publicly traded stocks. They are also exempt from having to provide the detailed information book, known as a Private Placement Memorandum, which would be required if the company were raising funds from any people who were not Accredited. As a result, there are no legal rules determining what—if anything—the company needs to give you. At the same time, there is no requirement for you to invest. So, for example, if you ask for next year's budget and the company refuses to give it to you, you simply won't invest.

That said, because of the risky nature of early-stage investing, it is typical for a company to give you anything and everything you ask for. I assure you that if any entrepreneur refused to give me *anything* I wanted (such as a cap table, customer lists, projected financials, and so on), there is no way that I would invest.

While there is an almost infinite amount of information that an investor can legitimately ask for when doing due diligence on a company, as a potential angel investor you should probably expect to see some or all of the following kinds of materials from an entrepreneur, depending on the style and venue of pitch meeting in which you participate:

Written Documents

- A one-page overview/teaser.
- A two- to three-page executive summary.
- A slide deck specifically designed to be handed out.
- A comprehensive business plan—either a traditional 10- to 20-page written plan or a carefully prepared and annotated *Business Model Canvas*.
- A finished (or prototype) marketing brochure.

For a Live Presentation

- A five-minute quick pitch.
- A 15- to 20-minute angel/VC PowerPoint/Keynote pitch.
- A sub-15-minute organized product/site demonstration.

Online

- A functional public website for the company.
- A short video pitch.
- A dedicated, controlled-access, investor-relations website.

Summary Financials

As angels, we want to see all of a company's past financial information to date and projections of three to four years going forward after funding. Five years would be completely mythical, and even four is really pushing it, but the idea here is to primarily do a gut check to see how large the business could get—or at least how large the entrepreneur *thinks* it could get. Investors need to know the specific financial status of a company before investing, because they are going to be part owners of the business. How much would you be willing to pay someone to take over their bank account if you had no idea how much was in it?

Therefore, it is standard practice for us as investors to require existing financials that document the current state of the company, as well as projected financial statements that give us some idea of what the entrepreneur believes he or she will be able to make, and what it will cost, if we invest.

These financial projections (including not just the operating budget, but also projected revenue and capital raises) will help answer important questions, such as:

- Is the game worth the candle? (Four years out and fully funded, if the company will only generate a couple of million dollars in revenue, it might be a nice business, but it's just not big enough.)
- Is the entrepreneur's operating plan realistic? (We look for reasonable, conservative projections about costs that mesh with what our experience has been. If the entrepreneur shows us a startup management team that costs an average of $250K per person per year, or projected Customer Acquisition Cost of 10 cents, we know that something is off.)
- Is the entrepreneur's revenue vision realistic? (If, four years out, the entrepreneur is showing us $200 million in revenue, we will have serious concerns about his judgment … even though there are companies that have pulled that off.)
- How much more capital will the entrepreneur need to get to breakeven? (Great businesses can always use more capital to fund their success. If the entrepreneur is asking us for a $250,000 investment but will require another $8 million before his business turns the corner, then he is betting everything on finding a VC to rescue us all, and that is unlikely.)
- What do the margins look like? (If the entrepreneur shows $20 million in revenue, but his costs to get that revenue are $19 million, it's probably not an angel-ready business because a small change for the worse could swing the company over the line.)
- How does this budget compare to industry standards? (We hope they show that the entrepreneur knows what he's talking about when it comes to areas like customer acquisition costs, lifetime customer value, revenue per employee, margins, growth rates, and so on.)

Of course, if the company is a brand-new startup which has spent nothing, received no income or investments, and has no assets, then the financial statements will be very simple. On the other hand, there might then be a question as to how much the company is actually worth.

The financial figures given at this point are generally understood to be subject to change over time—often radically so. How much are business plan numbers and revenue projections in initial pre-launch business plans off compared to actual post-launch figures? Oh... roughly the equivalent of the difference between, say, the Gutenberg Bible and *The Cat in the Hat*.

I don't think I have *ever* seen pre-launch projections that turned out to be in the same solar system as real world numbers. Out of 90-plus investments in my portfolio (including several that eventually generated 5–12x returns), not *one* beat its original projections.

So take the financial projections you receive from the founder with a giant grain of salt. But by all means take them! Impressive charts of future revenues and profits may be of doubtful accuracy... but a startup that hasn't thought through its business enough to even generate such charts (or that refuses to share them with you) is not one that a savvy angel should consider funding.

Look Under the Hood
and Lead a Deal

Coordinating Due Diligence
and Running the Show

ONCE YOU'VE DETERMINED that a startup has the qualities you seek in an investment—a great entrepreneur, a solid business idea, impressive growth potential, a viable plan for attracting customers and generating revenue—you should verify that appearance and reality are one. In the business world, this is called doing *due diligence*. The term is derived from a section in the Securities Act of 1933, which says that as long as broker-dealers exercise due diligence (i.e., appropriate care and effort) in their investigation into the company whose stock they are selling, they are not liable for nondisclosure of information that they did not discover. Over time, this was shortened to the two words, and today "due diligence" refers to the practice of carefully checking the details of claims made by any company.

Due diligence is not always a simple matter. In an investment round made up of Accredited Investors, there is no legal requirement for the entrepreneur to provide a prospectus or any specific disclosure schedule, and they are therefore rarely, if ever, provided for an angel round.

Where schedules and lists *do* appear, however, are in due-diligence requests or checklists from serious investors, which the investors' counsel provide to the company prior to closing. Depending on the size of the round and the size and professionalism of the investors (and the budget of their lawyers), the requested information may range from nothing more than a business plan and a slide deck (for an informal seed round), to a voluminous amount of material for a later-stage venture round from a top-tier VC fund.

The closing documents will then generally include a *representations and warranties clause*, in which the entrepreneur swears on a stack of Bibles (backed up by some severe economic penalties) that everything he has previously told you and the other investors is true ... including such promises as "We own all our code" and "We are operating perfectly legally."

In case you are thinking at this point that due diligence is some kind of arcane, technical thing that should be left to the lawyers, I refer you to a 2009 study by Professor Robert Wiltbank of Willamette University. Rob's analysis showed that angel investments in which investors spent more than 20 hours undertaking due diligence prior to investing had twice the likelihood of success as those who spent less time on the process.

What should you look for during your diligence investigation? There are three major categories:

Market diligence covers your independent review of the claims that the company makes regarding the industry into which it is entering. You should verify the market size, competitive players in the market, and industry trends that might affect the company's planned products and/or services roadmap. You do this by conducting online research, talking to people knowledgeable in the field (an excellent use of angel groups), reviewing the reports of analysts, etc.

Business diligence looks into specific claims that the company makes about its own operations. These include its customers (call some to verify that they are indeed customers, and that they are happy), revenues and expenses (look at their books), and the background of the founders. Although this last element is sometimes skipped, you should do as thorough a background check on any individual in whom you invest as you would on anyone you hire. Some angel groups arrange for online background checks on all founders prior to closing. I have included in

Appendix B the Business Diligence checklist that New York Angels uses. We don't require every answer on the list from every company in which we plan to make an investment, but use the list as a reminder of the things we should think about asking.

Legal diligence focuses on the company's structure, documentation, and history, making sure that everything is as claimed. The last thing you want to find out after the closing is that the company's entire source code is actually owned by some outside programmer because the company never effectively acquired ownership of it. Because legal diligence is factual and backed up by documents, this is one area where your lawyer can do much of the heavy lifting.

Here are the general areas we (and our lawyers) want to check:

- Corporate records, including the company's structure, ownership, voting agreements, past minutes of the board of directors meetings.
- Employee benefit plans and other employment matters, including the company's standard employment agreement, payroll records, benefit plans, new employee handbook, contracts for consulting or management agreements.
- Regulatory matters, including any correspondence with local, state, federal, or international governmental agencies.
- Properties, assets, and leases, including lists of all real property owned, leased, or used by the company and all intellectual property developed, whether filed or not.
- Material agreements and financing documents, including all paperwork created in connection with loans, grants, previous angel and venture financing, and bank accounts.
- Marketing, sales and operations background, including signed copies of all license agreements, contracts, promotional materials, and advertising.
- Accounting, financial, and insurance matters, including detailed financial statements for several years, budget and future planning for the next decade, all of the company's insurance policies, and prior insurance claims.
- Legal proceedings, including all litigation (and threats of litigation) against the company, its trademarks and patents.
- All other materials and documents involving the company that may, in your judgment, be material to the business of the company.

Leading a Deal

One of the delights of angel investing is the opportunity to get to know and learn from some of the smartest people in the business world—other angel investors. Within this universe, the lead investor in a particular business has a special role. If, in the context of a startup, the entrepreneur is the Leader, then the lead investor is the First Follower, and has the toughest and most critical role in the financing process. It is impossible to overstate how important this is, even in a world of ready capital and multiple funding sources.

It's a job you may find yourself occupying if you are the lead investor in a startup; in other cases, your role will be to work supportively and productively with another investor who has the lead position. Either way, it is useful to understand why this is such an important role.

Essentially, the lead investor functions as curator, funder, validator, negotiator, Sherpa, cheerleader, mediator, and communicator. Each individual function is like oxygen to a fire—necessary to make the combustion happen, but not sufficient to create fire by itself.

Curation. With hundreds of thousands of companies seeking startup funding every year, there is no way for any one investor to be fully aware of the market or to process personally the flow of available opportunities. The lead investor serves the purpose (relative to the other investors) of identifying the small subset of companies worth looking at. An indication of the value of curation is that on the Gust platform, companies that are listed in collections (such as accelerator Demo Days, or business plan competitions) receive 37 times as many views as do similar companies that have not been curated.

Funding. To be a lead investor, you have to be an investor first—and that means writing a check. Typically, the lead investor writes the first and biggest check in the round and makes it clear that there will be more money available in the future if necessary and appropriate. There is no way to lead a deal without making a direct investment. Angel deals cannot be led by consultants, brokers, intermediaries, or your mother. The lead *must* be a serious—and ideally, a well-known— investor.

Validation. Other angels (and, to an extent, VCs) expect that if I am leading a deal and putting in my own money, I will have done some level of due diligence investigation to confirm basic things including market opportunity, entrepreneur legitimacy, and customer references. When there are multiple investors in a round, the simple fact is that not everyone will check everything first hand, and everyone (officially or unofficially) relies on the deal lead to have done some hard work to validate that this is a great opportunity. While you may not be legally responsible for making good your followers' investments if the company goes out of business, there is a "moral hazard" issue. If the problem turns out to be something that everyone else assumes you, as the lead, should have picked up on, then you risk your reputation and your relationships.

Negotiation. Historically, every early-stage investment was a one-off deal, with every line of 120 pages of documentation negotiated by the parties and their lawyers. While this is changing with the availability of the model documents I'll discuss in Chapter 12, each investment still requires—at a minimum—agreement on the amount of the investment and the valuation. It is the responsibility of the lead to undertake this (often thankless) task, and to work with the entrepreneur to come to a meeting of the minds. The result is then presented to the other investors as a take-it-or-leave-it opportunity.

Sherpa-ing. In the vast majority of cases, an aspiring entrepreneur needs all the help he or she can get in finding additional investors. There are always a few deals that are over-subscribed, but even in the best cases, determining which potential investor to approach can be a challenge. In theory, the angel comes from this world and has much more familiarity than the entrepreneur in knowing which rocks to overturn in the quest for financing. Identifying (and often approaching) investors to fill out the round is a critical activity for the lead.

Cheerleading. Rounding up a gaggle of headless chick…oops, I mean, slightly distracted potential angel investors is a task to drive anyone to drink. The entrepreneur needs to devote most of the business day to actually making the company a success, so the task of keeping in touch with all the prospects (and jollying them along into writing the check) is often the job of the lead angel. The job can be greatly eased by using tools such as Gust to manage the deal book, keeping track of how far along in the process each investor is, but it is still a lot of work.

Mediating. During and after the investment process there will always be discussions, disagreements, requests and offers among the potential investors, and between the investors and the company. It is the role of the deal lead to intercede here, shielding the entrepreneur from bearing the brunt of the questions that inevitably arise from complex relationships. This also means acting as a "fair and neutral party." It means informing the other investors that "No, a 4x preference is not an effective deal structure," while simultaneously letting the company know that, "Yes, every preferred stock deal *does* include weighted average anti-dilution provisions."

Communicating. Once the deal is consummated, the lead investor has a responsibility to the other investors to serve as their primary representative to the company, and their primary or secondary vehicle for updates as to what is happening inside. Often, the deal lead will take a board seat that provides even more insights into what is happening, albeit sometimes at the cost of not being able to share confidential information with other investors.

Because all of this is tough, time-consuming, and takes work and skill (not to mention a solid reputation), it is difficult for any one angel (or VC, for that matter) to lead a large number of deals regularly. In one recent year New York Angels was named the most active angel group in the country. Of the 21 deals that the group did that year, we led six of them as the primary group. And of those six, I personally led four of the rounds.

While the effort is overwhelming, the results can be rewarding. I am not a big-ticket investor who writes giant checks. But because I am good at playing first follower to strong entrepreneurial leaders, I am often in the unique position where I can lead a large round in a cool company with a small personal investment. This gives me access to opportunities that I might not have otherwise had. Leading an investment round is not rocket science, but it often seems to require the same level of effort and stamina that it took to go to the moon.

If this sounds like work you might relish, by all means look for opportunities to be the lead investor on a deal that you find attractive. Meanwhile, in the more typical role of follower rather than leader, be sure you understand the special effort that the lead investor provides and do whatever you can to make his or her life easier. You, your fellow investors, and the company will all benefit as a result.

Valuations and Expectations

Discovering the
Secret Economics of the Angels

EVERYTHING DISCUSSED SO far, from finding new opportunities and identifying winning entrepreneurs to analyzing startups for their potential and carefully verifying the information they provide, serves one thing, and one thing only: making money from your investment. While this sounds obvious, getting the economics of a startup investment right is the most challenging aspect of angel investing, and the one in which most would-be angels go astray.

Unlike advanced books dealing with algorithmic, high-velocity day trading, I'm not going to delve into arcane subjects like Sharpe ratios, statistical mean reversion testing, and Black-Scholes equations. Instead, I will limit our discussion to the math that you learned in the fifth grade: multiplication, division, and a touch of exponentiation.

The Four Simple Numbers: Basics of Investment Math

The core of making money as an angel investor is to purchase an ownership share in a company when it is still young, unproven, and inexpensive, and to sell that share at a later date when the company has effectively achieved its vision and demonstrated that it is worth a lot more money. To take an example, if you invest $100 and receive a 10 percent ownership share of a company, you can calculate that after your investment the whole company is worth $1,000 (because $100 ÷ 10 percent = $1,000). If one year later a bigger company comes along and purchases the company for $10,000, you will receive $1,000 (because you will receive 10 percent of $10,000). Your Return On Investment (ROI) will therefore be $1,000 ÷ $100, or a 10-times return on your money. We abbreviate this as a 10x return.

Because you got this return exactly one year after you invested your money, one can say that the annual rate of return on your investment was 1,000 percent, because every year (even though in this case there was only the one year) you got 1,000 percent of your money back. We call this your Internal Rate of Return, or IRR.

The difference between the two terms is that ROI deals with the ratio between the money in and the money out, while IRR throws in the additional factor of time: how many years it took to generate that return. If it took two years to get to a sale, rather than one, the ROI on the theoretical sale would still be 10x, but the IRR would be only about 316 percent, because of the extra year we had to wait.

With a 316 percent per year return, at the end of Year One, your $100 would have turned into $316, and at the end of Year Two it would be $998.56—just a trifle less than $1,000.00. If it took three years to get that same +/–$1,000, however, your IRR would have been "only" about 215 percent: your $100 initial investment would be worth $215.00 at the end of Year One, $462.25 at the end of Year Two, and $993.84 at the end of Year Three.

You can now see that how much money you make from your angel investing is determined by four simple numbers:

1. The value of the company when you invest.
2. The value of the company when you sell.
3. The number of years between those two events, which, taken together, give you your rate of return.
4. The rate of return, multiplied by the amount of money you invest, will determine your ultimate angel investing bottom line.

Caveat: For purists, I will note here that there are in fact a bunch of other factors that will affect the outcome, including the extent to which your percentage ownership changes as other investors come in, known as "dilution"; and the priority of who gets paid how much in what order when the company has a liquidity event. However, if you understand the four simple numbers, you will have a solid foundation for everything that comes later.

How Much Should You Invest?

Since the rate of return you achieve through your investing activities will be multiplied by the number of dollars you put to work, determining the amount you are prepared to invest in each opportunity is the first step in your angel career. You can calculate this number by working backwards, based on some general assumptions.

First, keeping in mind that professional angel investing is a long-term activity, it is important to commit yourself to consistency over time. So let's say that you will be investing for five years (the typical active investing period of a venture capital fund). The amount you invest each year can be based on a percentage of your overall investment portfolio, a percentage of your annual income, or a combination of both. Most experts will suggest that because of the risk and volatility of private investments, you should devote no more than 10 percent of your investment portfolio to this asset class. John Huston, founder of Ohio Tech Angels and former Chairman of the Angel Capital Association, goes even further and suggests limiting your annual angel investing to no more than 10% of your annual Free Cash Flow (the amount you end up putting in your pocket each year).

Next, because we are following the Law of Large Numbers, it is important to commit to investing in many different ventures. Taking as your goal a portfolio of at least 20-25 companies (minimum), that means you will make at least five investments every year. And because every startup always needs more money, you'll want to reserve an additional amount so that you have the option of participating in follow-on rounds (see Chapter 13). Venture funds typically reserve the same amount as their initial investments under the theory that they will be betting heavily on the few big winners, but angels typically shave this a bit, and reserve roughly 50 percent of their original investment for follow-ons.

For an Accredited Investor with $5 million in investable assets, a reasonable amount to aim for as an initial check size for angel investments might be something like $5m × 10 percent ÷ (25 × 1.5) = $13,333, which rounds to an even $15,000 per deal. You'd end up at roughly the same amount if you had, say, half the investable assets, but were more comfortable with risk and were prepared to devote 20 percent of your assets to this high risk/high return class.

This $15,000 theoretical figure for a single investment is in the same ballpark as actual angel experience. According to several surveys by the Angel Capital Association and the Angel Resource Institute, the average investment amount per angel per company for members of organized angel groups is roughly $25,000, including participation in follow-on rounds.

What Target Rate of Return Should You Aim For?

The Kauffman Foundation released a report in 2007 entitled "Returns to Angel Investors in Groups." Written by Robert Wiltbank of Willamette University and Warren Boeker of the University of Washington, its findings were based on the largest data set of accredited angel investors collected to date, with information on exits from 539 angels—the best sample we have of serious angel investors. Those investors experienced 1,137 exits (including acquisitions or initial public offerings that provided positive returns, and firm closures that led to negative returns) from their venture investments over a 20-year period, with most exits occurring between 2004 and 2007. The average return of angel investments in the study was 2.6 times the investment in 3.5 years—an internal rate of return of approximately 27 percent.

Another study by Wiltbank, done two years later for the British National Endowment for Science, Technology and the Arts, analyzed 1,080 investments by 158 UK-based angels and reported an average IRR of 22 percent. Splitting the difference, it is therefore the premise of this book that serious angel investors, following a methodical, pragmatic approach in their investing activities, should aim for an annualized IRR of roughly 25 percent—a return that compares favorably to almost every other legal form of investment.

What Is the Company Worth When You Invest?

The valuation of startup companies before they have generated significant profits (or any profits at all) is a cross between black magic, hard math, market dynamics, investor return calculations, and entrepreneurial hubris. As a result, the single most important of the four simple numbers is the most confusing, debated, and variable number in the world of angel investing.

The entrepreneur wants the investor to value the company based on its (potentially sky-high) future value. The investor wants to value it based on its (much more modest) current value. Neither approach is objectively right or wrong. In most cases, the valuation of a company that is still in its early days but that both founders and investors think should grow, lies somewhere in between.

The number ultimately agreed upon reflects the number of current customers, the total revenues, the user and revenue growth curve, the business model, the market niche, the intellectual property value, and many other factors. It also reflects the relative bargaining power of those doing the negotiating. Which generally means—given the imbalance between the number of companies seeking investment funding and the number of investors with real money to invest—that, in the end, the valuation assigned to a company reflects the price that investors are willing to pay for it.

An investment in a startup is a market transaction, in which each side needs to believe that it is getting appropriate value for what it is giving up. Because the investor is putting in X amount of cash and getting Y percent of the company, the effect is to create a math equation that will let you figure out, for any given investment, what the value of the company would be today, before the investment. If you and the entrepreneur can agree on that, then you have a deal.

For example, let's say that you, as a potential investor, offer to invest $1 million in exchange for 25 percent ownership in a company. This means you are saying that, as of this moment, the founder has created something that is worth $3 million dollars.

"Huh?" I hear you ask. "If my million dollars gets a quarter of the company, doesn't that mean the company is worth $4 million? That's the way they do it on *Shark Tank!*"

That may be the way they do it on TV, but that doesn't make it right. Here's the math: If $1 million = 25 percent of the company, then the whole company *would* be worth $4 million. But since that would be after the investment—what is known as the *post-money valuation*—we have to back out the $1 million that just came in, because the company *after* your investment is worth whatever it was worth the day *before* your investment, *plus* your million dollars that is now sitting in the company's bank account! So $4 million − $1 million = $3 million ... which is the *pre-money valuation*, or what the company is worth today, before you arrive on the scene.

As an investor, you will decide how much a company is worth on the basis of many factors, including how far the business has come (Is it just a business plan? Is it already profitable? Is it somewhere in between?) and how far it can go (Does it have the potential to be a billion-dollar business? Or is it more likely to top out at $20 million?).

Further complicating the calculation is the question of incentive for the entrepreneur. If the real value of what the entrepreneur has created so far is $500,000, and the business needs $4.5 million to reach a point where the additional value would allow the company to raise more money at a higher valuation, then the math would say the investor should get 90 percent of the company. But since that would leave the entrepreneur with only 10 percent—and likely less, after taking in future investment rounds—the odds are that he or she would not be willing to take it, and instead would close the company and go on to do something else.

All of these factors make the valuation decision complicated and subjective—despite the various quantitative elements that play a role. That said, there have been many attempts to develop normalized models that can be used to provide a starting point for negotiation. The best summary of the different approaches has been written by my friend Bill Payne, the world's leading trainer of angel investors (who taught me much of what I'm now teaching you). Here, adapted with permission from his books, articles, and website, is an overview of the various valuation methods:

Scorecard Valuation Methodology. This method compares the target company to typical angel-funded startup ventures and adjusts the average valuation of recently funded companies in the region to establish a pre-money valuation of the target. Such comparisons can only be made for companies at the same stage of development—in this case, for pre-revenue startup ventures.

The first step in using the Scorecard Method is to determine the average pre-money valuation of pre-revenue companies in the region and business sector of the target company. Pre-money valuation varies with the economy and with the competitive environment for startup ventures within a region. In most regions, the pre-money valuation does not vary significantly from one business sector to another.

As of early 2014, the range of data aggregated from various surveys by the Angel Resource Institute, CB Insights, Gust and Bill Payne himself ranges from a low pre-money valuation of $500,000 to a high of $3.0 million for seed stage, pre-revenue companies. For our purposes, we will assume that the pre-money valuation of pre-revenue companies varies in the range of $1 million to $2 million and that a typical pre-money valuation for such firms is $1.5 million. (For context, CB Insights seed-stage valuation numbers for 2013 were an average of $1.9 million and a median of $600,000.)

The next step is to compare the target company to your perception of similar deals done in your region, considering the factors discussed in Chapter 7. In fact, the Screening and Valuation Worksheet in Appendix A was originally developed by Bill to assist in judging the relative strength of target companies.

To provide an example using the worksheet, assume a company with an average product and technology (100 percent of norm), a stronger-than-average team (125 percent of norm), and a significantly larger-than-average market opportunity (150 percent of norm). The company can get to positive cash flow with a single angel round of investment (100 percent of norm). Looking at the strength of the competition in the market, the target is weaker (75 percent of norm), but early customer feedback on the product is excellent (Other = 100 percent). The company needs some additional work on building sales channels and partnerships (80 percent of norm). Using this data, we can complete the following calculation:

Comparison Factor	Range	Target Company	Factor
Strength of Entrepreneur and Team	30 percent max	125 percent	0.3750
Size of the Opportunity	25 percent max	150 percent	0.3750
Product/Technology	15 percent max	100 percent	0.1500
Competitive Environment	10 percent max	75 percent	0.0750
Marketing/Sales/Partnerships	10 percent max	80 percent	0.0800
Need for Additional Investment	5 percent max	100 percent	0.0500
Other (great customer feedback)	5 percent max	100 percent	0.0500
Sum			1.0750

Multiplying the sum of factors (1.075) by the average pre-money valuation of $1.5 million, we arrive at a pre-money valuation for the target company of about $1.6 million (rounding from the calculated $1.61 million).

Venture Capital (VC) Method. Professor Bill Sahlman at Harvard Business School first described the VC method in 1987 in a case study. The concept is simple.

Since: Return on investment (ROI) = terminal value ÷ post-money valuation;

Then: Post-money valuation = terminal value ÷ anticipated ROI.

Let me address each of these terms and explain how they're calculated and used.

Terminal value is the anticipated selling price for the company at some point down the road—assume five to eight years after investment. The selling price can be estimated by establishing a reasonable expectation for revenues in the year of the sale and, based on those revenues, estimating earnings in the year of the sale from industry-specific statistics. For example, a software company with revenues of $20 million in the harvest year might be expected to have after-tax earnings of 15 percent, or $3 million. Using available industry-specific price-to-earnings ratios, one can then determine the terminal value; for example, a 15x price/earnings ratio for our software company would give an estimated terminal value of $45 million.

Another approach is to assume that, since software companies often sell for two times revenues, in this case the terminal value would be $40 million. Splitting the difference, we could arrive at a terminal value of $42.5 million.

Anticipated ROI: Since all angel investments must demonstrate the possibility of a 10x to 30x return, let's assume 20x for purposes of this example.

We can now use this information to calculate the *pre-money valuation* of the company—that is, what the company is worth before we invest in it.

Assuming our software entrepreneur needs $500,000 to achieve positive cash flow and will grow organically thereafter, here's how one calculates the pre-money valuation of this transaction:

Post-money valuation = terminal value ÷ anticipated ROI

$$= \$42.5 \text{ million} \div 20x.$$

Post-money valuation = $2.125 million.

Pre-money valuation = Post-money valuation − investment

$$= \$2.125 - \$0.5 \text{ million}.$$

Therefore,

Pre-money valuation = $1.625 million.

But what if the investors anticipate the need for subsequent investment? An easy way is to adjust the pre-money valuation of the current round, reducing the pre-money valuation by the estimated level of dilution from later investors. If investors in this round anticipate eventually being diluted by half, the pre-money valuation for the current round would be about $800,000.

Dave Berkus Method. Dave Berkus is a widely respected lecturer and educator and a founding member of the Tech Coast Angels in Southern California who has invested in more than 80 startup ventures. Dave's valuation model first appeared in a book published by Harvard's Howard Stevenson in the mid-1990s, and has been used by angels since. Here is the latest version, updated by Dave in 2009:

Start with a pre-money valuation of zero, and then assess the quality of the target company in light of the following characteristics:

Characteristic	Add to Pre-Money Valuation
Quality management team	Zero to $0.5 million
Sound idea	Zero to $0.5 million
Working prototype	Zero to $0.5 million
Quality board of directors	Zero to $0.5 million
Product rollout or sales	Zero to $0.5 million

Note that the numbers are the maximum for each class (not absolutes), so a valuation can be $800K (or less) as easily as $2.5 million. Furthermore, Dave reminds us that his method "was created specifically for the earliest stage investments as a way to find a starting point without relying upon the founder's financial forecasts."

Cayenne Valuation Calculator. The High Tech Startup Valuation Estimator is an online tool at www.caycon.com/valuation.php, developed by Cayenne Consulting. It uses 25 questions to assess the progress of the new venture and calculate a pre-money valuation for investment purposes. In many cases, the outcome from answering these 25 questions indicates that the company has not made sufficient progress in development to justify an investment at all. When a valuation range is provided, however, it could be as low as $480,000 to $580,000 or as high as $36 to $44 million, so this tool is clearly not limited to use on pre-revenue companies.

Users of the Cayenne Calculator are encouraged first to answer all 25 questions as conservatively as possible to determine a minimum valuation for the venture. It is easy for optimistic users to arrive quickly at unreasonable pre-money valuations for startup ventures. Users are encouraged to experiment with the tool to determine the most sensitive questions driving the calculated solution. Start with the most pessimistic responses to calculate a base valuation. Then repeatedly revise the assesment with increasingly more optimistic responses in an attempt to arrive at a reasonable valuation; one that is in line with other valuation methodologies.

The Risk-Factor Summation Method. This approach considers a much broader set of factors in determining the pre-money valuation of pre-revenue companies. The Ohio Tech Angels, who developed it, describe the method as follows:

> Reflecting the premise that the higher the number of risk factors, then the higher the overall risk, this method forces investors to think about the various types of risks which a particular venture must manage in order to achieve a lucrative exit. Of course, the largest is always "Management Risk" which demands the most consideration and investors feel is the most overarching risk in any venture. While this method certainly considers the level of management risk, it also prompts the user to assess other risk types.

The list of risk types to be considered when using this method includes:

- Management risk
- Stage-of-the-business risk
- Legislation/political risk
- Manufacturing risk
- Sales-and-marketing risk
- Funding/capital-raising risk
- Competition risk
- Technology risk
- Litigation risk
- International risk
- Reputation risk
- Potential lucrative exit

Assign a score to each risk as follows:

+2—Very positive for growing the company and executing a wonderful exit

+1—Positive

0—Neutral

−1—Negative for growing the company and executing a wonderful exit

−2—Very negative

The average pre-money valuation of pre-revenue companies in your region is then adjusted positively by $250,000 for every +1 ($500K for a +2) and negatively by $250,000 for every −1 ($500K for a −2).

Good practice suggests using at least three methods to estimate the appropriate pre-money valuation. If all three methods give approximately the same number, simply average the three. If one method seems to be an outlier (much higher or much lower than the other two), use the average of the other two. Alternatively, if one method is an outlier, calculate the pre-money valuation using a fourth method, in an attempt to find three methods in close agreement. If the three methods are uncomfortably different, use one—or even two—additional methods to arrive at a fair valuation.

Bill Payne and I both believe the Scorecard Method is the most useful approach to setting a baseline valuation. The Risk Factor Summation Method is good as a supplemental methodology because it considers factors not always included in investor considerations. The other three methods are also valuable, but should be used in combination with the Scorecard Method.

How Do Initial Valuations Affect an Angel's Ultimate IRR?

So far we have looked at valuations for each company on a stand-alone basis, the way we would if we were evaluating public stocks. However, in the case of a public stock, there is much more information available, much more of a track record for the company, and little chance of the company going out of business right after you invest. None of that is the case with startups. In fact, a *majority* of startups fail, and only a small minority become major hits. As a result, we need to return to the math exercises and conclude the valuation discussion by analyzing valuations and returns in the context of a full portfolio of angel investments, our expectations, and historical market experience.

Aside from rare exceptions like Instagram, which appreciated in value from $0 to $1 billion in 23 months, experience has shown that bigger successes take more time to reach fruition than bad companies take to fail. In fact, a recent study by the Angel Capital Association found that among its members, the average holding time for a company until a positive exit was nearly nine years. But let's be optimistic, and assume an average holding time of six years. If we then take our target IRR of 25 percent a year and run it out for six years, we get 1.25×6, or approximately 3.8. That means at the end of the day, after making all our investments, reaping all of our exits, and writing off all of our losses, we should end up with a target ROI of 3.8x on the total of our invested capital after six years.

That doesn't sound too onerous, does it? But let's dig a little deeper into the numbers and apply some industry norms. In the early-stage world, angels find that of every 10 investments, five are likely to fail completely, and two will eventually return just the capital that was originally invested. Of the remaining three successes, two will probably be solid winners, returning 2x to 3x the amount originally invested. Because each company represents only 1/10 of the portfolio's value, we need to divide each outcome by 10 in order to see what its overall contribution will be to the portfolio. This means that at the end of six years we will have the following results:

5 = 0x [1/10 × 5 × 0] = 0.0 of our total angel investment

2 = 1x [1/10 × 2 × 1] = 0.2 of our total angel investment

2 = 3x [1/10 × 2 × 3] = 0.6 of our total angel investment

Now we need to add up all the returns from the first nine companies and subtract the total from our target ROI:

$$3.8 - (0.0 + 0.2 + 0.6) = 3.0$$

This means we need that last company to return 3x the value of *our entire initial investment into all 10 companies.* But since that company itself only received one tenth of our original investment, simple math tells us that in order to hit our target 25 percent IRR, that one, single company needs to return 30x ROI! And because we won't know in advance which company will be That One, we need to make our initial investments under the theory that every one of the 10 must be at least theoretically capable of generating a 30x return!

Returning one final time to basic mathematics, we can see that there are two ways for a company to achieve that level of return. One of them is to make the initial investment at a post-money valuation for the company of, say, $10 million. In that case, we need to have the company either go public or be acquired within six years at a valuation of more than $300 million. I must confess that despite having had extremely positive exits to companies like Facebook, Google, Intel, Amazon, and others, not once have I had a $300 million exit.

Given the inexorability of math, therefore, there is only one other way to hit the 30x target: invest at a lower valuation. So if the initial valuation we agree upon with the company is, say, $1.5 million, our 30x target means that the company will need to be acquired eventually at a terminal valuation of $45 million. And guess what? It turns out that $30 to $50 million happens to be the range of the majority of private company acquisitions. Hmm ....

The math leads to a clear and definitive lesson for the angel investor: Investing in companies with reasonable initial valuations (typically in very low, single-digit millions) is a good way to increase your chance of achieving strong returns on your entire angel portfolio. Conversely, investing in companies at high valuations, regardless of how attractive, is the way to ruin—unless you hit the one-in-a-thousand megahit. Because the odds are not in your favor, reasonable valuations are one of the key secrets of professional early-stage investing.

Changing Valuations During a Round

Once a valuation has been agreed upon between the company and the lead investor for a given round, that valuation is generally regarded as fixed for the duration of that round. Changing valuation during a round is not usual, but also not uncommon. When it does happen, early investors typically get the benefit of the better of the valuation at which they commit (and the entrepreneur accepts) and whatever the final valuation given to later investors ends up being.

Sometimes an entrepreneur independently sets a valuation and gets an early Friends-and-Family investor to commit a portion of the cash, but then finds that professional investors have a different—that is, lower—view of the company's value. In that case, if everyone is closing as part of the same round, the Friends-and-Family investor(s) end up investing at the same price as the professional(s) or less, if they funded their cash under the terms of a convertible note with a predetermined discount.

A less-usual case (but it happens) is when a professional investor provides a company with a nonbinding term sheet at a given valuation, subject to due diligence, but during the diligence period things come to light (such as ownership problems with the intellectual property, big customers who aren't renewing, unexpected changes in the marketplace, and so on) that affect the valuation. In such a case, the investor might tell the company that he won't close at the agreed-upon valuation, but would be prepared to close at a lower number. The company then has the option to accept the new terms or not (although realistically, the company in such a case often doesn't have many other options).

An unusual case, but one that is beginning to gain currency in West Coast deals, is a *rolling close* on separately priced *convertible notes* (I discuss convertible notes in the next chapter). In this scenario, different investors come into the same round at different prices, based on either the order in which they commit (early birds get better prices) or their value to the company (Ron Super Angel gets a better value than Joe Six Pack).

But, in every case, unless there is explicit agreement in the documentation on revaluation or anti-dilution provisions, once the deal is closed and the money changes hands, the valuation for the money in this round is fixed and not renegotiable.

10

Investment Rounds and Their Forms

Common Stock, Convertible Notes, or Preferred Stock?

To make sense of the different ways in which startup investments technically get from the investors' bank account into that of the company, it is helpful to understand the role that investment money plays in a new venture. Let's take a step back to remind ourselves of the process by which a new business grows.

Our story begins when the founders of a young company realize they need more money if they're going to grow their business. To raise this money, they decide to launch an *investment round*—a set of one or more investments made in a particular company, by one or more investors on essentially similar terms at essentially the same time.

An investment round can take many forms. So if the brother of the founder lends her $25,000 to get her company off the ground with the understanding that the loan will eventually convert into an ownership interest, that would be a round. And if a year or so later, a group of professional angel investors get together and each put in $50,000 to buy another piece of the company, that, too, would be a round. And if the company did really well, and after another year a large venture capital fund came along and invested $2 million for preferred stock, that would be a round as well.

In the parlance of the business, the first round would be a *Friends and Family* round, the second a *Seed* or *Angel* round, and the third a *Series A* round. The Series terminology comes from the way successive tranches of preferred stock are labeled, because each round has specific defined rights and priorities relative to the other rounds.

How do these investment rounds happen? In an ideal world, an entrepreneur bootstraps a startup, gets traction in the marketplace, and gets noticed; a smart investor calls the company and says "Hey, I think you're doing great things, I'd like to invest a million dollars in exchange for 10 percent of your common stock;" the entrepreneur agrees; the lawyers quickly draw up the documents; the investor sends over a check; and the deal is done. However, to say this is a rare occurrence would be to overstate wildly the likelihood of it happening.

What does usually happen? A company gets started, gets some traction, and then starts talking to as many investors as it can find, ideally being introduced to them by mutual acquaintances. This is known as *starting a round*.

In all cases, the fundamental requirement is that the company and the investor agree on how much is being invested, and on what terms. These items are included in what is known as a *term sheet*. (What the terms end up being, and how a company and the investor(s) arrive at that term sheet, are discussed at length in Chapter 12.) If the entrepreneur is lucky, at least one investor will make a funding offer by presenting a term sheet. If he offers the full amount the company thinks it needs, and the terms are acceptable (perhaps after some negotiation), then the paperwork is signed, the money wired, and the round is closed.

However, if both sides agree on the term sheet, but the investor is willing to put in some, but not all, of the money needed, the company then has a *round in progress*, with a *lead investor* having been identified. At this point, the company (assisted in some cases by the lead investor) goes to other investors with the term sheet from the lead to fill out the round and get the full amount. Other investors will be invited to put in money on the same terms as the lead investor (as part of the same round).

In some cases the term sheet will provide that the round will be closed (that is, stop taking in new investments and have the investors transfer in their money) by a certain date, regardless of whether any other investors join in. Typically, however, the term sheet will provide for a minimum amount to be committed before anyone, including the lead investor, actually transfers the money. It may also provide for a maximum amount, beyond which no additional investors will be allowed to join in.

In either case, since the terms of the round have already been negotiated and agreed upon by the company and the lead investor, the decision for all the following investors is a simpler, take-it-or-leave-it choice based on the signed term sheet.

The challenge for the entrepreneur is that getting a lead investor is the single toughest thing in the startup world because it means that someone needs to take the first step, similar to getting the first pickle out of a tightly packed pickle jar. And because it is so difficult to get that lead investor, companies are often desperate enough to try shortcuts.

One of those is to draw up a term sheet themselves, setting a valuation, terms, and target amount. They then try to function as their own lead investor by presenting their term sheet to potential investors, getting quickly to the take-it-or-leave-it decision, and skipping the tough step-up-and-lead decision.

This rarely works, because it is just about guaranteed that an entrepreneur negotiating that self-proposed term sheet with him- or herself will not end up with the same kind of term sheet that a smart, tough, lead investor would have negotiated. And because the pseudo-term sheet will be less investor-friendly than a real one, and because there is no investor providing validation, support, and a good chunk of the funding for the round, the resulting easy take-it-or-leave-it usually becomes an even easier "leave it." In most cases, startups follow the traditional process for an investment round, with a lead investor providing the impetus.

Now let's examine the way various funding rounds operate, and start with some definitions:

A *seed round* means that, like planting a seed for the first time, this particular round is the first investment made into the company by someone other than the founder.

An *equity seed round* means that an entrepreneur sells a part of his or her business and therefore a proportional part of the good things (like profits) and the not-so-good things (like losses) to an investor.

In contrast to equity, *debt* means borrowed money that needs to be paid back. The entrepreneur rents the money for a specific period of time and promises to pay interest on the money for as long as the loan is outstanding.

Convertible debt means that the terms of the loan provide that the amount of money loaned may (or must, under certain conditions) be converted by the investor into shares of stock in the company at a particular price.

Angel rounds are traditionally the first money in a company after the founder's own money, and the founder's friends and family.

Series A rounds are usually the first professional outside money that is invested in exchange for ownership in a company, and typically are in the range of single-digit millions of dollars. Once the company has demonstrated potential for growth (usually evidenced by traction showing that people are willing to pay for whatever it has developed), it becomes attractive to fulltime, professional investors. These venture capital (VC) firms invest larger amounts of money (which had previously been invested in them by their limited partners—usually institutions, or very rich individuals).

If a company successfully uses the Series A money to grow and become more valuable, the original VC investors and/or new investors might be willing to invest even more money, usually at an even higher valuation. This next round is usually done as an issuance of *Series B* Preferred Stock, which, when the company is sold, gets paid out first, before the Series A (which in turn comes out before the angels' money). And if a company is growing quickly but needs increasing capital to fuel the growth, there might be additional rounds going through the alphabet. (One of my companies during the dot-com boom made it to Series F … but those were different times.)

Angel money typically enters the picture after the founder, friends, and family have invested in the company, but before venture capital firms get involved. The most fundamental division is between two ways one can put money into a startup: by purchasing part ownership in the company (equity) or by lending the company money (debt). Both equity and debt can be viable investment options. In the next few pages I will explain both, and the advantages and disadvantages of each.

How Equity Investments Work

When a corporation is established, its ownership is divided into equal pieces. These are called *shares of common stock*. That's what founders have, which is why it's also known as *founders stock*.

The company soon needs cash to fund its development and growth, so it turns to investors, such as angels, who purchase a part ownership of the company by paying cash for stock. But the stock we purchase is *not* the same common stock that the founders have—and that the employees have options on. Instead, the company creates and issues a different kind of stock called *preferred stock*.

While the name makes it seem to be all-around preferable to common stock, preferred is not inherently better, just different.

When the time comes to turn the value of the company into cash (during an exit), that cash may be more or less than the value that founders and investors agreed the company was worth at the time of the original investment. That is where the difference between the two types of stock is critical.

Preferred stock gets paid out *first* before any common stock gets paid—but it *only* gets back the amount that was paid for it (plus perhaps some dividends, which for this purpose act like interest). In contrast, common stock gets paid out only *after* all the preferred has been satisfied—but it gets its proportionate share of *all* the remaining value.

As an example, let's say that investors bought preferred stock for $200, and agreed that the value of all the common stock was $800. If the next day someone comes along and buys the company for $1,000, then it just confirms that everyone was correct in their assumptions, the investors get $200 and the common holders get $800.

But what happens if the company is sold for only $500? In that case, the preferred gets its $200 back first, after which the common splits up the rest—in this case $300—which is a lot less than the $800 value on which they raised their investment. On the other hand, what happens if the company is sold the next day for $2,000? The preferred stock investors still get their original $200 back, with the remaining $1,800 (including all of the newly created value) being divided among the common holders.

Based on this, you can see that it is much better to be a preferred shareholder in a down scenario, just as it is much better to be a common shareholder in an up scenario!

So, I hear you ask, if investors are putting money into a company precisely because they believe its value will increase dramatically, why would they want to buy preferred stock as I just described it?

The answer is, they don't.

What investors in startups buy is actually a hybrid type of stock, called *convertible preferred* stock.

The primary feature of convertible preferred stock is that, in an "up" scenario, it converts into common stock, and everyone is happy.

However, if the "down" scenario happens, then it works differently: the first money that comes in goes to pay off the cash that the investors paid (in the example above, the $200). Anything left over (in this case it would be $300) goes to the holders of common stock. The effect of this is to adjust retroactively the nominal value assigned to the founders' contribution.

That is why there are different classes of ownership in startup companies. At a basic level, the purpose of different classes is to ensure an appropriate match between risk and reward for founders and investors coming in at different times under different sets of conditions. Buying convertible preferred stock gives investors the best of both worlds and is rather like having your cake and eating it, too.

It starts as preferred stock, so if the company falls on hard times and is sold for less than it was originally valued at, we get the full amount of our investment back. But, if good things happen (as everyone hopes), then immediately before the sale of the company we get to wave a magic wand, and our preferred shares convert, one-for-one, into common shares, so that we can participate in the increased value along with the other common stock holders.

Investors can also benefit in other ways. Because the common and convertible preferred are separate types of shares, the company's charter and other documents can (and usually will) be amended to give different rights and privileges to the different types of stock.

The Discounted Convertible Note

So far, I have been focusing on the complexities of equity investing, but there's another way you can invest in a startup, and that's by lending money to the company for it to use in financing its growth.

The key difference is that debt results in a fixed payback regardless of whether good or bad things happen, while equity results in a variable payback from $0 (if the company goes under) to potentially billions of dollars (if the company ends up being worth a lot of money).

Debt has its advantages to a lender—primarily, the certainty of return. The borrower owes the money (plus interest) due on a specific date regardless of whether the company succeeds or fails. But startup investors aren't interested in ordinary debt with its attendant low returns. Instead, they always want to own an equity share of the company (and therefore its upside potential) rather than owning debt (which, no matter how successful the company gets, will only pay back the face amount of the loan, plus a relatively small interest payment).

There is one problem with this from the perspective of the startup founder. It happens that, for regulatory and other reasons, the legal costs of documenting an equity round can be high, often in the many tens of thousands of dollars. This is not a problem if a big venture fund is investing millions of dollars, but it can be problematic in the context of a small angel round of tens or hundreds of thousands of dollars.

To avoid the cost and complexity of documenting an equity round while still providing investors with the enticement of being able to participate in the upside of equity ownership, it is not uncommon these days for startup funding to take place with a hybrid investment vehicle known as a *convertible note.*

A convertible note carries with it the guarantee that, at some point in the future, the angel will be able to convert what started out as a loan into the equivalent of cash, and use that money to buy stock in the company. This can be useful, quick, and less expensive for the investor and the company, but it creates complications. Here's why.

If I'm putting $100,000 into Company A in the form of debt, the only thing we need to discuss is the interest rate that Company A will pay me for using my money until they pay it back. On the other hand, if I'm investing in the form of equity, then we need to decide what percentage of the company's ownership I will end up with in exchange for my investment. To figure that out, we use the following math equation:

[Amount I'm investing] ÷ [Company value] = [Percent ownership]

Since we can calculate any one of the three terms if we know the remaining two, and we already know how much I'm investing ($100,000), in order to figure out what my ownership percentage will be after the investment, Company A and I need to agree on what the company valuation is (or will be) at the time I purchase my shares of stock. We have already covered valuation methods in Chapter 9, and based on these, the company and I would negotiate a valuation figure we are both willing to live with. I'd give them the money today, they'd give me the appropriate percentage of the company's stock, and we'd be all set.

But that's not what I'm doing when I invest in a convertible note. Instead, I'm lending Company A the money today with the understanding that I will be able to convert that money into its equivalent in stock someday.

But because that conversion is going to be happening at some point in the *future*, while I'm giving the company the money *today*, we need to figure out a few things *today*, before I am willing to give them the money. Specifically, we need to decide (a) when in the future the debt will convert to equity, and (b) *how* we will determine the valuation of the company at that point in the future.

The answer to both turns out to be the same: we will wait until a richer, more experienced investor agrees to buy equity in the company. At that point we will convert the debt into equity (which answers question a) and use as the valuation whatever that other investor is using (which answers question b).

So far, so good. But we're not quite done. The fact is that I was willing to invest in Company A at a time when that other investor was not, and the founders used my investment to make the company more valuable (and therefore got a high valuation from the other investor). It doesn't seem fair that I should bear the early-stage risk, yet get the same reward as a later-stage investor.

We solve this problem by agreeing that I will get a discount to whatever the other investor sets the valuation at, which is why we call this a *discounted convertible note*. The discount is typically set at anywhere from 10 to 30 percent of the next-round pricing.

Although that sounds fair, it really isn't (or at least serious investors don't think it is). That's because the more successful Company A is at using my original money to increase its value, the higher the valuation the next guy will have to pay, and pretty soon the little discount I'm getting doesn't seem so fair after all. For instance, if that same investor would have valued Company A in its early days at $1 million, but is willing to invest in the now-much-more-successful company at a valuation of $5 million, that means the company founders were able to increase the company's value by 500 percent using my original seed money.

If my convertible note says that it will convert at a 20 percent discount to that $5 million, for example (which, if you do the math, is $4 million), I would seem to have made a very bad deal. Why? Because I end up paying for Company A's stock based on a $4 million valuation, instead of the $1 million it was worth in its early days when I was willing to make my risky investment.

We solve this problem by saying, "Okay, because I'm investing early, I'll get the 20 percent discount on whatever valuation the next guy gives you. But just to be sure that things don't get out of hand, we will also say that, regardless of whatever valuation the next investor is willing to give you, in no case will the valuation at which my debt converts ever be higher than $1 million." That figure is known as the *cap*, because it establishes the highest price at which my debt can ever convert to equity. And that's why we call this form of debt investment a *discounted convertible note with a cap*.

Over the past 20 years, the typical structure for seed/angel deals has shifted from common stock (in the mid-1990s), to convertible notes (late 1990s through early 2000s), to full Series A convertible preferred (mid 2000s), to convertible notes with a cap (late 2000s), to series seed convertible preferred or similar (present). This shows the increasing sophistication of investors and entrepreneurs, the increasing experience and publicity surrounding the advantages/disadvantages of various options, and the increasing availability of model documents and online term sheet generators for different choices.

Recently, Y Combinator, the leading accelerator program, unveiled a new type of equity called a SAFE, which stands for Simple Agreement for Future Equity. SAFEs have some of the good features of convertible notes, but because they are not actually a form of debt, they avoid some of the problems. Y Combinator has open-sourced the documents and published them at http://ycombinator.com/safe/. It remains to be seen if the industry will adopt these, and if so, for what types of transactions. My guess is that they make the most sense for very early investments, at low dollar amounts in pure startup companies, particularly in cases where seed investors are willing to wait for an expected future round for their protection. SAFEs are likely to find use in some hot deals where investors just want to be in the deal, but will probably not be adopted by angel groups or financially focused angels who are proactively leading an investment round.

Fine Points of Investing in Discounted Convertible Notes

Another factor bearing on the advisability of doing a convertible note is that it is debt, not equity, which is both good and bad for the investor. It's good because in a down liquidation scenario the note gets paid out ahead of anything going to the founder or any other equity holder; it's bad because, in an up-liquidation scenario prior to conversion, unless the note is carefully drafted, the company can just pay it off with interest, and avoid giving the investor *any* upside.

Notes typically provide fewer rights and protections for investors— those important details contribute to the cost of writing and negotiating an equity round. One further wrinkle is that while everyone investing in an equity round will be investing on the same terms at the same valuation, with a series of convertible notes a company can choose to raise money at different valuations from different investors.

The primary potential problem from an investor's point of view with using convertible notes (whether capped or not) for seed deals is not that the later Series A investors take advantage of the seed investors by making them second-class citizens. Rather, it is that the Series A investors don't want the seed investors to take advantage of the Series A. This can happen in one of two cases: either (a) the seed angels are greedy, and the negotiated discount to the Series A valuation is too large for the Series A's comfort, or (b) the convertible note has a valuation cap that becomes untenable in the unusual case of an enormous increase in valuation between the two rounds so that the seed investors are getting a much better financial deal than the Series A's, but end up with all the same rights.

Even in those cases, however, negotiated adjustments to the seed deal are more likely to be purely financial than anything else. Otherwise, and assuming that the total of the convertible notes is relatively small compared to the new money of the Series A (say, $400K of seed-convertible notes converting as part of a $2–$3 million Series A), professional venture investors are generally comfortable with the discount and welcome the seed investors' participation.

Because they are technically loans, all convertible notes have a maturity date on which the principal and any accrued interest must be repaid to the lender. But because convertible notes are designed to give investors an equity interest in a company that will eventually be worth much more than their investment, the intention is always to convert into equity. After all, if you were just after the interest on a loan, you could find less risky things to invest in than a startup.

Therefore, the only reason that an investor would not convert into the next round of equity would be if the company were doing so poorly that there was no such round. (Think about it this way: assuming a convertible note with a valuation cap, which is what all smart investors would do, it would always be to the investor's advantage to convert, regardless of whether the valuation of the round was high or low.)

The flip side is that if the company is doing so poorly that it can't raise another financing round, it is highly unlikely that it will have the cash on hand to repay the debt at maturity, so there would be no purpose served by the investor demanding repayment … you can't get back what doesn't exist.

Therefore, if the repayment-at-maturity clause is not used to get the investor's money back, what is it used for? In practice, it is used as an incentive (carrot/stick) for the investor and the company to sit down for a heart-to-heart talk, to figure out what to do next … with the balance of power this time in the hands of the investor, because the company was not able to deliver on its projections. As a result:

- If things are generally going well, the investor(s) will usually extend the note to give the company more breathing room, maintaining the status quo.
- If things are not going so well, and it doesn't look like there will be a follow-on financing round any time soon, the investor and company might agree to convert the note into equity at a lower than anticipated valuation (if there had been a previous round) or at whatever valuation they agree on.
- In a worst case, if the company is in really bad shape, the investor can dictate whatever terms she or he wants, using the implied threat of forcing the company into bankruptcy because it can't repay the debt. This is particularly the case if the note is secured by the company's assets.

While that last option sounds horrendous, in practice I have seen it used mostly for good. There are many permutations of what "good" looks like, but, essentially, holding a past-due note from a company that can't repay it is like holding a nuclear weapon: using it probably destroys all value for everyone, but having the ability to use it, as in the geopolitical theory of Mutually Assured Destruction, means that everyone is at least forced back to the table to negotiate a way of saving the company.

You hope the repayment-at-maturity clause will never have to be used in this way—but if the time comes when it is necessary, an investor will probably be glad it's there.

11

The Art of the Angel Deal

Negotiating a Win/Win Relationship with Your Entrepreneur

IN ECONOMICS AND in game theory, there are two classes of engagements: zero sum and positive sum. The former describes a contest in which there are a fixed number of resources and a fixed number of players. For one player to gain resources, or win, the other player(s) must give up resources, or lose. The combined total change of all players during the game is therefore zero. In a positive sum game, however, both sides can gain at the same time, and often gain more by cooperating than by acting on their own.*

If the negotiating version of a positive-sum game—the notion of a win/win outcome—applies anywhere, it applies to the crafting of an agreement between an angel investor and an entrepreneur. After all, what is being negotiated isn't a one-time deal from which both parties walk away without further interaction, but rather a long-term partnership whose goal is to produce value for both parties.

---

*Game theorists inform me there is also the concept of a negative sum game, in which both parties can lose, but we are optimistic angels, so we're not going there....

Negotiating investment deals can be simple or complex, easy or hard, enjoyable or agonizing. Which way the process goes is dependent on several variables including the participants' integrity, knowledge, relative power position, and personal style.

Integrity and Knowledge

The basic ground rule is that you should always be completely straightforward and honest in your interactions with entrepreneurs seeking funding. Always! As I counseled you in Chapter 6 to immediately walk away if you pick up the slightest hint of integrity issues with a founder, so would I counsel founders to run, not walk, if they sense anything other than rock-solid integrity on the investor side of the table.

This is a good rule for life in general, but it is particularly important in early-stage investing. Imagine a police officer making a dangerous undercover bust while not trusting her partner. Think how corrosive anything other than complete trust is to a marriage. You and the entrepreneur are, by definition, entering uncharted territory where bad things can (and do) lurk around every corner. The last thing either of you wants is to worry about the people on your team.

So make it a point never to lie, never to fib, and never to obfuscate when negotiating an investment deal.

What makes this rule challenging even for the most virtuous professional angels is the asymmetry of information that exists between the two parties, compounded by the complexity and intricacies of the subject matter. The majority of entrepreneurs are first-time founders who do not have the slightest clue about how the investment process works. In contrast, before you've made your 25th angel investment, you will have had so much experience in negotiating deals that you will be able to teach a course on the subject.

(That said, until you are comfortable with the ins and outs of the angel-funding process, it is imperative that you engage an attorney with experience in early-stage financing. This is not a situation where you want to rely on your family's personal lawyer, or on a local real estate attorney you happen to know. If you hire a skilled professional, the negotiation, term sheet, and documentation process will be much smoother than it might be otherwise.)

The first investor in my first tech company was one of the world's leading venture capital funds, Warburg Pincus. At that point I had not the foggiest idea of how venture deals worked, what was fair, and even what I should be negotiating. I was fortunate that every one of the partners with whom I dealt at the firm was a straight shooter and went out of his way to guide me through the process. Looking back at the deal terms today from the other side of the table, more than 20 years later, I am still grateful.

Because you will better understand the true ramifications of the provisions you negotiate (at least I hope you will, after you finish the next chapter), there will always be a tendency to take advantage of this when it comes to deal terms. Resist the temptation and realize that your long-term economic benefits will derive from how well you work with the entrepreneur and what she tells other entrepreneurs, in public and in private.

Relative Power Position and Personal Style

Given the asymmetry between the number of aspiring entrepreneurs and the number of active angel investors, in 9 out of 10 cases the lop-sided nature of the dynamics favors the investor. Angels typically look at 20, 30, or 40 opportunities before selecting one. At the same time, startups may be reaching out to the same number of potential investors, hoping to find one willing to write a check. The relationship during the courting stage is much like that of a supplicant and an almoner. In practice, this means that following the golden rule of early-stage investing ("the person with the gold makes the rules"), the tenor of the meeting, as well as its outcome, are often determined by the investor.

Because you will be meeting with so many founders seeking funding and because word spreads very quickly within the entrepreneurial community (there are entire websites and mobile applications—even satirical games—devoted to entrepreneurs' reviews of investors), it is in your own best interest to be respectful of, and helpful to, every entrepreneur with whom you meet. This is true even (especially) for those in whose companies you decide not to invest. Many of the most prominent angel investors with high public profiles—something that helps them get directly approached with hot deals—got that way because of their proactive support for entrepreneurs.

During negotiations with a founder, and despite the number of subjects that need to be hammered out before an investment is made, there are two issues that probably account for 80 percent of contention during discussions. The first of these is valuation, and in Chapter 10 we covered the theory and practice of valuation setting. The second issue is that of control of the company: who has it, now and in the future.

The Question of Control

Both investors and entrepreneurs often confuse the issue of equity ownership with that of control of the company. The two are not unconnected, but they are separate matters that need to be distinguished.

Ultimate control of a company, including the strategic direction it chooses, the decision to sell itself to an acquirer, the selection and compensation of the CEO—in short, everything—rests with the company's board of directors. Regardless of what percentage of equity the founder owns, if the founder controls a majority of seats on the company's board, the founder decides who is going to be the CEO, including hiring him or herself.

The number of members of a company's board is determined by its corporate documents, and technically each share of common stock gets one vote for the candidate for each seat. In practice, however, every investment round overrides this one-common-share-one-vote structure by a vehicle called a *shareholders' agreement*. That agreement, which is signed by all significant shareholders as part of the closing for the investment round, provides that everyone votes for directors according to agreed terms.

In seed-stage companies, it is not unusual to have a board of three people: one appointed by the founder (almost always him or herself), one appointed by the investors (typically the lead angel or VC in the round), and a third outside director unaffiliated with either the founder or the investor, but approved by both.

However, it is critically important to understand that investors in any serious investment round (not necessarily a friends-and-family round, but certainly a Series Seed or Series A from professional angels or VCs) will unquestionably insist on *negative* control provisions as a means to protect their investment from the actions of a board they do not control. Regardless of what the board chooses to do affirmatively, there are specified things that will require the agreement of investors (either all the investors voting as a class, or the approval of the director they appoint to the board).

In the actual investment documents, these provisions will be spelled out carefully and clearly, so that there is no wiggle room or way to game the system. In the real world of early-stage companies, though, these protective provisions can often turn into affirmative control provisions when the going gets tough ... provided that the investors are willing to play hardball. If, for example, the company needs to take in another round of investment, but the investors want the company to pivot its business model, they can refuse to approve taking the new investment unless the board votes to pivot the model.

When negotiating with an entrepreneur, keep in mind that equity and control are neither synonymous nor connected. The essence of equity is that by having an ownership interest, the investor shares in whatever good things or bad things come out of the company. By contrast, control is a defensive issue of protection. You are putting your fungible money under the control of an aspiring entrepreneur for use in a nonfungible enterprise. The last thing you want is for the entrepreneur to do anything other than use the cash in the best possible way forward for the business. The problem comes when your analysis of "the best possible way" diverges from that of the entrepreneur.

How control issues are resolved during negotiations is based on the relative negotiating strengths of the two parties. When Goldman Sachs invested one billion dollars into privately held Facebook, they did not get any control provisions for their money. On the other hand, if I were to invest $50,000 in a brand new startup company run by a brilliant but fulltime college student entrepreneur, you can be sure that I would want the ability to have 100 percent control of the company. I would then defer this control back to the entrepreneur for as long as things were heading in the right direction, but would reserve the right to step back in if necessary.

Red Flags in Deal Negotiation

In general, discussions between angels and entrepreneurs tend to be relatively smooth, but there are a few things to watch out for, so keep your eyes open.

- If you get the feeling that there is anything less than 100 percent honesty coming from the person across the table, politely finish the conversation, walk away, and don't look back.

- While it's not uncommon for entrepreneurs to resist the idea of stepping down as CEO at some point in the future, if you find yourself faced with a founder who makes his most important stand on maintaining absolute control in perpetuity, I suggest you think hard about whether you are comfortable leaving yourself in the hands of this entrepreneur, regardless of the economics.
- If you receive any push back on the subject of reporting, board meetings, or access to company information, the cause may be innocent, but you should redouble your diligence to find out what is causing this reluctance.

Just remember that throughout your meetings your goal should be to establish positive incentives for everyone involved, including the entrepreneur and the management team. The more fully engaged and committed they are, and the more wholeheartedly they are dedicating their time, energy, and creativity to growing the business because of the amazing benefits they expect to accrue as a result, the better the odds that the company will become the world's next big economic sensation—and create value for everyone in the process.

12

Term Sheets and Closing

Trust Everyone ... but Cut the Cards Anyway

ALL INVESTMENTS BY angels (and everyone else) in a company are made according to detailed legal documents that specify everything about the relationship among the various parties, the terms of the value exchange, and the various rights and responsibilities of everyone involved. The paperwork can range from three to five pages for a simple, nonconvertible note, to 120 pages or more for a full convertible preferred stock round. Because these are legal documents, both parties—the company and the investor—have their own lawyers, who work together to develop the actual agreements signed by the principals.

The collection of documents that together constitute the investment agreement are typically summarized in a much shorter document (anywhere from one to half a dozen pages, depending on the type of investment) known as the *term sheet*. Think of the term sheet as a shorthand way of documenting an agreement in principle that will take many pages of legalese to implement. Because it deals specifically with all of the major points of the relationships, it allows both sides to determine quickly whether or not they want to enter into a deal in the first place.

A term sheet is usually (although not always) drafted by the investor and presented to the entrepreneur with a defined date by which it needs to be accepted. If the entrepreneur signs and returns it within that period, then the deal is in motion, and the lawyers for each side go back and forth on the actual documents that will be signed at the closing. Alternatively, the entrepreneur might respond by declining the terms as presented, but indicate that he or she would be receptive to a deal at a higher valuation, or with a larger investment, or fewer board seats, or something else. In that case, the ball is back in the investor's court and they may simply walk away, or come back with a revised term sheet.

The period between when an investor has presented a signed term sheet to an entrepreneur and the expiration date of that offer, is a critical time for everyone. Since the entrepreneur is not bound by anything in the terms until he signs it, he is free to do whatever he wants with it, including taking it to other potential investors and saying, in effect, "Look! Here is a signed term sheet that I've been given by Tom. Dick, would you be interested in matching or beating it? Just so you know, I'm also speaking with Harry, who has expressed interest as well." While it wouldn't happen in exactly that way, I can guarantee you that the Holy Grail of fundraising from an entrepreneur's perspective is having more than one term sheet from which to choose. And since market competition is one of the main drivers in early-stage finance, one term sheet often brings others who might have been sitting on the fence.

Because of the possibility (if not likelihood) of their term sheet being shopped around to other investors and used as a stalking horse, investors typically try to make the consideration time as short as possible. The ultimate version of this is the ridiculous (and, frankly, offensive) 24-second shot clock that some of the cast members on the TV show *Shark Tank* pull on entrepreneurs. In most cases, however, investors have several conversations with companies to figure out the range of terms they are likely to accept. They may also send over an unsigned draft of the sheet, which is not binding on them, to get some feedback. But after the real one is delivered with a signature, the company will usually have one to three days to accept or decline the offer.

Once the entrepreneur has signed the term sheet, it is binding— not just legally (for at least some parts of it) but also ethically. If either party backs out of a signed term sheet without a *very* good reason, word will almost certainly get around, and the action will have long-term repercussions: a hard-to-erase stain on the entrepreneur's or investor's reputation.

After both parties have signed, the lawyers get to work on the full documentation for the round. One lawyer (usually specified in the term sheet) will be responsible for the base drafting, with the other making comments, although in virtually all cases the documents are based on more-or-less standard industry models. The timing of the actual payment of moneys committed during the investment round depends on the nature of the round. In Friends-and-Family rounds, the entrepreneur will probably be able to get funds as they are committed. In a traditional angel round, there will usually be a targeted range that the entrepreneur is trying to reach as well as a minimum amount to close. Once that minimum is reached, a simultaneous closing is held at which the funds are released to the entrepreneur.

In the past, the closing typically involved sending paper back and forth for signatures and using overnight delivery services to send checks to the company's bank. Today there is a trend toward fully electronic/ digital closings, in which the requisite documents are electronically signed by all parties and funds are wired directly into the company's bank accounts.

Depositing funds into an escrow account is often required during a large funding round involving several investors, in cases where investors only want to fund if the company can be sure to get all the money it needs to execute its plan. Otherwise, if the money came in as dribs and drabs, the company might get part way down the road, run out of money, and go broke. So investors say, in effect, "Okay, I'll put the money in escrow with your lawyer (or an online platform like Gust), so *you* know that you'll have my money, but you can't get your hands on it until *I* know that you will be successful in raising the full amount you say you need."

Another situation in a round like this is that everyone wants to invest simultaneously with everyone else, but logistically the signatures will be coming in at different times, and there may be changes in the paperwork up until the last minute. So everyone signs the signature pages, and the signatures are held in escrow until everyone gives permission to release, at which time the deal is closed.

Term Sheet for Convertible Notes

In Chapter 10 I discussed the two primary forms that angel investments take: convertible notes and convertible preferred stock.

For several years in the early days of the professional angel world, investors used a very simple form of convertible note that needed little explanation and effectively punted on everything (valuation, conversion, protections, and other provisions) until the next institutional venture round. As angels became smarter and recognized the anomalies in the risk/reward ratio, they insisted on a valuation cap. And then as they got burned in various edge cases (such as an acquisition happening before they converted), they started to add certain limited protections which made the once-simple note a tad more complicated.

In Appendix C I have included the full text of the standard Gust Convertible Note Term Sheet, which you are free to use when you lead your own investments. An electronic version is available online, together with its supporting documents, at http://gust.com/termsheets/.

We developed this based on hard-earned experience, and I personally have used it on several investments that I have led. It is easier and cheaper to negotiate, document, and close than it is to do a full equity round, but it still provides a cap on valuation and some limited protections for investors during the period up to the next financing.

Term Sheet for Convertible Preferred Stock

When it comes to a full equity round using convertible preferred stock, the majority of U.S.-based venture capital funds historically have used a standard term sheet model developed over a number of years by all of their law firms working together under the coordination of the National Venture Capital Association. This term sheet, known as the NVCA Model Venture Capital Financing Term Sheet, is a free download, together with the deal documents backing it up, from http://tinyurl.com/NVCAmodel. It is annotated with comments that explain the various company- and investor-favorable terms, as well as those which are generally neutral and agreed upon by both sides.

Professional angels, especially those investing in groups, initially followed the lead of the VCs and used the same documents, which made it much easier to do follow-on investment rounds when VCs would typically join in. The problem is that the NVCA term sheet alone is 17 pages, which in turn expands into 120 pages of additional documentation. Negotiating these documents—with lawyers on both sides of the table—can become expensive, and it is not unusual to see legal fees reaching $50,000 or more for a full convertible preferred round.

As more and more companies began to get funded by angels and as the market changed to make much of the NVCA content seem like overkill for a small investment (such as many pages about registration rights during an initial public offering, which is, frankly, a highly unlikely occurrence), there emerged a need for something easier to use for angel deals. A much shorter and simpler set of documents was therefore developed on a pro-bono basis by attorney Ted Wang of Fenwick and West and is available online, together with its backup documents and annotations/discussion, at www.seriesseed.com. This term sheet is really simple, reducing the 17 pages of the NVCA version to just over one! The challenge with this approach, however, is that it manages this shrinkage by removing all protections for the investor and pushes off the major issues until the next round.

We at Gust therefore took the liberty of coming up with a middle-ground approach that I believe is most useful for serious angel investors who are likely to read this book. Over the course of a year, we worked with lawyers for investors and companies and iterated the result with some of the leading professional angel investor members of New York Angels. Under the guidance of Lori Smith of White and Williams (one of the country's top corporate lawyers who serves on the legal advisory committee of the Angel Capital Association), we started with Ted Wang's bare bones Series Seed documents and added back in the bare minimum of investor protections that sophisticated investors would insist upon.

I've now used this approach with several recent investments that I've led, and it seems to be, as Goldilocks would say, "Just right!" It's thoroughly annotated (by me) and designed to be a middle-of-the-road document, scrupulously balanced between the needs and interests of investors and entrepreneurs. The full term sheet is included in Appendix D, and can be found in an electronic version, along with all of its supporting documents, online at http://gust.com/seriesseed/.

13

After the Investment

Managing Your Portfolio and Adding Value as an Active Angel

THE MINUTE YOUR investment is transferred to the bank account of a startup, the relationship between the two of you enters a very different phase. Up until that moment, in most cases you are Lord or Lady Bountiful, and the entrepreneur is an obsequious supplicant. But from that moment forward, how you interact with your portfolio company lies somewhere on a wide spectrum that is defined by the relative power positions, maturity, and sophistication of both parties.

On the one hand, if you are a small investor tagging along as part of a syndicate and don't have many explicit rights as part of the investment terms, you may literally not hear from the entrepreneur again until you get an email telling you that the company has been acquired or shut down ... and you may not even hear about that! This may happen despite what is almost certainly your right to receive annual reports.

On the other hand, if you are the lead investor with a significant equity interest in the company and the right to a board seat (or even board control) through a shareholders' agreement, then you have a great deal of influence on the company, and will likely be in communication with the CEO on a monthly, weekly, or even more frequent basis.

In most cases, however, the relationship will fall somewhere in the middle ground: the company will send you annual—or perhaps even quarterly—financial reports about its progress, you may be invited to an in-person annual shareholders meeting, and you will likely receive occasional legal notices for things requesting your signature or vote, such as future financings, bylaw changes, and the like. Let's walk through the company's post-investment activities, and see what an appropriate relationship should look like.

Monitoring Your Company

Because you are a serious angel investor and are *not* treating this as throw-away money (right?!), it is important that you keep track of your investment, particularly because it is likely to be volatile and illiquid and because there will be occasions where you will be required to make decisions relative to further investments. You may also have annual tax reporting requirements if the corporate form of the company is an LLC or partnership rather than a C corporation.

Fortunately, as an angel investor, part of what you negotiate during the investment round is access to an array of performance data about the companies in your portfolio. This always includes annual numbers, and often narrative reports from the CEO. Many financing rounds provide for a class of Major Investors (typically the ones with the largest amounts invested) who are entitled to a superset of rights. These rights would include at least quarterly financials and often monthlies, periodic calls with management, and access to the company's books and records. The cutoff line for the level of investment defining a major investor will vary, and could be as low as $25,000 for a small round with sophisticated angels, and as high as $500,000 for a larger round led by a venture capital fund.

As you might imagine, keeping track of information from all companies in a serious angel portfolio can be daunting. This is one place where an investor-relations platform like Gust can be helpful. What Gust does is to greatly simplify the bidirectional relationship and communications process between startups and investors. Because the startup uses the platform to keep in touch with all of its investors and to post all of the required documents, reports, and updates, it makes life easy for the entrepreneur. Similarly because you, as the investor, can use Gust to track all of your investments, it means that you can always check your investor dashboard to see the status of each of your portfolio companies.

The degree to which a particular investor scrutinizes the actual financials of a company, or even asks questions of management concerning what the company is doing, is generally a product of three factors: how active/passive that investor is or wants to be, how good the CEO is in reaching out to and communicating with investors, and how well the company is doing.

In the case of passive investors where the company is perceived to be doing well, they may not even ask for an annual report, although they're certainly entitled to one. But active (or scared or would-be-active) investors in a company that is in a rocky period where its survival is at stake may feel driven to place weekly calls to company headquarters asking for the latest information.

It can be difficult to decide how proactive you should be as an angel investor. Is it your job to scrutinize details of the business's operations, looking for inefficiencies that could be remedied or strategic break-throughs that may be overlooked? Or is it smarter to wait, and have faith in the business acumen of the entrepreneur whom you were at such pains to vet and approve before casting your lot with him or her?

In general, your involvement with a portfolio company as a small investor should be to support the management team, providing a level of interaction that is comfortable for the CEO. The smartest entrepreneurs, in my experience, understand that they have a great resource in their investor base, and will provide regular updates while not being hesitant to ask for help when needed. Typically, that help will involve sales leads or introductions to potential partners or investors or assistance in recruiting executives. Rarely will it involve discussions about the company's strategy and virtually never will it involve specific operational questions.

That is because if you start taking a close look at the day-to-day operations of a company in which you've invested, you may find it hard to resist the temptation to micromanage—especially if you notice patterns of spending or management that strike you as dubious. You may find yourself pondering the metaphysics of such unusual financial questions as, "Is purchasing office jellyfish a good use of my investment money?"

Before you jump to any conclusions, consider that it's important to look at questions like this holistically. Remember, you're putting money behind an entrepreneur and his or her particular vision, team, and operating skills. If the entrepreneur believes that having office jellyfish is a good thing for company morale and will foster a work environment conducive to a more productive startup team, then you need to decide whether you believe in and support that choice. If you sincerely find it impossible to support that choice, then there needs to be a heart-to-heart talk about what is appropriate and what isn't, for a given stage of a company.

While wise counsel (and ongoing support and introductions) are usually welcomed by entrepreneurs, there are cases in which angel investors begin to live the entrepreneurial life vicariously and become too involved in the inner workings of the business. This can create an awkward situation for the entrepreneur who finds himself continually second-guessed by a well-meaning angel whose advice is more intrusive than helpful.

In such a situation, I know of one smart company founder who, faced with a particularly persistent small angel who was taking up hours of his time, resorted to sending all of his investors the following letter:

Dear NewCo Investors,

We have been blessed with an amazing group of value-adding investors during our company's seed phase. In turn, we have established a virtually unprecedented communications program with our investors, including weekly reports, monthly in-person meetings, and frequent phone calls. This has been a great boon for NewCo during our formative period, and we look forward to continuing our frequent and regular investor communications as we continue to grow. However, we have now come to a point where I need to be able to focus directly on running the business rather than spending nearly a full day a week on the phone with my wonderful investors.

Therefore, beginning this week, we will need to limit our investor communications to the weekly reports and monthly meetings. Of course, if anything urgent arises requiring your advice, I will be sure to reach out to you immediately. But otherwise, I respectfully ask your support in allowing me to dedicate my full time to enhancing the value of your investment.

Warmly, and with great appreciation for your support,
John Doe
CEO

From that point on, the CEO actually refused to take calls from the angel investor who had made daily conversations a part of his routine, and in this was quietly applauded by the remaining—more restrained—investors.

Thinking About Your Portfolio as a Whole

Aside from the Law-of-Large-Numbers motivation to diversify your funds across a substantial portfolio of angel investments, there are two schools of thought when it comes to the concept of portfolio building.

One of them mirrors the standard advice concerning an overall investment portfolio: carefully distribute your investments over a range of different risk/reward opportunities, and diversify across uncorrelated industries, time horizons, geographic regions, and company stages. This would suggest that you invest in some risky, pre-seed deals with potentially enormous payoffs, which might be balanced by an investment in a non-sexy business with a clear and ready market.

The challenge in applying this approach to startup investing is that experience has shown that there is a low correlation between the size of a potential outcome and the risk of an early failure, at least when it comes to newly created businesses. *All* startups are risky, and it is difficult—if not impossible—to trade off the risk factor against anything else.

My approach, therefore, is the opposite: I have decided that since angel investing already represents a small, specific part of my otherwise-diversified investment portfolio, it does not make sense to diversify further within my angel investments. I approach angel investing with a particular investing thesis, find companies that fit that thesis, and distribute my risk by investing in a number of them.

One aspect of thinking in terms of your portfolio rather than in terms of one-off investments is considering the possibility of conflicts among the companies you own. The reason is simple: why have part of your investment in one company be used for the sole purpose of fighting against part of your investment in another?

The best way to mitigate conflicts between portfolio companies is to avoid investing in direct competitors in the first place. While this can be difficult for seed funds with large portfolios and limited direct day-to-day involvement, most investors are careful to avoid directly competitive investments.

Once the investments have been made, and assuming that (as in 99 percent of all cases) they are minority investments, the operative approach should be the same as the Hippocratic Oath: "First, do no harm." If two portfolio companies are competing in the same space, the investor has to be excruciatingly careful about not sharing confidential information across the two companies, or in any way advising or guiding one of them based on privileged knowledge of the other.

This is done by avoiding service on the two different boards, or recusing oneself from voting or discussions, if board-level deliberations verge into specifically competitive areas.

A good example (albeit on a much larger scale) is the case of Apple and Google. The two companies had similar outlooks, close relations, and shared board members. This was fine so long as one was making computer hardware and the other was running a search engine, but when the business models began converging, they had no choice but to go their separate ways.

Making Follow-On Investments

Most novice angels (and, to be fair, many experienced ones as well) expect that they will write one check up-front, and sit back until the initial public offering (IPO); however, in the majority of cases the real world intervenes, and additional funding is required. When this happens, there are not typically a lot of other sources of cash immediately at hand, so all eyes turn to the original angels. Here is where *follow-on investments* become important.

A follow-on investment is simply an additional investment in a company by a current investor. It can be structured in a number of ways depending on the particular circumstances (inside/outside, up/down/flat, bridge/equity, and so on). In general, however, it takes its cue in form, if not valuation, from the previous round.

Take the example of a company that completes a convertible preferred stock financing round labeled Series C, with investors putting in
$10 million. If an investor putting in an additional $2 million follows
this round, the follow-up investment might be structured in one of the
following ways:

- All of the existing preferred investors (Series C and earlier), the
  new investor, and the company agree to "re-open" the Series C,
  with the same equity sold at the same valuation to the new investor.
  Depending on how much time elapses between the two investments, it would likely be considered part of the same round. This
  would be used primarily in a case where the same investor had all
  of the original Series C, because by purchasing the same equity
  (the Series C preferred stock), the new investor's liquidation preferences would be *pari passu*—that is, side by side in liquidation
  preference—to the earlier investors. (In many sequenced financings, the repayment order in a liquidity scenario is often last in, first
  out, so this would have the effect of benefiting the original Series C
  at the expense of the later investor, because the later investor would
  be getting money out at the same time as the original Series C, not
  ahead of it.)
- The company could issue a Series D convertible preferred stock
  identical to the Series C, except that it has liquidation priority
  (remember, last in, first out). This might be used in a case where
  a follow-on investor did not own all of the C shares and wanted
  to be sure to get all the new money out before the C holders were
  paid back. This would generally be considered a new, follow-on, *flat
  round*.
- If the company is doing well, it could issue a new Series D identical
  to the C, except for its liquidation priority and a higher valuation.
  This would be considered a new, follow-on, *up round*.
- If the company is doing poorly, but the investor still has faith that
  the company can improve, it could invest in a Series D at a lower
  valuation. This would be a follow-on, *down round*, and would not
  be a good thing for anyone. It would probably trigger the (almost
  inevitable) antidilution clauses in the Series A, B, and C rounds,
  providing partial (but not total) protection of their value, and the
  result would be the common stockholders (that is, the founders)

taking an even bigger hit than the new investment by itself would warrant.

- A last case would be if everyone believes that in the not-too-distant future the company will be able to raise a new round from some third-party investor—hopefully at a higher valuation—but needs operating cash to keep it going until that investment closes. Then the investor might be willing to put in the $2 million as a convertible note to *bridge* the company to the outside Series D. In this scenario, the money would go in as a loan and convert (probably at a discount) to whatever form of equity would be sold to the new investor. The $2 million would thus (eventually) be considered a follow-on investment in the new round.

A *pay-to-play down round* may occur when a company has not met expectations and needs to raise additional capital to keep going. But because it isn't doing well, the valuation of the company used for the new investment is lower than the valuation used for the prior round of investment. This is a down round, which means new investors buy more shares of the company for their dollars than did the earlier investors.

While this seems like a good incentive to get the company's existing investors to put in more money, it often is not enough. Many investors are quick to cut their losses in troubled companies, and might regard this as throwing good money after bad or "trying to catch a falling knife." So an additional incentive is needed.

The company, together with whichever investor(s) is/are prepared to commit cash in this round, thereupon issues an ultimatum, such as the following, to all the other investors.

Every current investor is expected to invest new money as part of this round, in the same proportion as the amount of equity you currently own (known as your *pro rata*).

And just to provide you with a little incentive to do the right thing, we are going to up the ante: If you are an existing investor, you currently own shares of convertible preferred stock. Those have all sorts of good features, both economic and protective. If you do *not* participate in this round (which of course is your prerogative) then we are going to convert your preferred stock into common stock, taking away all of your protective and control provisions. And, in addition you will suffer dilution of your ownership in favor of those who do invest.

Now, would you like to reconsider your decision?

The result is to set up a situation where, if existing investors want to continue to have a meaningful interest in the future of the company ("playing"), they need to cough up new cash to invest in this round ("paying").

Hence, this is known as a *pay-to-play down round.*

Adding Value to Your Investment

Part of the beauty of angel investing is the opportunity to do much more with your investments than simply monitor them (actively or passively) or even participate in subsequent investment rounds. Because startups are small, often scrambling for resources of all kinds, informally managed, and open to input and ideas from all sources, angels can contribute to the success of their portfolio companies in a host of ways—which can be enormously gratifying and beneficial for everyone involved.

The ideal angel investor spends a great deal of his or her time working on behalf of the company in support of the CEO in every way other than being a fulltime employee.

The baseline expectation is that an angel investor will at least do things that anyone (employee, friend, parent, founder, or anyone else involved in the startup) could do: refer potential customers, tweet out company news, suggest ideas, check out competitive sites, point out relevant news articles, provide moral support, and so on.

The best angels, however, provide the same categories of contributions that well-run, not-for-profit institutions look for when recruiting board members: the three Ws of Wealth, Work, and Wisdom. Let's consider all three in turn.

First, wealth. The likelihood of additional investment rounds in *every* company means that serious angel investors reserve additional capital (known colloquially as "dry powder") for just that purpose. There could be a good carrot (the opportunity to invest your pro-rata amount in an up-round because the company is doing very well and you want to bet more on a winner). There could be a bad stick (the previously discussed "pay or play" scenario). Or, as happens in most situations, the company might just need more cash to execute its plan. In all cases, you want to have enough cash in reserve so that you can make the decision yourself, rather than have one made for you because you have no option.

When it comes to work for the company, angels can be most productive with the types of unique contributions only they can provide. These might be skill-based, such as presentation coaching for the CEO (something I do a lot of), or helping write or revise the business plan. More typically, they are network-based, with the angel offering to connect the startup with resources, partners, investors, or acquirers that would otherwise fall outside the company's reach. In fact, the first thing that super angel Ron Conway does after making an investment is to give the new portfolio company a large binder containing the names of every person Ron knows in the industry, with the offer to make whatever introductions are needed. While this is worth Ron's weight in gold, for the rest of us, connecting a portfolio CEO to your LinkedIn network can be a decent substitute.

As for wisdom, one good angel can be worth a boatload of industry consultants, and great CEOs take advantage of this. The average serious angel in the United States has had over 15 years of entrepreneurial experience and personally started two or three companies. As a result, angels can provide insights and experience impossible to obtain elsewhere. I know angels (including some who didn't even serve on the company's board) who meet weekly with startup CEOs for executive coaching sessions. And others who facilitate off-site management meetings, provide a much-needed perspective from outside the company, or keep the entrepreneur focused on real-world metrics and financials.

All of the above items are some things that truly committed angels do for some of their startups. In the real world, it should be obvious that no one human being can simultaneously do everything I've described for each of the dozens of companies I suggest you have in your portfolio.

Realistically, a good angel investor will:

- Intelligently understand the entrepreneur's vision.
- Provide early-stage funding based on that understanding and faith in the entrepreneur.

- Respond quickly whenever approached by the entrepreneur, both before and after the investment.
- Try not to get in the way or be a pain in the neck.
- Reserve at least some additional cash to re-up during a follow-on round if appropriate.
- Do at least some of the things I've listed under the Three Ws.

If you become an angel who does every one of the items on the list above, then you are a truly committed investor and the entrepreneurs you choose to support will be lucky to have found (or been found by) you.

Serving on a Company Board

Many new angels wonder about serving on the boards of directors of the companies in which they invest. Is this a normal part of being a significant investor in a startup? Is it a fringe benefit? A punishment?

As with so many questions related to angel investing, the answer is "it depends." A board seat in and of itself has no particular value, and is often something to be avoided rather than sought. It usually doesn't give you more cash compensation or more direct control over the operating business. In recent years, as angels have become more professional and best practices have emerged, the Angel Capital Association has suggested that one-quarter to 1 percent in equity (subject to vesting) may be an appropriate additional compensation for an angel undertaking board service. Nonetheless, there are circumstances in which serving on a board can be a great way to strengthen the business in which you've invested and to create value for yourself and everyone else involved in the startup.

The legal role of the board is to make strategic and corporate-level decisions, hire and fire the CEO, and represent all of the stockholders of the company. Being a member of the board of directors means that you have a legal, fiduciary responsibility to all the other investors, and you are required to put the stockholders' interests ahead of your personal ones.

So the question you need to ask yourself is "Why do I want to be on the board?" If you are going to be a true partner of the founder, owning a significant share of company equity (in the range of 20 percent or higher) and sharing overall decision making about company direction, strategy, financing, staffing, and so on, with one or more cofounders and you see that role continuing in the future, then being on the board might make sense.

On the other hand, a seed-startup board would typically have only three members (often one founder, one investor serving as Chairman, and one independent member approved by the other two), expanding to five around the time of a full Series A venture round. If you are not the CEO (who is also presumably a founder and who really needs to be on the board), then you'd effectively be taking the single investor seat. Ask yourself if you are the person best qualified to fill that important role.

If you do decide to become a board member, one of your roles will be to monitor the strategy of the company as it evolves over time. You will need to apply your best judgment to the thorny question of when and how the company's approach to the market should change from the vision that originally won your support.

As an investor, you put your money behind the entrepreneur and her company, not behind a specific product or service. As such, your expectation should be that over time there will be other products, extensions, and changes to the company. However, technically speaking, depending on the documentation used for the investment (such as a Series A preferred stock financing, or a convertible note with protective provisions), the money raised is intended to be used for relatively specific purposes as laid out in the business plan, and major budget deviations need to be approved by the company's board of directors. If the entrepreneur you've supported raises money on the premise that she is going to invest it in creating a social network and then turns around and uses it to open a hot dog stand, it's your job as a board member to ask hard questions about what's going on.

One hopes problems like those won't arise for the simple reason that you and your fellow investors will maintain a line of open connection with the entrepreneurial founder. You should expect to hear in advance when any dramatic change in company strategy is contemplated, and you should have the opportunity to offer feedback and advice before such a change is made.

In other cases, the board may have to drive the process of change when a company is heading in the wrong direction. This may include replacing the CEO or pushing the CEO to make changes in the executive ranks below the CEO's level. Handling such changes is one of the trickiest situations a startup faces.

In large part it comes down to the integrity and personality of the CEO. If he is a straight-shooting professional, then a full, private, direct discussion and negotiation over serious management issues is in order before any personnel decisions are made. If you occupy a board seat as an angel investor, you can play a key role in making sure that such transitions are handled with fairness and professionalism so that the company is able to get back on the right growth track quickly.

14

Exits and Other Unicorns

Getting Your Money Out
Makes All Things Right

THROUGHOUT THIS BOOK, I've talked about the ancillary benefits of being an angel investor: the opportunity to be an entrepreneur once removed, the chance to work with many of the most interesting businesspeople you'll ever meet, the ability to contribute to the growth of the economy through the creation of world-changing new companies, and more. But the central goal—the outcome that attracted you to angel investing in the first place—is the possibility of making money by having the foresight and opportunity to invest in a company whose revenues, profits, and equity value soar through the roof. That's the happy ending we all dream about—the ending that makes the hard work, long wait, and risk worthwhile.

How often does that happen? In the real world, what can you expect when your investment winds up and it's time to take your money and go elsewhere? It would be great if I could give you a completely sourced, definitive answer based on the specific outcomes of the last 10,000 angel investments in the United States. Unfortunately, angel investing—dealing as it does with private companies and Accredited Investors exempt from most regulation and tracking—is carried out almost entirely away from public view or reporting. That, in turn, means that there are few reliable statistics (despite what you may hear or read in the press), and those that exist are high-level numbers of either economic outcomes or complete write-offs.

In the real world, moreover, things are not always black and white. Company sales that appear on the surface to be great successes may actually be face-saving wind-ups, and transactions involving unheralded, no-name companies that are ignored by the media may generate hundreds of millions of dollars. But it's my job to serve as your guide through the labyrinth of this new asset class, so I'll take a shot at the *real* answer. Here, in a purely anecdotal and totally subjective answer with numbers pulled out of the air (but based on my personal investments in over 90 companies, New York Angels' involvement in several hundred others, and nearly two decades of familiarity with active angel investors), is my best guess of what *really* happens: the most common angel exit scenarios and the frequency with which they occur.

Outcome	Percentage
Goes out of business	50.0
Sale to a larger company	20.0
Acqui-hire	15.0
Walking dead	7.0
Soft landing with a competitor	3.0
Bought out by a later investor	2.0
Bought out by a lifestyle entrepreneur	1.0
Becomes part of a roll-up	1.0
Disappears	0.9
Initial public offering (IPO)	0.1

This table reinforces a lesson I've emphasized several times in this book: Investing in early stage, pre-profitable companies is risky, with only a small minority of companies having significantly successful outcomes. And because it's impossible to tell up front exactly which of the companies will be the home run with the 20x return, it means that all of the companies in an early-stage portfolio must at least have the possibility of becoming that home run.

These realities explain why long-term investments are not the goal of angel investors in startups. They certainly happen, but it is not what we are hoping for when we first make the investment. Why is a 3- to 5-year exit strategy more desirable than a 10- to 20-plus-year time frame? Because seed-stage investments in private startup companies are not Warren Buffett-type investments which are perfect for the buy-and-hold strategy beloved by low-risk investors.

Returning to the math lesson, let's assume that we as angels want to target a 20 percent annualized return from our investments into 10 companies, and we know that statistically only 1 out of those 10 is going to be our portfolio-maker home run. This means that every individual company in our portfolio needs to be at least theoretically able to return the profit for all ten.

Each investment needs to be able to generate 200 percent of the initial investment each year. Of course, 9 out of the 10 won't get there, but we hope that one will.

Because that 200 percent is an annualized return, if we are going to hold for four years before an exit (taking the midpoint between three and five), the company needs to be able to generate $2 \times 2 \times 2 \times 2$ at exit, or a 16x return.

If, on the other hand, the money must patiently wait for its payoff for 15 years (taking the midpoint between 10 and 20), the math goes: $2 \times 2 \times 2 \times 2 \times 2 \times 2 \times 2 \times 2 \times 2 \times 2 \times 2 \times 2 \times 2 \times 2 \times 2$ at exit, or 32,768 times. Which means that a $100,000 investment today in a long-term play has to payoff with a future value of over $3.2 billion ... and that's just the angel's share, assuming no other investment into the company during those 15 years (a near impossibility). If we purchased, say, a 20 percent interest in the company for our $100,000, that sets the required IPO valuation of the company at around $16 billion, or roughly the value at which Twitter went public. (The math is intended primarily to illustrate the challenge of long-term, risky investments.)

For precisely this reason there is a shift underway toward the concept of *early exits*, a term popularized in an influential book and workshop series of the same name by Basil Peters, an experienced Canadian angel investor. According to Peters, because there are so many myths and misperceptions about startup exits, much of what one hears in the press is dangerously wrong. He maintains that the traditional venture-capital model does not always work for angel investors.

Peters further asserts that in the entrepreneurial environment of the early twenty-first century:

- It has become much more difficult to raise expansion funding of $5 million and more.
- Corporate America is loaded with cash and is choosing to acquire small companies in lieu of expanded internal R&D.
- The valuation sweet spot for many large U.S. companies is $15 to $30 million, selling prices of great interest to entrepreneurs and angels, but not generally to traditional VCs.
- Building companies with a valuation of $15 million or more takes much less time with lower risk than building companies with a valuation of $150 million, the average VC exit in recent years.

Peters therefore counsels startups and their angel investors to consider a company's exit strategy before the initial investment is made, and then work diligently to complete such an exit within a few years.

Peters's analysis seems to me well-grounded. So how should these realities influence our goals for an angel exit? The options are rather limited.

For example, it is possible—but unusual—for VC funders to acquire the interests of early-stage investors at a significant profit. I've seen this happen only when the company was a blowout hit, with a venture valuation high enough that it was worthwhile for the VCs to pick up small interests from early angels.

It does happen, though, and some early-stage investors are very good at structuring things this way. For example, the investors in India's Mumbai Angels have managed this on more than one occasion. And there have been a few cases in New York Angels' portfolio where later-stage investors wanted to clean up the company's cap table, and therefore made attractive offers to the angels. But this is rare—and not something an investor or an entrepreneur can or should rely upon.

Another way for a startup to multiply its value is by growing to the point where an IPO is possible. But in practice, any startup these days that is "targeting" an IPO as its exit strategy is so out of touch with reality that it is unlikely to succeed.

In fact, the whole concept of an IPO as a planned exit strategy was an aberration born of the global insanity of the turn-of-the-century dotcom boom. When that world came crashing down, so did the IPO window for ambitious startups. To put things in perspective, there were about 750,000 incorporated employer businesses founded in the United States in 2012, according to the U.S. Bureau of Labor Statistics. In the same year, there were exactly 128 IPOs. And of those, a majority (including major high flyers like Facebook, Groupon, and Zynga) were unable to maintain their opening prices.

The question of a deliberate exit strategy for a startup (as opposed to throwing oneself into the hands of the Fates) boils down to two possibilities: the sale of the company as a high-growth business to another company or to a major investment organization, or its sale to the company's founder who might be seeking a lifestyle-supporting, income-generating, business. And if those are the only two realistic possibilities, this means that startups can logically follow one of two strategic paths.

Businesses designed for sale at a later, sharp valuation increase will be purchased with an eye to their future growth and profitability, rather than their current earnings, or even revenues. They should thus be willing to take bigger risks, accept outside equity and debt capital, and swing for the fences, focusing on growth above all. This is a typical angel-tech deal, and buyers for these types of companies fall into two categories: strategic and financial.

A strategic buyer acquires the company because of its synergies with the parent and believes that adding the target's customers, products, technology, brand, or expertise will leverage assets the acquirer already has and create more value than the cost of the acquisition. A financial buyer looks at the company's numbers on a stand-alone basis, and calculates the transaction's potential economic return by looking at the company's future projected cash flow compared to its acquisition cost.

In contrast, a business that the founder intends to own and manage for the long haul as a cash-generating sinecure should focus primarily on generating near-term profitability and avoiding debt, while retaining most or all of the equity in the founder's hands. This is the typical Main Street small business, which is generally not the type of company that makes sense for an angel seeking high returns.

When a Company Fails

The reality of startup investing is that most companies do not attain the phenomenal success their investors and founders are hoping for.

Most, in fact, will eventually close their doors. When this happens, venture and angel investors will typically not see any money at all. That is because the definition of bankruptcy is what happens when liabilities (what you owe to creditors) are greater than assets (the monetary value of everything you have that could be used to pay your debts).

Because investors are not creditors but equity owners of the business, in a full bankruptcy 100 percent of the assets are liquidated, and the money they generate is used to pay off as much of the debt (loans and trade payables) as possible. By definition, there will be nothing left (remember, liabilities are greater than assets), so equity holders (investors and founders) get wiped out.

In some cases, however (my experience tells me about 25 percent, but I doubt there are any accurate numbers), the company reaches a point where the value of the business (either as an operating company, or its technology, people, customers, or intellectual property) is worth more than its accrued debt, but less than it was valued when the investment was made. If the board and management think that the company is unlikely to be able to recover, then they will try to find an acquirer "to take the body off the street."

In that situation, the acquirer may pay some fraction of the value of the original investment, in cash or in stock, and all of that will almost certainly go to the investors (who own preferred stock) before a penny goes to the founders (who own common stock). I've seen cases where this was one or two pennies per dollar of investment, and cases where it was dollar for dollar, so the investors didn't make any money, but didn't lose anything either.

Sometimes a company that goes bankrupt will retain some assets with significant value. For example, when a dot-com goes bust, what happens to its source code (the program containing the data and relationships that provided services or activities to customers)?

The answer is that all assets of a bankrupt company, including not just source code but the computers, desk chairs, domain name, office lease, and so on—continue to be owned by the entity that bought or created those assets until either it is explicitly disowned by such entity (as by gifting it to another entity, selling or trading it, deliberately abandoning it, or releasing it to the public domain (in the case of intellectual property such as source code), or ownership is transferred or eliminated by action of law (such as passing through inheritance on a person's death, being transferred during a court-supervised bankruptcy hearing, or passing automatically into the public domain at the expiration of a patent or copyright).

When a company declares bankruptcy, the court will usually distribute its assets among the company's creditors. In most cases, the bankruptcy of a company you've invested in will be a total financial loss. The only real upside lies in the intangible values you may have received from the experience—knowledge, industry insights, personal connections, and so on.

Note that although theoretically a company either has assets worth less than its obligations (and thus should technically be bankrupt) or has assets worth more than its obligations (and thus should be of some net positive value), in practice the amounts involved with a small, failing business (either positive or negative) are usually too small for anyone to fight over. As a result, in most cases a failed company will simply file a Certificate of Dissolution with the state, which is enough for investors to write off the full amount of the investment against their income for the year.

Occasionally one hears about an entrepreneur offering free stock in a new startup to former angel investors who lost money in a former failed startup. It's neither required nor expected, but it is a classy thing to do and is greatly appreciated, even if the former investors decline to accept the offer.

It's also very rare. Out of the few dozen failed companies in which I've invested, my guess is that 25 to 30 percent of the entrepreneurs have gone on to start another company. Of those, exactly one gave me stock in NewCo (although most of the others kindly offered me the opportunity to *invest* in NewCo …).

If you are lucky enough to receive such a gift of stock, there's no question of due diligence or negotiation. The entrepreneur is likely to make it a gift of common stock with whatever features they choose, thereby minimizing the downside risk to them. Your sole job is to say a sincere "Thank you" and hope that NewCo will fare better than OldCo did.

When a Company Is Acquired

The most common way a positive outcome occurs for an angel-financed startup is through an acquisition of the company. For a startup that has a product that is a natural extension of the acquirers' own products, or traction in a market that the acquirer needs to enter, the startup is typically folded in to the larger company.

If it's a big acquisition (such as Mint, the web-based personal finance service that was purchased by Intuit in 2009 for $170 million, or Instagram, the photo-sharing service purchased by Facebook in 2012 for $1 billion), the startup is generally kept in one piece, and the CEO can take on an important role in the acquirer. If it's a smaller acquisition, often the startup's product is simply abandoned and the startup team members are added to the company's existing teams working in a similar area. If the key reason for the purchase was one or more specific people in the startup, that's colloquially known as an *acqui-hire*, and often the original startup is shut down and some or all of the employees are put to work on other projects for the bigger company.

There are a few cases where the motivation for the acquisition is purely or primarily for its intellectual property, and in those cases the startup team may not even go to the new company ... but those situations are relatively rare.

A more important question to you as an investor is what happens to the money that changes hands when the acquisition takes place? Since all companies are ultimately owned by individuals and/or other entities, usually through the ownership of stock, the acquirer is buying the target company from its owners, not from the company itself. As such, the founders of—and early investors in—Instagram made a lot of money on the sale to Facebook because Facebook purchased the company from them for cash and stock.

Pure cash exits (particularly for founders, as opposed to investors) are typically restricted to cases where the acquirer is looking for value that the startup has already created, as opposed to the people who will likely create more value in the future. That could be high-value users (i.e., subscribers paying big dollars on an automatically recurring basis, as with mobile phones or cable television), monopolistic market rights (such as a transferrable exclusive license to a patent, brand, or sales channel), or technology that would be expensive or time-consuming to replicate (such as a high-frequency trading system or a complex predictive algorithm). From these descriptions, it is obvious that in most cases a "startup" wouldn't have been around long enough to create that kind of value.

So why the acquisition?

In the case of the vast majority of tech startups acquired by large industry players in the range of $10 to $40 million, the larger company is looking to bring on the team, the ideas, and the fresh blood of the upstart to augment its activities, or to serve as the core for a new product offering or line of business. In that case, little value is assigned to the company itself and most of the value is attributable to the team. As such, the last thing the acquirer wants is to give the founders of the company "walking-away money," because the goal is to lock them into contracts with the company for at least the next one to two years.

In most cases where the acquisition is for all cash, a majority of the cash that the founders would receive is locked up, and payable only after they've spent some years working for the acquirer. The investors, however, would get their cash up front (except for a small hold-back percentage to cover any post-closing surprises).

In the case of a company acquiring a startup for stock, either:

1. The company is a large one (Google, Facebook et al.), where the stock is liquid, has determinable value, and is therefore effectively the same as cash, or
2. The company is small (perhaps only a bit larger than the target), where cash is tight, and the stock they're paying with is the only way they can do the deal. In that situation, everyone effectively becomes partners and is incentivized to help the combined company grow rapidly.

Occasionally, a startup is acquired for less money than it raised from its investors, and in that case what happens is straightforward. Every investment round in a company is made on the basis of extensive paperwork (often upwards of 100 pages), with the most important part specifying precisely what happens when it comes time to pay out the proceeds (if any) from the sale or dissolution of the company. Since all prior investors sign such agreements (or are otherwise legally bound by them) with every new financing, there is never *any* confusion about what will happen under any particular outcome.

In many, if not most, seed- and early-stage funding scenarios, the investments are structured in LIFO order: last in, first out.

The technical term for this is the *liquidation waterfall*, because in a liquidation—whether good, as in a large buyout, or bad, as in a distress sale—investors and others are paid out in a specified order. After one pool of investors (say, all those in the Series A round) is filled up, any remaining cash falls down to the next pool, until that pool is filled up, and so on all the way down the line.

Here is the typical payout order, from first to last.

1. Transaction costs, including legal and investment banking fees
2. Salaries owed to employees
3. Debt owed to secured creditors
4. Debt owed to unsecured trade creditors
5. Debt owed to note holders (convertible and other)
6. Management carve-out (if any)
7. Senior Preferred stock and warrants
8. Any preference multiple on the senior Preferred stock and warrants
9. Junior Preferred stock and warrants
10. Any preference multiple on the junior Preferred stock and warrants
11. Common stock (including any Preferred that converted to Common, any exercised options, and all Founders' stock) and Common stock warrants

If a company hasn't taken in any outside financing and is current on its payment obligations, things are simple because the liquidation waterfall jumps directly from step 1 down to step 11. But for a company with multiple rounds of equity and/or debt funding, things can rapidly become so complicated that the only way to figure out who gets what and in what order, is to use a specialized computer or web-based program (see Figure 14.1).

As indicated in step 6 of the payout order, in some cases the investors may choose to provide an incentive to the management team in order to ensure that the sale goes through quickly. That is done by setting aside either a fixed amount, or a percentage of the purchase price, which gets divided up among the management team and gets paid out before the investors start getting paid back. In some cases, all preferred investors are treated *pari passu*, so steps 7 and 8 are combined into one, as are steps 9 and 10.

Once you have received your compensation from an exit, you can take the cash and move on, or you can enter once more into battle and

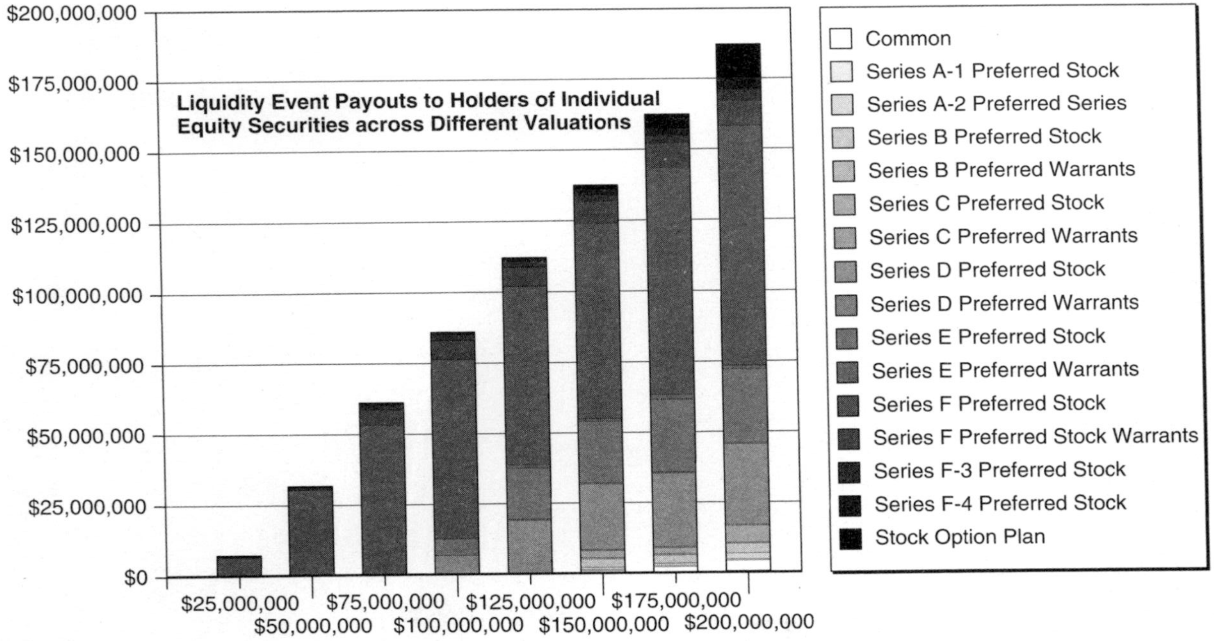

Figure 14.1 Liquidation Waterfall for a Company with Six Equity Classes

Source: Shareholder Insite, Inc.

deploy that cash into more startups. The ideal situation for a serious angel is to invest in a broad range of companies, have at least one serious exit which returns all of the invested capital and continue finding and supporting innovative companies, but from then on playing with "house money."

May we all be so fortunate!

PART

III

Your Place in the World of Angels

15

The Entrepreneurship Financing Ecosystem

Grants, Venture Capital, Accelerators, and Other Players

THROUGHOUT THIS BOOK I've touched on some of the other participants in the world of startup investing—individuals and organizations that in some cases may be viewed as competitors with angel investors for the funding of startup ventures, but that—far more often—complement what angels do. As in any vibrant ecosystem, a variety of organisms has evolved over time, and the result is a complex, continually changing world in which resources of all kinds—not just money, but also ideas, talent, knowledge, connections, opportunities, and energy—have a good chance of finding their way to the fledgling companies that need them most to fuel their transformation into large, successful businesses.

In Chapter 4, we looked at the financial life of a startup and identified the typical sequencing of different types of capital. Now it is time to take a closer look at these other players and how you are likely to interact with them.

Government Grants

The closest thing to "free money" for a company is when the government gives it cash and doesn't expect it back. Governments at virtually all levels, in virtually all countries, provide grants of some type to small companies with the goal of supporting entrepreneurial development.

In the United States, the Small Business Innovation Research (SBIR) program, established in 1982, encourages domestic small businesses to engage in federal research and development (R&D) that has the potential for commercialization.

The theory, according to the program's enabling legislation, is that "by including qualified small businesses in the nation's R&D arena, high-tech innovation is stimulated and the United States gains entrepreneurial spirit as it meets its specific research and development needs." Each year, federal agencies with outside R&D budgets that exceed $100 million are required to allocate 2.5 percent of that budget to these grants.

As of 2014, eleven federal agencies participate in the program. SBIR enables small businesses to explore their technological potential and provides the incentive to profit from its commercialization. Through the end of 2013, over 140,000 awards had been made, totaling more than $38.44 billion, and over 2,400 of the companies that received grants went on to receive venture capital financing. The program's goals are fourfold:

1. Stimulate technological innovation.
2. Meet federal research and development needs.
3. Foster and encourage participation in innovation and entrepreneurship by socially and economically disadvantaged persons.
4. Increase private-sector commercialization of innovations derived from federal research and development funding.

The SBIR program issues grants to a company in two phases. The objective of Phase I, which offers grants up to $150,000, is to establish the technical merit, feasibility, and commercial potential of the proposed R&D efforts and to determine how well the company can deliver on its promises. Phase II grants, up to $1 million, are used to continue the R&D efforts, and funding is based on the results achieved in Phase I, as well as the scientific and technical merits, and commercial potential, of the project proposed in Phase II.

A second federal program, run parallel with SBIR, is the Small Business Technology Transfer (STTR) program for technology-transfer grants. The two programs are similar, except that STTR projects must be done in conjunction with a university and the program does not require the principal investigator to work fulltime at the company (which SBIR grants do).

Each agency administers its own program, designating general research and development topics in its solicitations. They accept proposals from small businesses (which to them means under 500 people), and awards are made on a competitive basis. What's interesting (and not widely known) is that the award rate is roughly 25 percent... which means that a company with a viable proposal is 10 times more likely to be able to get an SBIR grant than it is to get angel funding, and 100 times as likely as venture funding!

What this means to you as an angel is that you should (1) encourage your portfolio companies to apply for one of these grants if there is a reasonable likelihood that they might qualify, and (2) consider looking through the list of companies that have received such grants as possible investment targets, since they have already had non-dilutive capital applied to the riskiest stage of the business. The Small Business Administration maintains an online, public database of all SBIR/STTR grant winners at www.sbir.gov/past-awards, and a commercial database from InKnowVation has even more information at http://inknowvation.com.

Economic Development Agencies

All states and many local governments have economic-development agencies dedicated to assisting new and established businesses start, grow, and succeed. Services provided by these agencies typically include startup advice, training and resources, business location and site selection assistance, employee recruitment and training assistance, and, of interest to us as angels, financial assistance. Including loans, grants, tax-exempt bonds, and—in many instances—state-funded seed and venture capital funds, these agencies expend great time, money, and effort trying to help new businesses get off the ground.

As just one example, New York State has announced an initiative called StartupNY, slated to begin in 2014. The program will designate

68 zones across the state in which new businesses can operate tax-free for 10 years. That means no business, corporate, state, local, sales, and property taxes or franchise fees … and no state income taxes for the startup's employees!

In other states, such as Wisconsin, investments by angel investors into qualified early-stage businesses are eligible to receive a tax credit equal to 25 percent of the amount of the equity investment, whether the startup succeeds or fails. This means that fully one quarter of your financing risk in angel investing is being subsidized by the state. Not a bad deal.

Business Plan Competitions

As discussed in Chapter 4, many schools and other organizations have adopted the idea of business competitions to spur entrepreneurship. What's fascinating is that these reach increasingly diverse populations, from high school students to senior citizens. In most cases, there is a cash prize for the winner(s), and this is sometimes enough to enable the team to delay seeking outside investors until they have had the opportunity to develop their product and gain traction.

This was the case for CourseHorse, which won $75,000 at the NYU Business Plan Competition in 2011. That money enabled them to complete their online platform connecting users to local classes and positioned them for a $500,000 investment round led by New York Angels a year later.

Accelerators

The concept of the venture accelerator burst on the scene in 2005, when serial entrepreneur and angel investor Paul Graham founded a program called Y Combinator as a new model of startup funding. Twice a year, Y Combinator invests a small amount of money (for 2014 the amounts range from $14,000 to $20,000 plus a note for $80,000) in a large number of startups (most recently 52). The startups move to Silicon Valley for three months, where they work intensively to put the company into the best possible shape and refine its pitch to investors. Each cycle culminates in *Demo Day*, when the startups present their business to a large audience of angel and VC investors. Since 2005,

Y Combinator has funded over 630 startups, including big hits such as Airbnb, Dropbox, Disqus, Reddit, Loopt, Wufoo, Scribd, Heroku, Hipmunk, and Codecademy that in total have created over \$7.8 billion in value.

The success of Y Combinator spurred an explosion of similar programs, many of which—TechStars, DreamIt!, Wayra, Founder Institute, Seedcamp, and 500 Startups, among others—run networks of accelerators in major cities. According to the online website F6S.com, as of February, 2014, there were over 2,000 different accelerators or equivalent startup programs around the world.

While the value of the companies nurtured by the accelerators is impressive, perhaps the biggest impact of these programs has come from their role as curators in the startup world. The best known ones, including Y Combinator and TechStars, accept only 1 to 2 percent of startup teams that apply, which means that angels who attend an accelerator Demo Day see an extraordinarily refined selection of companies, let alone companies that benefited from the intense mentoring and support of the program itself. As a result, according to the *New York Times*, fully 72 percent of all companies that graduated from Y Combinator raised venture capital rounds following their Demo Day.

While investor competition at Demo Days for the top-ranked programs is so fierce that seed valuations reach extraordinarily high (some investors would say "insane") levels, the sheer number of programs around the world, and the fact that they each churn out two to four classes of dozens of companies every year, means that there are a large number of pre-vetted and accelerated startups for angels to consider, even if you didn't get an invitation to the Demo Day itself. Accelerators post public lists of their graduating classes, and platforms like Gust provide easy access to collections of graduates from the various classes who are actively seeking investments.

Funding Platforms

Until the passage of the JOBS Act of 2012, private companies were not allowed to generally solicit investments. While they were allowed to raise money from Accredited Investors, they weren't allowed to tell anyone that they were doing so! As you might imagine, this made it tricky for startups to find funding and was one of the things that spurred the formation of angel investor groups.

But as of September 23, 2013, all of that changed. With companies now allowed to trumpet publicly the fact that they are looking for funding (provided they ensure that the only people who invest are Accredited Investors), dozens of online websites have emerged where companies can list themselves and where investors can search for them. They are somewhat like fishing holes where the fish very much want to be caught.

Gust, the official deal flow and collaboration platform of most of the world's federations of organized angel investors, is the oldest and largest equity funding platform. But there are many other platforms—general purpose and specialized, regional, and international, open and curated—where angels can seek investment opportunities.

Among the better-known sites are AngelList (general), CircleUp (consumer brands), Seedrs (UK and Europe), Funders Club (accelerators), WeFunder (general), Bolstr ("Main Street" businesses), EarlyShares (general), RockThePost (general), Slated (films), SecondMarket (general), RealtyMogul (real estate) and MicroVentures (general).

Intermediaries

Prior to the JOBS Act and the emergence of online platforms, one way that investors without significant independent deal flow could find investment opportunities was through intermediaries engaged by a startup to find investors. These *finders* span a wide range, from unregistered individuals operating in the gray area of the financing world, through SEC-registered broker/dealers, to large, well-known investment bankers. It is important to note that these intermediaries are not investors themselves, but instead are compensated by the company based on the amount of money they raise from strategic or financial investors.

Because of the relatively small financial numbers involved in angel financing, it is not particularly cost effective for a startup company to engage an intermediary, and most angel groups and venture capital funds prefer to work directly with a company. That said, the more desperate a company is for funding, the more it may be willing to seek whatever help it can. Once you develop a reputation as an investor, it is likely that you will be approached by brokers or others soliciting your investment in a "hot new company."

There is nothing illegal or otherwise wrong with this, provided that you deal with an SEC-registered broker/dealer—the only intermediary authorized to solicit investments for a fee. However, the likelihood is that you will find the opportunities they offer priced significantly higher than ones you find yourself, and with significantly less investor-friendly terms.

Super Angel Investors

Media coverage of the early stage world often contains stories about people described as *super angels*. If after reading this book so far you are somewhat confused about exactly who these folks are, it's not surprising. That's because the people generally referred to as super angels may well be "super," but very few of them are actually angels. Most would be more correctly described (and describe themselves) as *micro-VCs* or *seed funds*, in that they have raised pools of money from—and invest on behalf of—limited partners, just like larger venture capital firms. In contrast, true angels are, like you, individuals investing their own cash.

While it may seem from the blogs and adoring coverage as though the "supes" are all over the place, there are fewer than three or four dozen of them on both coasts combined. If their average fund size is somewhere between $10 million and $40 million, that means all of them together are roughly the size of one—more traditional—venture fund (and significantly smaller than any of the major top-tier funds). Nonetheless, because many of these investors (people like Josh Kopelman and Howard Morgan, Jeff Clavier, Mike Maples and Ann Miura Ko, Dave McClure, Ken and Ben Lerer and Eric Hippeau, Aydin Senkut, Josh Kushner, Bill Lohse, Charlie O'Donnell, Dusan Stojanovic and others) are serious, rational investors targeting a market segment that is difficult for the larger funds to reach, the likelihood is that they will be around for a long time and generate good returns on their portfolios. In addition, each of the people I've listed started out with a small fund, often of their own money plus some from their friends and family, but has proven successful enough to have raised additional, larger funds and is becoming increasingly institutionalized.

As for real angels—the ones investing their own funds—they are probably best described with terms such as *active* if they make lots of investments, *deep-pocketed* if they write large checks, *well-connected* if they can introduce their entrepreneurs to good people, *well-known* if they have high name recognition, *smart-money* if they are great strategic advisors, *experienced* if they're willing and able to lead a round, and so forth. Someone who scores high in many or most of these categories could legitimately be described as an all-around Super Angel—but anyone who fits that definition is probably already figuring out how to raise a fund!

An even more significant trend than the emergence of the micro-VCs or super angels is the appearance of a new crop of high profile, true angels: young, energetic, cashed-out tech entrepreneurs, chiefly in the San Francisco Bay Area, New York City, and other tech hubs, who are leveraging their respective networks and connections to find and vet potential investments. This group is enthusiastic, fast-moving, often valuation-insensitive, and operating to a large extent on the basis of *social proof*—the identity of other, well-known people who are supporting the company.

Their stated approach to investing is oriented exclusively toward companies with blockbuster potential, and leads them to a distinctive attitude about valuation: "It's a hits-based business, and as long as I'm in a hit deal it doesn't matter at what valuation I invested." As a result, they have had the effect of driving up valuations dramatically for many seed-stage investments, particularly on the West Coast, to the point that many of the micro-VCs and traditional angels now often sit on the sidelines (or at least wring their hands while writing checks).

What is unclear, however, is what will happen in the near future when the seed financing for many of these companies runs out and no follow-on rounds or exits are available, something that is colloquially known as the *Series A Crunch*. There may end up being a mismatch between the time horizons of these new angels who are used to instant gratification and the reality that the current average holding period for an angel investment in the United States is nine years.

Angel Groups

In contrast, traditional angel groups are made up of a different class of investors. While most group members are also entrepreneurs (a recent ACA study showed that the average member of an accredited U.S.

angel group has 15 years of entrepreneurial experience and has started 2.7 companies), they are not tied in to the Silicon Valley *mafias* (in this context, a term used colloquially to refer to the early investors, founders, and employees of highly successful tech companies such as PayPal, Google, LinkedIn, and others). Angel group members are typically not quite as tech-oriented and have longer time horizons and often more subdued expectations than the brash newcomers. These groups have among them tens of thousands of members, investing hundreds of millions of dollars annually.

The number of groups and the number of active, professional angels are growing rapidly, and as they improve their game, collaborate with each other, and make use of increasingly sophisticated online tools, the odds are that they will be a more significant source for early-stage financing in the coming years. In the next chapter, I delve more deeply into the nature of angel groups and the important role they can play in jump-starting your own investment success.

Venture Funds

Venture capitalists (VCs), like other fund managers, are professional financial managers who raise large pools of money to invest. The professionals who run the venture firm and make its investments are referred to as *general partners*, while the outside investors whose money the VCs manage are called *limited partners*. The VCs reinvest the funds they've raised in early-stage, private companies that they hope will return many times the original investment, either through being acquired by a larger company or by going public, which will allow the VC fund to sell the shares that it received in exchange for its investment. The investment strategy followed by most VCs bears a strong resemblance to that followed by professional angels (or vice versa), and many early-stage VCs and seed funds, in fact, invest in companies directly alongside angel investors.

VCs find potential investments from their extensive networks of contacts as well as through referrals from angel investors, portfolio CEOs, and other VCs. Because they believe that proprietary deal flow is critical to their success, VCs spend much of their time hunting down deals that they hope other VCs may not yet have seen. In this way, too, they resemble angel investors.

The typical investment fund raised by a VC has a life of 10 years, with investments made during the first 5 years and then harvested during the next 5.

Limited partners in U.S. venture funds need to be either Accredited or Qualified Investors according to the regulations of the U.S. Securities and Exchange Commission. Because of this, they fall into one of two categories: rich people (typically worth many millions of dollars themselves), or institutions with cash on hand (such as pension funds, insurance companies, and university endowments). Because of the high risk/high return nature of the venture capital field, investments in such funds usually account for a small percentage of the investor's overall portfolio (+/− 10 percent).

VCs are compensated by their limited partners for operating the fund (that is, *trying* to make money) and for generating a good return on investments (actually *making* money for their investors). The first form of compensation comes as a management fee, in which every year the VC gets to take 2 to 3 percent of all the money committed to the fund. This covers salaries for the VCs and their staffs plus operating expenses such as rent and travel.

As large as the management fee may be (2 percent on a $500 million fund is $10 million a year), the bigger returns for successful VCs (theoretically) come in the form of what is called their *carried interest*. This means that when companies in the fund's portfolio have a *liquidity event*—that is, they are either acquired or taken public—the general partners keep 20 percent of the profits for themselves, after returning the amount of the original investment to their investors.

Like many angel investors, most VCs believe that the value they bring to their portfolio companies is much greater than only money. VC investors typically take a very active role in helping the company grow so as to increase the value of their investments. This takes the form of serving on a company's board of directors, mentoring the CEO, helping the company raise future rounds of investment, and using the investors' networks to help the company with recruiting, sales, business development, and, eventually, the company's exit.

As you can see, VCs and angels have a lot in common. So how exactly do they differ? The chief difference, of course, is that angel investors are investing their own money, while venture capitalists are professional investment managers who invest other people's money.

In general, experienced angel investors are more tolerant of smaller markets than VCs because of the math involved. VCs invest from large funds, often hundreds of millions of dollars. When divided into the number of partners in the firm, who have limited bandwidth for supporting portfolio companies and serving on their boards, this means that a typical VC Series A investment would be $3 million to $5 million, or more. When you factor in the follow-on rounds, it is reasonable to assume that a VC might have upwards of $10 million invested into a startup by the time it exits.

Since VCs do not want to own a majority of a company, that means the post-money valuation of the company at the time of their investment(s) would be $10 million to $20 million or more. Because VCs need their companies to target at least a 10x return on the investment (many companies in their portfolios will fail, and even for those who don't, it typically takes five to seven years for a successful company to get big enough for a healthy exit), that means the company needs to be acquired by a strategic player for upwards of $100 to $200 million. For that enterprise value to be created, in most cases the company would need to operate in a market where potential annual revenues would be at least at that number.

By contrast, angels invest from their own—much smaller—pockets, and a typical angel round (from a group of angels, or a super-angel fund) might be a total of $250,000 to $500,000, with a postmoney valuation of $1 million to $2 million. Even if the angels target a higher ROI (say, 15x to 30x), they can achieve that with a strategic sale of the company at only $30 million: the sweet spot (+/− 50 percent) where the great majority of acquisitions are done. It is possible to create a successful $30 million company with much lower revenue targets, and to do so in many smaller markets.

So VCs and angels often focus on different categories of companies, at different stages in their life-cycle. Nevertheless, there is enough overlap that it would not be surprising for you, as an angel, to find yourself considering an opportunity to invest in a business that is simultaneously being scrutinized by one or more VC funds.

Venture Debt Lenders

Venture debt refers to debt financing offered to companies that have a professional investor as a significant equity holder in the company.

The reason the venture investor is important is because high-growth companies in the market for a significant loan often do not have the underlying levels of financial performance (namely, a history of profitable revenues) that a traditional lender (read: regular commercial bank) requires when underwriting a loan.

Venture-backed companies tend to be cash rich after raising a round of funding, but often have plans to burn through a portion (or all) of the round of equity financing in order to grow product development or (hopefully) sales rapidly. In general, normal commercial lenders are scared by the idea of a company planning on burning through their cash. Over the past 25 years or so, a variety of institutions have popped up that understand the dynamics of the venture world and have gone out of their way to carefully cultivate relationships with the venture capitalists and entrepreneurs who are part of the ecosystem. By leveraging the relationships and understanding the dynamics at play with venture-backed companies, venture lenders can effectively provide loans to companies who are burning cash while minimizing loan losses, leading to a workable business model. This alternative form of capital for entrepreneurs is venture debt.

Private Equity

Private equity investors are a very different group from angels or VCs. These investors typically concentrate on later-stage investments— profitable companies with real cash flow. They will often seek to acquire complete control of a company (something that almost never happens with angels or VCs) and they are highly unlikely ever to be looking at the same type of deal flow as their early-stage colleagues.

Corporate Venture Groups

An increasing number of large companies are devoting part of their assets to investing cash in other companies in much the same way as a venture capital fund. While they are certainly trying to get a financial return on their investment just as the VCs do, in virtually all cases their more important goal is to identify and exploit synergies between the big company and the new venture, to help with additional growth within the parent firm. They want to keep up to speed on new technologies, to enter new markets, to identify acquisition targets, and/or to access new resources.

The good news for startups and their angels is that corporate venture investors are usually willing to invest at higher valuations than pure financial players. On the other hand, the corporate investor is not always completely aligned either with the company's other investors or with the company itself. Corporate venture money can be enticing—and valuable for all parties—but it is crucial to understand where everyone's interests lie.

As you pursue your angel investing career, you will encounter most, or all, of these different players in one or more of the investments you make. Understanding the role they play in the ecosystem will give you the background you need to deal with them appropriately, helping turn your investments (and theirs) into win/win situations.

16

Building Your Angelic Reputation
Getting the Best Deals to Come to You

In Chapter 5, I discussed the critical first part of angel investing: seeking exciting potential companies in which to invest, and building your top-of-the-funnel deal flow. We went through a host of places you could visit proactively to find investment targets, from personal connections and meetups to angel groups and Demo Days. But while the world's best VCs and "super angels" spend serious time prospecting for deals, they have an even easier way to find cool companies: they sit back and wait for the companies to find them.

How (and why) will companies come looking for you as an angel if the ecosystem—as we saw in Chapter 15—is so big and has so many things going on? Precisely because you will jump right in and take an active part in that same ecosystem! In an age of online communication, 24-hour news sources, and social networks that tie together a majority of the planet's population, there are myriad opportunities for you to establish such a presence for yourself that companies will seek you out. Here are some ways that you can build your reputation as an angel investor.

Create Your Profile

If you want to be found, start by raising your hand! Companies looking for funding are searching for potential investors as least as actively (and usually more) than you are searching for them. Make yourself easy to find by writing up your background, your investing thesis, and your contact information and disseminating them widely in the places that cool startups will be looking.

Setting up your free investor profile on Gust is the logical first step in this direction, but why limit yourself? You should also create (and keep updated) profiles and entries for yourself in reference sources such as Wikipedia (if you are notable enough) and Crunchbase, social networking sites such as LinkedIn (mandatory), Facebook, and other funding platforms such as AngelList and CircleUp. The more relevant information you include, the easier you will be to find.

Write a Blog

Some of the best known VCs and angel investors earned that distinction because of their original writings related to the startup world. While you may not think that you have as much to offer to entrepreneurs and to your fellow investors as industry thought leaders like Fred Wilson, Mark Suster, or Naval Ravikant, the fact is that, to a large extent in this connected world, "If you write it, they will read it." Of course not every entrepreneur is going to read every blog, but you would be amazed at how much name recognition you can develop simply by writing regularly, intelligently, and helpfully about an area in which you have something useful to say.

Startup founders are thirsty for advice and guidance about business in general and startup funding in particular. Writing a regular blog (you need to write *regularly*, not sporadically) is an excellent way to show entrepreneurs (1) that you are smart, (2) that you are helpful, and (3) that you are interested in hearing about companies in specific areas or industries.

I've included a list in Appendix H of a selection of blogs written by and about angel investing, which will provide you with good examples of investors doing exactly this, and give you invaluable insights into the thoughts of some of the industry's leaders.

Answer Questions Online

For many people, blogging can be intimidating. They find it frustrating to stare at a blank screen and wait for inspiration to strike. Luckily, the Internet can save the day. There are many websites where entrepreneurs and others in the startup world congregate to have discussions with, or—even better—ask direct questions of, investors. In virtually all of these cases, the normal Internet participation metrics of 90/9/1 apply: roughly 90 percent of visitors simply read the contents, 9 percent ask questions or participate by voting on the quality of answers, but only 1 percent of users will actually take the time to write an answer. The interesting statistic, however, is that for every one person who writes an answer, 99 people are likely to see it and be influenced.

The most popular and useful of these question-and-answer websites is Quora.com, founded in 2010 by two former Facebook employees. With millions of users, many of them interested in the world of startups, it has become a great source of information about early-stage company building, angel investing, and venture capital. Among the investors who have answered questions on Quora are Dave McClure (500 Startups), Mark Suster (Up Front Ventures), Marc Andreesen (Andreesen Horowitz), Shervin Pishevar (Sherpa Global), and Reid Hoffman (Greylock), as well as dozens of active angels.

In fact, that's how this book came about. I regularly answer startup and angel investing questions on Quora, and the folks at Wiley realized that scattered among my 2,000-plus answers was probably enough information to make a book—which is what you're now reading.

Attend Events in Your Local Startup Community

To see and be seen by local entrepreneurs, hang out in the same places they do. Whether by attending local startup-related Meetups, going to lectures and events featuring entrepreneurs or investors, or participating in open houses and demo days at incubators or accelerators, the more visible you make yourself, the more founders will think of you when it comes time for them to raise money.

Participate as a Judge, Mentor, or Panelist

Every business-plan competition needs judges, every accelerator needs mentors, and every startup event needs panelists and speakers. Because of the desire for information and updates on the world of early-stage investing, there is an equivalent need for speakers, judges and panelists on the topic. If you seek out the organizers of such events, you will find that they will likely welcome your participation and be grateful for it. The more you speak, the more you will become known as a speaker, and the more invitations you will receive to speak. It's a virtuous circle of reputation enhancement. Speaking and judging not only expose you to entrepreneurs with interesting startup companies, but also establish you as an authority (why else would you have been chosen to speak or judge?)

Pay It Forward by Advising Startups

Perhaps the best way to develop your reputation as a value-adding investor for startups is to add value to startups. Brian Cohen is now a well-known angel investor (he was the first angel to discover Pinterest), but his initial steps into the field were as a pro-bono advisor. When he first joined New York Angels, he offered to help any of the group's portfolio companies that might benefit from his advice and extensive experience as an entrepreneur and strategic communications expert. Quite a few companies took him up on this, even though he had not invested in them and had no financial interest in their success. But word spreads quickly, and soon other startups were approaching him directly, looking both for his wisdom *and* his investment.

What is absolutely critical about giving advice, however, is that it be done with no direct expectation of financial return. There are many self-proclaimed advisors/mentors/Sherpas who pitch their services to startups in exchange for fees, equity, or other compensation. While I'm sure that they make a few bucks from this, I guarantee you that it does nothing whatsoever to enhance their reputations, either with startups or with other investors. But those people who are genuinely helpful to entrepreneurs even when they do not receive direct financial benefit soon develop a significant reputation, find themselves invited into interesting opportunities, and get to play with the cool kids. Besides, it is usually quite gratifying.

17

Joining an Angel Group

Increasing Your Opportunities and Reducing Your Risks

IF YOU'RE A new angel investor, whether you're interested merely in dipping a toe into angel waters or serious about making a long-term commitment to angel investing, I strongly recommend considering membership in a local angel group. There are over one thousand such organizations around the world, with at least one in every state in the United States, and at least one in more than 75 countries. Major metropolitan areas typically have more than one (there are currently over a dozen in New York City alone!).

What all these groups have in common is bringing together active Accredited Investors interested in putting capital to work in this asset class, supporting young startups, and assisting each other. The benefits of joining a group include pooling deal flow, capital, domain expertise, and investing experience. Most groups run regular education sessions for new members and provide mentoring for less experienced investors from those with many deals under their belts.

Angel groups over the past decade have become very sophisticated, with professional trade associations, standardized best practices, extensive syndication, a global, web-based investment management platform, and a generally strong track record. New York Angels, for example, has invested over $70 million in more than 100 startups over the past several years, and companies in which we've invested have been acquired by Google, Intel, Amazon, AOL, Living Social, CBS, Kodak, and other major firms.

In selecting a group to join, the first thing to do is to make sure that it belongs to its national federation of professional angel groups. In the United States, that would be the Angel Capital Association (ACA); in Canada, the National Angel Capital Organization (NACO); in Australia, the Australian Association of Angel Investors (AAAI), and so forth. I've included in Appendix G a list of all the national federations with some of their leading groups.

How Angel Groups Operate

In working with an angel group, it's important to understand what makes the experience different from being an individual angel or investing in a professional venture fund.

As an individual angel investor, you are responsible only to yourself (and your spouse) for your investment decisions. This means you could, in theory, meet an entrepreneur at a cocktail party, hear a three-minute elevator pitch, and write a check for a full investment round on the spot. This has happened, but it's not necessarily the best way to make an investment decision. The biggest problem with investing solely as an individual is that, without a personal introduction from someone who knows both you and a great entrepreneur, it can be difficult to ensure that you're in the right place at the right time to hear about the most promising opportunities.

Venture capital funds, at the other end of the spectrum, are commercial organizations whose business it is to find the 5 to 20 companies each year that they believe have a chance of being one of the only 80 companies a year that will ultimately exit in a sale of over $50 million. Because funds are highly visible and listed in the phone book, every other entrepreneur in town is vying to get in front of them for funding. As a result, the major VC funds each receive between 5,000 and 10,000 funding requests a year.

Angel groups are in the middle between the two extremes. Unlike individual angels, they make themselves available to entrepreneurs (including having a website, soliciting funding applications even from entrepreneurs they don't personally know, running events, and so on), but unlike venture funds they typically receive hundreds of applications a year instead of thousands. This means that angels who are members of a group have the opportunity to be exposed to a healthy but manageable flow of investment opportunities every year.

The typical U.S. angel group will receive a dozen or more funding applications from startups or referrals from members each month; the most active ones, such as New York Angels, will receive over 100. Groups also often syndicate investments, working cooperatively to fund larger rounds that are bigger than one group can handle alone. A typical group member invests in one or two companies each year, putting in $25,000 to $100,000 in each. Most groups expect this level of investment from members; some even require it.

That said, angel groups don't have the budgets or staffs that venture funds do. Instead, they're composed of 25 to 250 individual people (many of them former entrepreneurs themselves) who volunteer their time and effort to work together on funding startups. They have to coordinate a group of Type-A personalities, while organizing (and personally funding) a process that will let them review hundreds of opportunities each year so they can fund typically 5 to 10 of them.

In practice, most angel groups work on a monthly cycle, reviewing all the submissions that have come in during the previous 30 days and choosing 5 to 15 of them for screening. The selected companies, who usually will not have had a previous relationship with anyone in the group, meet with a screening committee of 2 to 20 angels, who will usually spend at least half an hour hearing the company's pitch. Thus the percentage of companies who get in front of real investors for a real pitch is very much higher than it is for individual angels or venture funds.

The screening committee will then invite three to five companies to return a few weeks later to present their pitch formally to the whole group, usually in a 15- to 30-minute session including questions and answers. During that meeting, dozens of legitimate Accredited Investors will listen to the company's presentation, hoping to find interesting companies in which they can invest. (Remember, unlike VCs, who do this as a job, angel group members are voluntarily spending their time and money because they want to invest in startups. No one does this just for fun with no intention of investing.)

If enough of the angels in attendance are interested in hearing more about the company, there will usually be a series of follow-up meetings and due-diligence sessions, resulting (everyone hopes) in either a term sheet for an investment (if the company doesn't already have one outstanding, and the group can corral enough members to come up with a reasonable total investment amount), or one or more angels agreeing to invest alongside other investors that the company has found.

With the world changing rapidly and an increasing number of new vehicles emerging to facilitate direct investments in startups, many angel groups are not proud of the time their traditional processes take (typically two to three months from submission to funding). Speaking from experience, however, I can tell you that herding 75 cats is a nontrivial exercise. The good news is that the groups—as an industry—are continually trying to reduce the length and complexity of the process. The ACA and its affiliate, The Angel Resource Institute, hold annual summits, training sessions, and leadership conferences for its members, and many groups now routinely work together to syndicate investments that are larger than a single group has the resources to fund.

Some angel groups specialize, investing primarily in life sciences or tech or space companies, or women- or minority- or GLBT-led ventures, or social impact or platform-based or university-affiliated companies. Other angel groups are wide open, investing in everything from real estate to films. Most are somewhere in between, focusing primarily on early-stage, high-growth companies with scalable business models. These are typically Internet-enabled, or consumer products or medical devices.

Finally, the development of the Gust platform as the near-universal infrastructure for the global, organized angel industry means that much of the administrative burden is lightened for startups. An entrepreneur can now create a single investor-relations website for his or her company at no cost using Gust, and then share it with any angel group that might be a good match for the business (in the United States and internationally). Each group's screening committee will review the information and use it as the basis for their internal collaboration as they move through their process. And if more than one group syndicates the investment, they'll all be working off the same site as well.

For all of these reasons, organized, professional angel groups account for well over $100 million annually in seed funding. The major groups will typically see many—if not most—of the current deals in their area (even the "hot" ones), but one of their main advantages is that they are often the best approach for getting an unbiased hearing for entrepreneurs who may not be quite as connected as some others. In addition to the United States, other countries with active, organized business angel communities include Canada, France, Australia, New Zealand, the UK, Ireland, Portugal, Spain, Scotland, India, The Netherlands, Germany, Turkey, Russia, and Belarus. (In Europe, angel groups are typically referred to as *angel networks*.) To find the angel groups near you, use the Gust investment group search engine at gust.com/find-investors.

It would be interesting to document whether angel groups enjoy consistently superior financial returns and reduced risk compared with individual angel investors (which is what the prevailing wisdom says). Unfortunately, there's no definitive way to test this hypothesis because all of the academic surveys on outcomes to date have been based on angels who *are* in groups.

That said, anecdotal and personal evidence indicate that investments in the context of professional angel groups have moderate to strong correlation with improved outcomes over independent personal investments.

How Smart Entrepreneurs Work with Angel Groups

The main issue for entrepreneurs who work with angel groups as opposed to individual investors is simultaneously obvious and underestimated: the entrepreneur whose company is selected for support by an angel group is dealing with a group of small investors at one time. This might be anywhere from 5 to 25 investors, each putting in somewhere between $10,000 and $100,000 (depending on the group).

From the entrepreneur's perspective, the good side is that there are now 5 to 25 smart, connected people rooting for the success of the venture. Handled correctly, they can be a major asset for the business when it comes to introductions, connections, advice, and follow-on funding.

The not-so-good side for the business founder is that there are now an equal number of people with a legitimate interest in the details of the business, and the entrepreneur has a fiduciary responsibility to safe-guard the investors' money and keep them informed. While this usually works out well, I've seen cases where a couple of small investors can aggravate the CEO by constantly calling with questions, intruding with operating advice, and generally being a pain in the neck. So, as a pro-fessional angel collaborating with others in a group, you are *not* going to do that.

The solution, however, is straightforward, and it's one that most smart entrepreneurs and experienced angels are careful to practice.

First, the entrepreneur and the lead angel should make sure that they have a good working relationship, particularly if the lead angel will also be a board member. The lead angel is normally the entrepreneur's primary interface with the group.

Second, the entrepreneur should communicate early, often, and fully with all the investor members. If the term sheet calls for quarterly reports to investors, the entrepreneur should send them, accompanied by a management letter explaining what's actually happening. The entrepreneur should also use an investor relations platform (like Gust) to keep all the investor material, reports, and contact information up to date, as well as hold a regularly scheduled conference call with the angels to keep them in the loop and to let them ask questions. Quarterly is probably too frequent, but semi-annually may be just about right.

The smart entrepreneur also makes it a point to reach out to investors when she needs something, including introductions, leads, team members, and so on. In turn, it is the angel's responsibility to reply to requests, and deliver real value to the company. Money is fungible, and despite the asymmetry in the number of startups and investors, a strong company will always be able to find capital, so angels really need to earn their wings. Right from the beginning, all the parties involved with a venture need to be clear as to what they expect from the relationship. In the best company and angel relationships, both sides are comfortable accepting regular communications *to* investors in exchange for putting rational limits on communications *from* them.

Does every entrepreneur live up to these expectations? No—but an increasing number do. It's useful for you as an angel to have these benchmarks in mind as you enter into a relationship with a business partner. Being a member of an angel group can significantly smooth the waters and make it much easier for each side in the relationship to feel consistently satisfied.

Angel Group Money Matters

Some people wonder how angel groups support themselves financially, and whether they accept any funding from entrepreneurs themselves. In most legitimate cases, the answer is a resounding no. The only legitimate revenue model for angel networks is one where the revenue comes, in one form or another, either from the angels themselves, or from a sponsor who contributes cash in return for exposure or other benefits.

In probably 75 percent of the cases this means straight-up dues payments from angel investor members, which typically run between $500 and $5,000 per year. In the remaining cases, the group is usually organized as a fund, with similar economics as a traditional venture fund, and the group's operating budget would come out of the fund's annual management fee. Most angel groups and networks augment their members' personal contributions with sponsorship fees from professional service providers, such as law firms, accounting firms, or banks. These sponsorships can run into the tens of thousands of dollars annually.

The outlying cases, which can often be problematic from a legal and/or ethical perspective, include the group taking a *success fee* when a deal closes, or charging entrepreneurs more than a nominal amount for presenting, screening, or training. The great majority of angel groups (90 percent or more) do not charge application fees to entrepreneurs who want to apply for funding, and the Angel Capital Association has a policy prohibiting any fees over $500. In practice, the vast majority of angel groups are not-for-profits (as a group, of course—the angels themselves are certainly trying to make a return by investing in startups), and the small application fees that some of them charge are not a profit center, but are used to cover the expenses of operating the group (unlike venture funds, where the partners are paid hefty management fees by their limited partners).

When entrepreneurs ask me about the application fees charged by some angel groups, I tell them that, as a general rule, application fees of under a couple of hundred dollars to an ACA-accredited angel group are not a problem. From a couple of hundred up to the $500 limit, they should make a reasoned decision as to whether they are a good match for that particular group, and whether the odds of getting funded are worth the fee.

Over $500, the entrepreneur needs to be very careful and do a lot of checking to make sure that a group is legitimate (as does any potential angel investor considering membership in such a group). The big player in this range is Keiretsu Forum, a non-ACA network of 27 groups that typically charges $3000 or more to present to each of their chapters. The group's administrators run it as a for-profit enterprise, but the angel members themselves don't profit from the fees, and they *do* write checks. Keiretsu Forum has engendered a lot of controversy, but they have invested over $110 million into over 180 startups during the past decade, so the issue is by no means clear-cut.

The Future of Angel Groups

The bottom line on angel groups recalls what Winston Churchill said about democracy: "It's the worst form of government there is … except for all the others." In the same way, angel groups as currently constituted are far from perfect—but they offer an invaluable service, particularly to novice investors—and they certainly have the potential to become dramatically better in the years to come.

Angel groups play a significant role in the early-stage financing ecosystem. They bring new investors into the market, provide a generally open framework for funding submissions that don't rely on who you know, aggregate capital to help organize investment rounds that would not be done by later-stage investors, often provide amazing mentorship to young companies, and much more.

At the same time, however, they have earned a reputation for being process-bound, time-wasting, nitpicking, and occasionally unprofessional. The problem lies in the inherent contradictions and realities surrounding the concept of angel groups. If an angel group is actively led by an investor member, the fact that he or she is an Accredited Investor with other interests means that there's no one to do the day-to-day work; but if it is led by a professional manager, that person is not an actual investor and can neither commit to an investment nor control the members to whom he or she reports. If an angel group's manager is not particularly good, then the group will be ineffective at best, and dissolve at worst; but if the manager is great, he or she will eventually face the overwhelming incentive to leave the group, become a professional VC, and raise a real venture fund.

All of the leading angel groups are, I assure you, well aware of this, and all of them spend significant amounts of time trying to improve their processes. There is an annual summit organized by the Angel Capital Association, and an annual leaders' workshop for angel group leaders at which these issues are discussed exhaustively, best practices are shared, common documents are drafted, and joint activities are undertaken.

In the coming years, I believe that we will see increasingly prominent roles played by local angel groups in the on-boarding of new investors who will learn best practices, defray their risks, and augment their capital by investing alongside more experienced angels. Once they become more involved, I would not be surprised to see the now-experienced angels spread their wings and move on to individual investing, facilitated by online platforms, while maintaining ties to their local angel group through which they, in turn, will mentor the next generation of angels.

18

Impact Investing
Doing Well While Doing Good

WHILE TRADITIONAL ANGEL investing has always been primarily an economic activity designed to generate above-market financial returns, in Chapter 2 I discussed the multiple reasons that individuals put money into high-risk, innovative startups. Many of these were related either to professional benefits or to personal fulfillment and fun. One of them, however, is perhaps the fastest-growing segment of the early-stage finance world: *impact investing*. This involves putting your money behind companies that strive to produce social or environmental benefits for society even as they work to generate profits, equity growth, and financial benefits for investors.

A popular description of impact investing, or *social venture capital* (as it is sometimes called) is that investors are targeting a *double bottom line*. In addition to the financial bottom line of generating economic profit, investments also target a second bottom line of social good. This is different from traditional 'socially responsible' investing, where the goal is generally to minimize the negative impact of an investment on society or the environment. Here, the goal is intentionally to benefit society.

The spectrum of impact investing runs from simply "doing no harm" on one end (i.e., avoiding investments in tobacco companies or arms manufacturers), to proactively "doing good" on the other (for example, developing inexpensive mosquito nets in Africa or operating health-care clinics in Peru). See Figure 18.1.

The problem, however, is that it is mathematically impossible to optimize independently for two variables at the same time. That is, the focus of your investing can be to maximize your financial return without regard to social impact, or you can maximize the social impact of your investment without regard to the rate of return you achieve. You can also try to solve for them both together, and come up with the highest absolute value achievable, maximizing as best you can each of the two axes. The problems with this double-bottom-line approach, however, are that (1) financial returns and social impact are assessed on two different scales, and there is no objective mathematical system that relates the value of one to the value of the other, and (2) even if there were a way to integrate the two scales, a double optimization would mean that the investor would need to be willing to accept a less-than-maximized outcome for either or both scales, in the service of maximizing the overall value on two scales.

It is critically important, therefore, for would-be impact investors to understand explicitly where they are on the impact-investing matrix.

In Figure 18.2, you can see that all impact investing falls in the upper-right quadrant, combining targets of high-financial returns with targets of high social and/or environmental impact. But in order to be an effective impact investor, you must decide for yourself whether you are a "financial first" investor, optimizing for financial returns while setting some baseline on the amount of impact your investment will generate, or an "impact first" investor, optimizing for the maximum societal impact while setting some baseline on the financial returns you are targeting.

For my part, I fall squarely in the first category. I try to do good through outright charitable contributions and volunteer activities, and I try to make money as an investor. However, I am very conscious of whether a company in which I invest is doing things that benefit the common good—as I define it. That is why I have made startup investments in fields such as health care (from telemedicine for returning

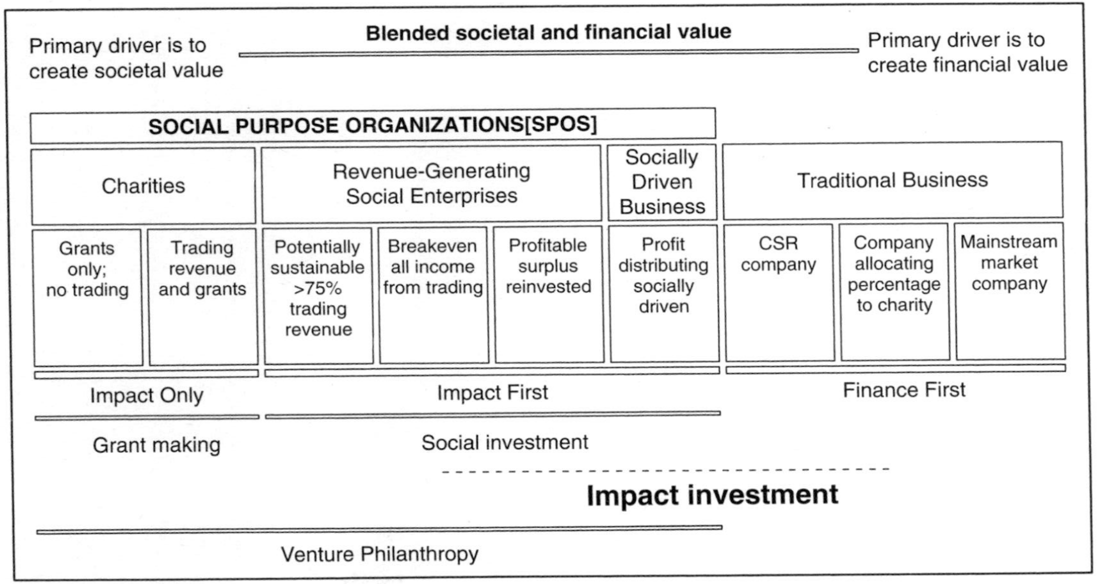

Figure 18.1 Impact Investing and the Business-to-Philanthropic Spectrum

Source: Shaerpa and EVPA.

The figure contains the following labels:

Primary driver is to create societal value

Blended societal and financial value

Primary driver is to create financial value

SOCIAL PURPOSE ORGANIZATIONS[SPOS]

| Charities | Revenue-Generating Social Enterprises | Socially Driven Business | Traditional Business |

| Grants only; no trading | Trading revenue and grants | Potentially sustainable >75% trading revenue | Breakeven all income from trading | Profitable surplus reinvested | Profit distributing socially driven | CSR company | Company allocating percentage to charity | Mainstream market company |

Impact Only — Impact First — Finance First

Grant making

Social investment

Venture Philanthropy

Impact investment

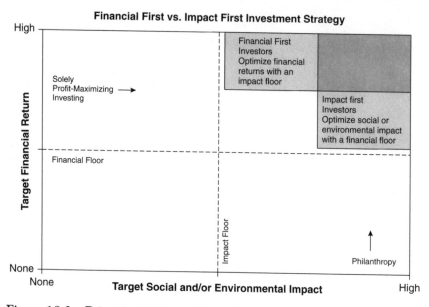

Figure 18.2   Priorities in Impact Investing

Source: Monitor Institute.

veterans with posttraumatic stress disorder (PTSD) to street corner clinics for the uninsured population of Lima, Peru); education (from collaboration websites for parents and teachers to platforms helping teachers raise money for classroom needs); and finance (from payment systems for workers without bank accounts to crowdfunding platforms that help entrepreneurs finance their visions).

A good example of how all this can come together is a company called LearnVest. After graduating from college, Alexa von Tobel worked at Morgan Stanley for two years before leaving to manage business development for Drop.io, one of my portfolio companies that was eventually acquired by Facebook. As a young woman with a strong finance background, she was dismayed to find that many other women she knew seemed to have a complete lack of understanding when it came to their personal finances. Whether it was understanding the different types of investments that made sense for different goals, or even such basics as how to manage bank accounts, credit cards, and automatic payroll deductions, it was clear that personal finance education was a major challenge for people of her generation and she felt passionately about trying to meet it.

Coming up with the idea for a business based around an online, budgeting and advice platform for young women that would make personal finance education fun and available to everyone, von Tobel enrolled at Harvard Business School to learn the skills that would enable her to build a serious company. But fate has a way of intervening in life, and von Tobel had barely settled into her Cambridge apartment when her nascent little startup won a national award and mainstream media began to give her tremendous press coverage. Following the dictum of *carpe diem*, she took a leave of absence from HBS, returned to New York, and began the process of fundraising for her fledgling venture at the age of 25.

Knowing what a force of nature von Tobel was and knowing from my own children the challenges of personal financial education, I signed on to her vision of creating a free, local, online personal finance community for women with access to experts for personal financial support. LearnVest drove user adoption with comparison tools for women to see where they stood against their peers, and then provided access to educational videos, newsletters, and financial services. With the help of my associate at the time, Bronson Lingamfelter, we were able to assist her in bringing in other early angels, including members of Golden Seeds, a women-focused angel group that had recently been founded by my friend and fellow New York Angel, Stephanie Newby, as well as Paul Sethi, another active angel in New York. Von Tobel closed out her seed round with over $1 million in angel financing, and was off to the races.

In the four years since that original investment, LearnVest has expanded its focus beyond women to become a full-fledged financial advisor with a staff of certified financial planners. The company today is worth over $100 million, and has raised additional capital from top tier investors such as Accel Partners and Claritas Capital. One of the participants in the company's latest round was American Express, which now works closely with LearnVest to provide joint financial products to their respective customers.

For me as an angel, what value can I put on the fun of supporting an impressive young entrepreneur *and* helping regular people get control of their finances *and* seeing the value of my investment increase by a factor of 50x?

It's priceless.

Whether by investing in socially oriented seed funds, seeking direct investments in commercial startups whose products or services are designed to solve societal problems, or applying one's business acumen and free-market economics to eleemosynary, cultural, or political agendas, opportunities abound for investors to make money while making a difference. For many entrepreneurs who approach the angel world after fulfilling business careers of their own, this is as good as it gets.

As more and more investors seek to give back and pay it forward through impact investing, a number of organizations and angel groups have emerged to support them. The most prominent such group is Toniic (toniic.com), founded by the dynamic duo Charly and Lisa Kleissner, based in California but with chapters and investors around the world. Other substantive impact-oriented angel groups are ClearlySo (clearlyso.com) in the UK and Investors Circle (investorscircle.net) in the United States. An annual series of conferences called SOCAP, produced by Social Capital Markets (socialcapitalmarkets.net), is "dedicated to accelerating a new global market at the intersection of money & meaning."

19

Sit Back and Let Someone Else Do the Work

Investing in Startups through Seed Funds and Venture Funds

THROUGHOUT THIS BOOK, I've been hammering home the importance of approaching startup investing with a serious, professional attitude. It's the only way to get involved in this high-risk/high-return game with a reasonable chance of success. If you're not interested in doing the homework and legwork necessary to learn about the entrepreneurs, companies, and industries in which you'll be investing, and then putting your money to work calmly and steadily over a long period of time while your assets are completely illiquid, I suggest you reconsider the idea of directly investing in startups.

However, that doesn't necessarily mean you should just walk off and play somewhere else. As the early-stage entrepreneurial sector becomes an ever increasing part of the global financing world, an industry is rising around it to service the financial needs of a wide variety of investors, including those who don't have the time or expertise to make their own direct investments but still want exposure to the asset class.

The first venture capital fund was founded in the United States in 1946, when Georges Doriot, the Dean of Harvard Business School and future founder of INSEAD (the leading international business school) created American Research and Development Corporation with Ralph Flanders and Karl Compton (a former president of MIT), to encourage private sector investments in businesses run by soldiers who were returning from World War II. It was the first private equity fund to raise capital from institutional limited partners and individuals, and its flagship deal was $70,000 invested in a startup company called Digital Equipment Corporation in 1957. When the company went public in 1968, ARDC's stake was worth $355 million.

Other venture funds soon followed, including J. H. Whitney & Company, Draper and Johnson, and Venrock. For a fascinating and enjoyable look at the early days of the VC industry, from Fairchild Semiconductor (which produced the first practical integrated circuit) to Apple Computer, I recommend the wonderful film *Something Ventured: Risk, Reward and the Original Venture Capitalists* (somethingventuredthemovie.com).

As I've explained, the essential operation of a venture capital firm is simple: investors, known as Limited Partners (LPs), put money into a fund under the control of a professional investment manager (the VC), known as the General Partner. The VC then acts much as an angel investor would, except playing on a much larger scale, with much more money. The VC puts the LP's investments to work in backing young, private companies with high growth prospects. When those companies are eventually either sold to larger companies, or become publicly traded through an initial public offering, the profits are returned to the Limited Partners.

As compensation for doing the heavy lifting, the General Partner receives both a percentage (1 to 3 percent) every year of the total amount committed to the fund, and then 20 percent of the profit from each investment, after returning the investors' original capital.

Because companies used to require a large amount of money to get started, and even larger amounts to grow to scale, venture capital funds began to grow in size. During the dotcom boom in the late 1990s, over $200 billion of capital flowed into U.S. venture funds within a two-year period. Following the dotcom crash, venture funds found themselves with enormous amounts of cash that needed to be deployed, and a disinclination and inability to deploy it into startups. (If a multi-hundred-million-dollar fund has three or four partners, each of whom does one or two deals a year, each deal needs to be at the scale of multiple millions of dollars.) So venture funds started moving rapidly up-stream, with a majority of their investments being made into growth-stage companies at the Series B, C, D, and pre-IPO stages.

This left a hole in the market at the earliest stages, and in the early 2000s a number of successful angel investors began creating a new class of venture capital fund to fill it. One of the earliest of these was First Round Capital, established as an experiment in 2004 by Josh Kopelman and Howard Morgan. Josh, a serial entrepreneur, had co-founded Half.com, which was acquired by eBay, and Howard had a distinguished career as an investor and co-founder of companies including Renaissance Technologies and Franklin Electronic Publishers. Both were members of New York Angels at the time, and they believed that there was an opportunity to create a new kind of fund to invest in companies at their earliest stages.

According to Josh, the goal of a seed investment is "to validate, de-risk, or disprove the entrepreneur's hypothesis as quickly and cheaply as possible." Since the cost of starting a company was beginning to drop exponentially, this could be done with small amounts of money compared to traditional venture funds. The initial First Round Capital fund, therefore, was in the single-digit millions of dollars—a dramatic departure from the average venture fund at the time, which was $149 million. The combination of this novel thesis, a superb nose for sniffing out promising companies and the ability to provide a great deal of post-investment support to its portfolio teams, quickly established the fund as the leader of a new breed of microVC or seed funds.

Over the next decade, First Round Capital continued to focus on early-stage deals, but with IPOs and acquisition successes of companies like Mint, Mashery, BazaarVoice, and StumbleUpon, it is now one of the busiest venture firms in the United States and is not accepting new investors.

With the cost of founding a startup continuing to drop and the number of startups continuing to expand, there are a host of other seed funds that have followed in First Round Capital's footsteps, putting to work small amounts of money at the earliest stages of a company's life—precisely the stage at which angels typically invest. Because these funds are so small (often in the $5 million to $50 million range), they are not appropriate for the institutional investors who are the usual limited partners in larger funds. Instead, they are just the right size for individual Accredited Investors who would like exposure to early-stage deals without having to do all the work themselves. These funds typically take investments from individuals in the range of $250,000 to $5 million.

Because they have small staffs and are directed by only one or two general partners, these funds tend to specialize in particular parts of the early-stage world. For example, SocialStarts, based in San Francisco, invests in startups related to social media; Brooklyn Bridge Ventures has a sweet spot for new ventures coming out of Brooklyn's blisteringly hot startup scene; and True Global Ventures invests in international startups where its entrepreneur-partners can add specific, direct value.

Note that, as with all venture funds, investments in these seed funds are still illiquid: once your money goes in, it won't be coming out for many years. But at least you will get regular accountings and updates from the General Partner, and you'll be able to live vicariously part of the life of an angel. Indeed, one feature of some—but by no means all—of these funds is that, as a Limited Partner, you may be invited (or allowed) to invest your own money as an angel alongside that of the fund. This can be tricky because of the carried interest issue—if you are piggybacking alongside all of the work of the fund it is only fair that the fund should receive its usual carried interest on your investment into the target company. But those funds that allow this have worked out ways of dealing with the problem.

When microVC funds first appeared on the scene, it was challenging for them to find investors, and for investors to find them. But the same change under the JOBS Act of 2012 that allowed general solicitation for startup companies also allowed it for investment funds themselves, so we are now entering a whole new world of opportunity. As an Accredited Investor, you can search on Gust for seed and venture funds that are currently accepting new Limited Partners and indicate your interest in participating. For a new investor with more cash than time, this can be an intriguing and potentially profitable way to stick your toe in the early stage waters.

20

Crowdfunding and the Global Revolution

Angel Investing for Everyone

In 1884, THE PEOPLE of France donated the Statue of Liberty to the United States. It was a gift of the heart, but it came with a condition: the United States was required to fund construction of the pedestal on which the statue would stand. When the U.S. Congress and New York State declined to allocate money for the project, newspaper publisher Joseph Pulitzer started a campaign that ultimately raised over $100,000 from more than 120,000 supporters, with 80 percent of the total being raised in sums of less than one dollar.

This was the first major *crowdfunding* campaign. It would take another 120 years and the emergence of the Internet before the concept of raising money from many small donors hit the mainstream. You've probably heard about crowdfunding in connection with some of its best-known online platforms—sites like Kickstarter, IndieGoGo, RocketHub, ArtistShare, and Sellaband—and may have wondered whether this approach could be used to fund startup companies. Under the crowdfunding model, supporters of a project contribute funds to support something they believe in, and receive various levels of rewards or perks in exchange.

The key thing to understand here is that in "traditional" online crowdfunding, as it has existed in the United States from 2003 until 2014, supporters are *not* in any way, shape or form purchasing ownership in the company or project, nor will they receive any benefit from the success of the project other than receiving the promised product or thank-you gift.

I have funded over a dozen crowdfunded projects myself across several of these platforms during the past decade, for nearly as many reasons. In no particular order, my motivations have included: pure philanthropy, product pre-purchase, brand sponsorship, making something I want happen, providing encouragement, getting a special perk, or doing a friend a favor.

As you can see, "hope for financial return" and "interest in owning a portion of a growing business" do *not* appear on this list—which is why, through the beginning of 2014 (when this book was written), crowdfunding, whether through IndieGoGo, Kickstarter, or any other site, was not yet available as a form of equity investing.

Another activity conducted using online platforms that is sometimes confused with crowdfunding is *peer-to-peer lending*. Like crowdfunding, peer-to-peer lending is not a form of equity investment, since you do not acquire an ownership interest (and thus a share of the profits and losses) in a company. Instead, you are simply lending money to a person at a fixed interest rate. Technically the only way you *won't* get your money back is if the borrower turns out to be a deadbeat or files for bankruptcy.

As these strictures make clear, an entrepreneur cannot use Kickstarter or other traditional crowdfunding sites to raise equity capital for a business, nor can you, as a potential investor, use them to acquire stakes in high-growth startups. Currently, crowdfunding is based on the concept of contributions and rewards, so that the money raised on Kickstarter belongs to the people making the appeal (assuming they raise at least the full amount they are looking for). But they are expected to finish the project in some finite time frame, and then provide some type of tangible reward (like products, or name recognition, or T-shirts or whatever) to those who contributed. But that's *all* they are allowed to receive … not shares of any company that may have been supported by the money.

But Wait! Here Comes Equity Crowdfunding!

The most important change in startup financing since the establishment of the U.S. Securities and Exchange Commission in 1934 happened on April 5, 2012, when the Jumpstart Our Business Startups Act was signed into law by President Barack Obama. Known as the JOBS Act of 2012, this landmark legislation had three major components.

The first, Title I, made it easier for companies to stay private for a longer period of time and easier to go public at a later date when the time was right. These provisions went into effect immediately upon the president's signature, and had a significant impact on later-stage private companies, but little effect on startups.

The second component, Title II, for the first time made it possible for startups to let everyone know that they were seeking funding (known as *general solicitation*). Companies were still restricted to taking investments only from Accredited Investors, but now they didn't have to do it behind closed doors. Title II went into effect on September 23, 2013, and has had a major impact on startup financing, with companies filing to raise over $25 billion just in the first two months (how many will actually be successful is another story). The ability to solicit generally is what allows the full operation of online equity funding platforms for individual Accredited Investors, as discussed throughout this book.

Note, however, that angel groups using a platform like Gust to manage their internal collaboration with potential investments, or startups using Gust to manage their direct, private communications with potential investors with whom they already have an existing relationship, have always been permissible, and will remain so. What changed for startups with Title II is the ability to advertise publicly the details of a funding round.

But that change did come with a cost: startups that plan to use the new provisions and publicly advertise their raise are now required to verify specifically that all of their investors are, indeed, Accredited. Under the old provisions (which are still applicable if you do *not* advertise), all that you need to do as an angel is sign a form provided by the company confirming that you meet the qualifications to be an Accredited Investor. But for a company choosing to solicit generally, you may now find yourself asked to supply a signed confirmation from your banker or broker testifying to your net worth or income. Or you may find a startup requesting your tax returns or W2 forms before you can invest. Yikes! That's one reason that many companies are trying to follow the older, more restrictive rules of fundraising *without* generally soliciting. To help ease this burden, Gust and other platforms for Accredited equity investing are developing ways to separate the verification process for the investor from the investment into the startup. With these services, you will be able to establish your Accredited status once, and use that verification for multiple investments so that you will not need to provide personal details to each startup in which you invest.

Then there is Title III of the JOBS Act.

Title III for the first time says that the "crowd"—that is, regular people who are not Accredited Investors—will be allowed to invest in private companies—that is, startups. It also explicitly states that this must happen either through a specific class of online venues that are defined in the Act as a *funding platforms* or through a traditionally registered broker/dealer. So as not to do away completely with all securities regulations of the past 80 years, the JOBS Act places strict limits on how much companies will be able to raise this way, and how much in total people will be able to invest each year if they are not Accredited Investors.

According to the initial draft rules issued by the SEC, companies will be able to raise up to $1,000,000 in any 12-month period from non-Accredited Investors using either a FINRA-registered Internet Funding Platform or a broker/dealer. They can also raise money at the same time from other sources, such as angel groups or on Gust, under the old rules. Any investor can invest a total of between $2,000 and $100,000 in a 12-month period. The 12-month investment limit is based on the greater of annual income or assets: 5 percent of that amount if less than $100,000 (but not less than $2,000), 10 percent if greater than $100,000 (but not more than $100,000). Investors will self-certify their income, assets, and other investments.

What is the bottom line of all these changes? For now, it means:

- As of the writing of this book there has been no change yet for non-Accredited equity crowdfunding, although there are rules proposed that will make it possible, but potentially tough and expensive for small companies.
- Companies selling only to Accredited Investors can now begin to solicit investors generally, although, if they do so, they will need to verify their income and/or net worth officially.
- Soliciting in this context means virtually any kind of public communication, from ads on the sides of buses to Twitter blasts to Facebook posts.

What Can We Expect to See with Equity Crowdfunding?

As you have seen in the course of this book, serious angel investing is challenging, risky, and requires a great effort over a lengthy period of time to be done correctly. And that's not to mention the leverage held by investors writing large checks and insisting on term sheets with significant investor protections. In contrast, crowdfunding for non-Accredited Investors will be a different type of activity, much closer to traditional, project-based crowdfunding than to traditional early stage, Accredited, angel investing. While the JOBS Act of 2012 and its proponents envisioned crowd investments as primarily direct equity purchases (similar to angel investing), in the long run, I believe that the viable models for equity-based crowdfunding are likely to be most effective with one of the following two approaches:

1. Revenue-backed, interest-bearing notes with a kicker multiple. Under this model, the funds go into the company as a loan, and get repaid with interest by distributing a fixed percentage of gross revenues (say, 5 percent) among all the note holders. Once the base plus interest has been returned to the investors, the company continues to pay out a percentage of revenues (perhaps at a lesser rate, say, 2.5 percent) until the investors have received a fixed multiple of their original investment (say, 5x). At any time, the company may retire the note(s) by paying off the base plus interest

plus 5x kicker. Some sites will use a similar approach, but limit the repayment by time (say, 5 percent of revenues for the first three years) rather than a multiple of the investment, but this is problematic for a number of reasons.

2. Single-holder, special purpose vehicles with a professional manager. Under this model, entities will hold the individual crowd-funded investments and aggregate them, from the company's perspective, into a single entity on the company's cap table. The professional manager of the vehicle will handle all administrative work for both investors and the company, and will contractually be obligated to abstain from any shareholder votes.

Whatever happens with equity crowdfunding, there is no question that the world of early-stage financing will remain in flux for the next several years as new technologies, platforms, business models, and legislation come into play. Regardless of whether you are a multimillionaire super angel, or a $2,000-a-year crowdfunder, internalizing the underlying lessons in this book will be equally as vital when it comes to generating long-term results.

■ ■ ■

If you've read this far, you've probably noticed that I am a committed believer (as well as an enthusiastic participant) in the social, economic, and personal value of angel investing. As a crucial cog in the machinery of entrepreneurship, angel investing plays a vital role in launching and nurturing the businesses that will shape the world of tomorrow—the companies that will help millions of people live richer, longer, healthier, more prosperous, and more enjoyable lives, even as they build significant assets for their founders, their employees, and, yes, their investors.

I hope the information you've gleaned from this book has convinced you that angel investing can be an amazingly rewarding practice—and if you're ready to take the plunge into this exciting business arena, I wish you a lifetime of adventure and success!

A

Angel Screening and Valuation Worksheet

Company _____ Date _____

Weighted Ranking	Factors and Issues Relevant to the Viability of Pre-Revenue Start-Up Companies for Angel Funding	
0–30% (x3)	**Strength of the Management Team**	
	Impact	*Founder's business experience*
	+++	Experience as a CEO
	++	As a COO, CTO, CFO
	+	As a product manager
	0	Many year's business experience
	−−	Sales person or technologist only
	−−−	Straight out of school
	Impact	*Founder's domain experience*
	++	Successful experience in this space
	+	Experience in directly analagous space
	−	New entrant to this space

(continued)

Weighted Ranking	Factors and Issues Relevant to the Viability of Pre-Revenue Start-Up Companies for Angel Funding (*continued*)	
	Impact	*Willingness to step aside, if necessary, for a new CEO*
	++	Willing
	+	Somewhat willing
	0	Neutral
	––	Somewhat unwilling
	–––	Unwilling
	Impact	*Is the founder coachable?*
	+	Yes
	–––	No
	Impact	*How complete is the management team*
	+++	A complete and experienced management team
	+	Rather complete team
	0	Good start
	–	Somewhat incomplete
	––	Very incomplete
0–15% (x3)	**Size of the Opportunity**	
	Impact	*Size of the specific market for the company's product or service*
	++	>$500,000,000
	+	>$100,000,000
	–	>$50,000,000
	––	<$50,000,000
	Impact	*Potential for revenues in five years*
	++	>$100,000,000
	+	>$50,000,000
	–	<$25,000,000
	Impact	*Strength of competition in this marketplace*
	+	Weak
	0	Modest (or none)
	–	Strong

Weighted Ranking	Factors and Issues Relevant to the Viability of Pre-Revenue Start-Up Companies for Angel Funding (*continued*)	
0–15% (x3)	**Product or Service**	
	Impact	*How well is the product/market defined?*
	+	Clear, focused, and succinct
	0	Some definition, needs focus
	– –	Poorly defined
	Impact	*Is the product/service compelling?*
	+	Product is a pain-killer with no side effects
	0	Product is a pain-killer
	–	Produt is a vitamin
	Impact	*What is the path to product acceptance?*
	+	Product is an easily understood and adopted improvement
	0	Product is an innovative approach to a known market
	–	Product defines a new industry or category
	Impact	*Can product/service be easily copied?*
	++	Solid, issued patent protection
	+	Product is unique and protected by trade secrets
	–	Duplicated or replaced with difficulty
	– –	Easily copied
0–10% (x5)	Impact	**Sales Channels**
	++	Channels established and moving product
	+	Initial channels verified
	0	Narrowed to one or two channels
	– –	Channel strategy not yet established
0–10% (x5)	Impact	**Stage of Business**
	++	Customers generating significant revenue
	+	Positive, verifiable acceptance by beta sites
	0	Product ready to market
	–	Product in prototype
	– –	Only have a plan

(*continued*)

Weighted Ranking	Factors and Issues Relevant to the Viability of Pre-Revenue Start-Up Companies for Angel Funding (*continued*)	
0–5% (x5)	Impact	Size of This Investment Round
	+	$250,000 to $750,000
	0	$750,000 to $1,500,000
	— —	Over $1,500,000
0–5% (x5)	Impact	**Need for Subsequent Funding**
	+	None
	0	Less than $2,000,000
	— —	Over $10,000,000
0–5% (x5)	Impact	**Quality of Business Plan and Presentation**
	+	Excellent
	0	OK
	— — —	Poor
0–2.5% (x2.5)	Impact	**Location of Business**
	+	Within driving distance
	0	Within the same country
	— —	Elsewhere
0–2.5% (x2.5)	Impact	**Type of Industry**
	+	Meets investor's specific thesis
	0	Scalable consumer or B-to-B
	—	Capital intensive
	Raw Score		**Intangible (±25%)**		**Final Score**

Angel Investment
Due Diligence Checklist

Internal Due Diligence Checklist
Company Overview
<ul><li>Articulate the "equity story" here (i.e., why the company is on to something and why its stock will appreciate greatly). Is it compelling?</li><li>Does the company engage in thorough business planning?</li><li>Does management have a clear understanding of the challenges it faces and a realistic plan to address them?</li><li>Are there any skeletons in the company's closet from previous activities (e.g. outstanding liabilities, unassigned IP)?</li></ul>

(continued)

Management Team

- Are all resumes and personal references available?
- What key strengths does the management team have collectively and individually?
- What holes are there in the team and how/when might they be filled?
- Have there been any disgruntled employees and, if so, why? Do these employees cause any tangible risk going forward?
- What strengths does the Board bring to the company? How might it be augmented?
- Is there a Board of Advisors, and, if so, how active is it?

Marketing

- Does the company have a well-defined sense of what its true market is?
- Is this market sufficiently large and fast-growing to be attractive?
- Is the company's market generalized or niche?
- If generalized, does the company stand out from competitors?
- If niche, will the company dominate sufficiently either to build attractive cash flow or be bought by a larger firm?
- Is the company the leading firm in its market? Market share?
- What barriers to entry does the company enjoy? How long-lasting are they?

Marketing
■ Does management understand the key metrics to measure its business and does it track its progress effectively? How do the metrics compare to similar firms? ■ Does the company have a sensible business model?

Sales
■ Do customer reference calls bear out claims management makes about demand for their products/services? ■ Is the company pipeline attractive? What is the probability that it will hit its targets? ■ Does the sales strategy make sense? What could be done to improve it? ■ Can the company acquire customers profitably? ■ Is the company's sales cycle better or worse than its competitors and is it attractive?

Competition
■ Does the company know who its competitors are, including indirect competitors? ■ Where does the company stack up versus competitors? Can it win business from them? ■ Has the company focused its business plan narrowly enough to limit its competition? ■ How well-funded is the competition?

(continued)

Product Development

- Is the product a need-to-have, a nice-to-have, or a luxury? Does it solve a critical problem or enable growth (if B2B)/provide entertainment (if B2C)?
- Describe the customer demand in detail.
- Has the company proven adept at product development? Does it have an adequate technical team?
- Did product development flow from perceived (or, better yet, researched) customer demand or from some other impetus? Explain.

Intellectual Property

- Does the company have an appropriate IP strategy? Explain.
- Are there any issues relating to patents or intellectual property?

Production/Operations (HR, Customer Support, Fulfillment, Returns, Distribution Logistics)

- Do the management team and other employees enjoy appropriate incentives to run the company for the long term?
- Are the interests of management aligned with ours?
- Are total labor costs appropriate?
- Does the company have a realistic plan for managing its back office and customer support? Will it be able to handle customer growth while maintaining customer satisfaction?

Financing Strategy

- Is the valuation attractive? What is the projected times money returned and IRR (if calculable)? Is the risk-adjusted return attractive?
- Does the company have a thorough plan as to what it will do with our money? Is it sensible?
- Is the company raising the right amount of money?
- What financing risk exists in the business plan? How much additional money must they raise and how flexible (in amount and timing) can they be in raising it?

Financials

- Does the company have a realistic set of projections based on reasonable assumptions?
- Are the projections bottom-up (good) or top-down (not so good)?
- Does the company have good operating leverage?
- Are the margins attractive (absolutely and relative to competitors)?
- Has the company met, exceeded, or fallen short of its previous budgets? Analyze variances.

Assets and Property

- Are there any issues here?

(continued)

Customer References

- Write up summary of reference calls.
- Do customer reference calls bear out claims management makes about demand for their products/services?
- Are there any issues flagged by customers? Does management recognize and admit to (without prompting) these issues?

Contracts and Agreements

- Review all contracts with legal counsel and flag any issues, risks, or omissions.

Corporate Documents

- Review all corporate documents with legal counsel and flag any issues, risks, or omissions.

Taxes

- Review company tax situation and analyze effects on cash flow over next several years.

Insurance

- Assess adequacy of insurance coverage and analyze risk to investment thesis of any insurance gaps.

C

Gust Convertible Note Term Sheet

**TERMS FOR CONVERTIBLE NOTE BRIDGE
FINANCING OF NEWCO, INC.**
_____, 20__

The following is a summary of the principal terms with respect to the proposed Convertible Note Financing of NewCo, Inc., a Delaware corporation (the "**Company**"). Except for the sections entitled "Expenses" and "No Shop/Confidentiality," such summary of terms does not constitute a legally binding obligation. Any other legally binding obligation will only be made pursuant to definitive agreements to be negotiated and executed by the parties.

Securities to Issue:	Convertible Promissory Notes of the Company (the "**Notes**").
Aggregate Proceeds:	Minimum of $_____ and maximum of $_____ in aggregate, including the conversion of any prior Convertible notes outstanding as of the Closing.
Lenders:	Nice Guy Angels, LLC (the "**Lead Lender**") who will lend a minimum of _____ and other lenders acceptable to the Company and the Lead Lender.

Purchase Price:	Face value.
Interest Rate:	Annual 5% accruing cumulative interest, payable at maturity.
Term:	All principal, together with accrued and unpaid interest under the Notes, is due and payable on the date that is 12 months from the Closing (the "**Maturity Date**"). The Maturity Date may be extended by the consent of holders of the Notes that hold a majority of the aggregate outstanding principal amount of the Notes (a "**Majority Interest**").
Note Priority:	Notes shall be senior to all other indebtedness. All unsecured indebtedness of the Company for borrowed money will be fully subordinated to the prior payment of all principal and interest on the Notes.
Prepayment:	The Notes may not be prepaid without the consent of a Majority Interest.
Conversion:	The "**Conversion Sales Price**" shall be a price per share equal to the lesser of (i) 80% of the lowest price per share paid by any other party purchasing Common or Preferred stock upon a Conversion Event as defined below, and (ii) the price obtained by dividing (x) \$_____ (the "**Valuation Cap**") by (y) the number of Fully Diluted Shares outstanding immediately prior to the Conversion Event. "**Fully Diluted Shares**" shall mean the number of shares of Common Stock of the Company outstanding at the applicable time assuming full conversion or exercise of all then outstanding options, options reserved for issuance, warrants, and convertible securities (other than the Notes).

A "**Conversion Event**" shall mean any one of the following events:

(i) *Qualified Financing*. The Company consummates, on or prior to the Maturity Date, an equity financing pursuant to which it sells shares of a series of its preferred stock (**"Preferred Stock"**) with an aggregate sales price of not less than $_____ (excluding all indebtedness other than the Notes that is converted into Preferred Stock in such financing) with the principal purpose of raising capital (a **"Qualified Financing"**).

(ii) *Non-Qualified Financing.* The Company consummates, on or prior to the Maturity Date, an equity financing pursuant to which it sells shares of a series of Preferred Stock, which is not a Qualified Financing (a **"Non-Qualified Financing"**).

(iii) *Change of Control.* On or prior to the Maturity Date and prior to the consummation of a Qualified Financing, the Company consummates a change of control or sale transaction of its common stock (**"Common Stock"**).

(iv) *Maturity.* The Company has not consummated a Qualified Financing or a change of control or sale transaction on or prior to the Maturity Date, and the Maturity Date has not been extended by a Majority Interest.

Conversion under (i) shall be automatic. Conversion under (ii)–(iv) shall be at the option of a Majority Interest.

In the event of a Financing conversion described in (i) or (ii) above, the Notes shall convert into a series of Preferred Stock that is identical to the securities issued in the Qualified or Non-Qualified Financing and on the same terms as the other parties purchasing such stock upon the Conversion Event, except that for the purposes of the Notes, the Original Issue Price in such financing shall be the discounted price actually paid per share by the noteholder.

In the event of a Change of Control conversion described in (iii) above, the Notes shall convert into Common Stock.

In the event of a Maturity conversion described in (iv) above, the Notes shall convert into non-participating convertible preferred stock with a 1x liquidation preference, customary dividend preference, customary broad-based weighted average anti-dilution protection, and customary protective provisions which will entitle the holder to customary contractual preemptive rights and other customary contractual rights (each as provided in the Seed Series Convertible Preferred model documents maintained at gust.com/seedseries) (**"New Preferred Stock"**).

Special Approvals: So long as a Majority Interest is entitled to elect a Lender Director, the Company will not, without Board approval, which approval must include the affirmative vote of the Lender Director: (i) incur any aggregate indebtedness in excess of $50,000; (ii) make any loan or advance to any person, including employees, subject to customary exceptions; (iii) make any expenditure not in compliance with the annual budget approved by the Board including the Lender Director (other than expenditures within 25% of budget, individually, and in the aggregate); or (iv) approve or enter into any related party transactions (including any amendment of agreements with the founders).

The Company will not, without the consent of a Majority Interest: (i) approve the voluntary liquidation or dissolution of the Company (or any subsidiary), a sale of all or substantially all of the Company's assets, a merger or consolidation of the Company with any other company, or a lease or exclusive license of the Company's assets (each a "**Liquidation Event**") (other than a Liquidation Event in which net proceeds exceed $_____); (ii) authorize, create (by reclassification or otherwise), or issue any new class or series of shares (including in connection with a Qualified Financing) or debt security; or (iii) declare or pay any dividend or distribution or approve any repurchase of capital stock.

Use of Funds: Proceeds shall be used for general corporate operations, and not for repayment of any existing debt obligations of the Company.

Documentation: Transaction documents will be drafted by counsel to Lenders.

Financial Information: All Lenders will receive quarterly financial statements and narrative update reports from management. Lead Lender will receive such information monthly.

Board of Directors: Following the initial Closing, the Company's board of directors (the "**Board**") shall include one representative designated by the Lead Lender (the "**Lender Director**"), so long as any principal or interest remains outstanding under the Notes.

Expenses: The Company shall pay the reasonable fees and expenses of a single counsel to the Lenders up to $5,000 if the financing closes. If the financing is not consummated, each party will bear its own legal fees and expense, unless the financing is not consummated by reason of the Company's refusal to proceed, in which case the Company shall pay the Lenders' out-of-pocket expenses, including legal fees.

Founder/Employees: Founder(s) and all employees and contractors as of the Closing shall have assigned all relevant IP to the Company and shall have entered into nondisclosure, noncompetition, and non-solicitation agreements in a form reasonably acceptable to Lenders, with such covenants to be applicable during the term of their employment by the Company and for one year after the termination thereof.

No-Shop/
Confidentiality: The Company agrees to work in good faith expeditiously towards a closing of this note financing (the date the earliest Note is issued shall be the "**Closing**"). The Company and its officers and founders agree that they will not, for a period of 30 days from the date these terms are accepted, take any action to solicit, initiate, encourage, or assist the submission of any proposal, negotiation, or offer from any person or entity other than the Lenders relating to the sale or issuance, of any of the capital stock of the Company or the acquisition, sale, lease, license, or other disposition of the Company or any material part of the stock or assets of the Company, or the execution of any debt instruments of any kind, and shall notify the Lenders promptly of any inquiries by any third parties in regards to the foregoing. The Company will not disclose the terms or existence of this Term Sheet or the fact that negotiations are ongoing to any person other than officers, members of its board of directors, and the Company's accountants and attorneys and other potential Lenders acceptable to the Lead Lender, without the written consent of the Lead Lender.

Expiration: This Term Sheet expires on _____, 20__ if not accepted by the Company by that date.

This Term Sheet may be executed in counterparts, which together will constitute one document. Facsimile or digital signatures shall have the same legal effect as original signatures.

NEWCO, INC.

Name:

_____

Title: Founder and CEO

Date: _____

NICE GUY ANGELS, LLC

_____

Name:

Title:

Date: _____

D

Gust Series Seed Term Sheet

This term sheet for financing early stage companies with investments from sophisticated angel investors was developed by Gust, the platform powering more than 90 percent of the organized angel investment groups in the United States. The goal was to standardize on a single investment structure, eliminate confusion, and significantly reduce the costs of negotiating, documenting, and closing an early stage seed investment.

For those familiar with early stage angel transactions, this middle-of-the-road approach is founder-friendly and investor-rational, intended to strike a balance between the Series A Model Documents developed by the National Venture Capital Association that have traditionally been used by most American angel groups (which include a 17-page term sheet and 120 pages of supporting documentation covering many low-probability edge cases), and the one-page Series Seed 2.0 Term Sheet developed in 2010 by Ted Wang of Fenwick & West as a contribution to the early stage community (which deferred most investor protections and deal specifics until future financing rounds).

TERMS FOR PRIVATE PLACEMENT OF SEED SERIES PREFERRED STOCK OF
[*Insert Company Name*], INC.
[Date]

The following is a summary of the principal terms with respect to the proposed Seed Series Preferred Stock financing of _____, Inc., a [Delaware] corporation (the "*Company*"). Except for the sections entitled "Expenses," "No Shop/Confidentiality," and "Special Terms," such summary of terms does not constitute a legally binding obligation. Any other legally binding obligation will only be made pursuant to definitive agreements to be negotiated and executed by the parties.

Shares of stock are only applicable to an incorporated company (which means that this term sheet is only applicable to a C Corporation. Angel investments in a Limited Liability Company are more complex, and require a different structure.) Delaware is the favored state of incorporation for U.S. businesses (including more than half of the Fortune 500) because it is considered "corporate-friendly" with well-established case law. While not required either by law or by this term sheet, incorporation of the company in Delaware is strongly advised. Recently, Nevada has developed a similar reputation, and is sometimes used as the incorporation venue for companies based on the West Coast.

This term sheet is, for the most part, "nonbinding," which means that it is used only to document the general meeting of the minds between the two parties, and not to serve as the legal basis for the investment. However, this paragraph makes clear that the three specific sections referenced, "Expenses," "No Shop/Confidentiality," and "Special Terms" (if such a section is included), ARE legally binding, and once this term sheet is signed by both parties, those sections [only] are immediately in force. Therefore, regardless of whether or not the investment is ultimately made, any breach of things such as the confidentiality provisions, or the requirement to pay legal fees, can subject the breaching party to legal action by the other.

Note that the company name should be inserted in both the title and in this paragraph, the state of incorporation should be inserted where indicated, and the brackets should be removed. If there is a Special Terms section added to the document, the brackets around that phrase should be removed, otherwise delete the whole bracketed phrase.

Offering Terms

Securities to
Issue:

Shares of Seed Series Preferred Stock of the Company (the "*Series Seed*").

In exchange for their financial investment, the investors under this term sheet are acquiring shares of stock in the company. Unlike Common Stock (which is what is usually purchased on the public stock markets), this term sheet specifies Preferred Stock. The difference is that in the case of a sale, liquidation, or winding up of the company, the Preferred Stock gets paid back first, before any Common Stock (which is typically what Founders and employees of the company hold). However, because Preferred Stock gets back ONLY the amount invested, all of the upside goes to the Common Stock holders. For that reason, a subsequent section of this term sheet provides for the option of the investors to convert the Preferred to Common, if such conversion would be in the investors' interest.

Note that the class of stock being purchased in this investment round is named "Series Seed." This is a purely arbitrary name, for reference purposes. Traditionally, a first, relatively small, investment round from angel investors or a seed fund would be called a Series Seed. The first institutional investment round from a venture capital fund would be called a "Series A," with each subsequent round incrementing one letter (Series B, Series C, etc.).

Aggregate
Proceeds:

Minimum of $_____ [and maximum of $_____ in aggregate].

This sets forth how much money the company is planning to raise in this round. Investors typically would not want to fund their commitments until they are sure that the company will receive enough money to be able to achieve its objectives for this round. As such, even if the investors and the company sign the term sheet today, no money will change hands until at least the minimum amount is committed by adding additional commitments from other investors. If the company and investors have agreed upon a maximum amount to be raised, insert it here and remove the brackets. If there is no maximum, delete the bracketed phrase.

Lead Investors: _____ who will invest a minimum of $_____

> This sets for the identity of the investor(s) who are signing this term sheet and committing to invest in the company. While other investors may participate in the funding, the primary investor (whether individual, fund, or group) may (but need not) be granted additional rights in the term sheet. The amount here is the minimum amount that the Lead investor(s) are committing to this round, and is distinct from the minimum amount required to consummate the investment.

Price Per Share: $_____ (the **"*Original Issue Price*"**), based on a pre-money valuation of $____, calculated based upon the capitalization of the Company as set forth in Exhibit A inclusive of an available post-closing option pool of 15 percent after receipt of maximum Aggregate Proceeds.

> The price that investors will pay for each share of Preferred Stock is calculated on the basis of the other factors noted in the term sheet, as well as the number of shares that the company has authorized (or will do so as part of this round). This price is usually filled in last, with the important number in this paragraph being the "pre-money valuation." This is the amount that the Founders and investors agree that the company is worth as of the date the term sheet is signed, before the investors' money is received by the company.
>
> To make this section absolutely clear for everyone, it refers to Exhibit A to the Term Sheet, which is a Capitalization Table for the company, showing in names and numbers exactly who owns what shares, both before and after the investment.
>
> In the second part of the sentence the parties agree that before the investment happens, the company will set aside extra shares of Common Stock that will be used to attract and compensate future employees. This is known as the "unallocated, post-closing, option pool." The important thing to understand here is that the 15 percent for the option pool is what will exist AFTER the investment, but the calculation is done BEFORE the investment is made. That means all of the shares for the option pool come out of the Founder's shares, not the investors'.

> Here is an example: A founder owns 100 percent of a company. Investors put in $350,000 in exchange for 35 percent ownership. That means the "post money" valuation of the company is $1 million, and the "pre-money" valuation (after subtracting out the $350,000) is $650,000. However, as the term sheet indicates, there needs to be a pool of 15 percent of the stock available for employee options. This means the post-closing Cap Table shown in Exhibit A will show 35 percent for the investors, 15 percent for the option pool, and 50 percent for the Founder.

Dividends:

Annual 5 percent accruing cumulative dividend payable when as and if declared, and upon (a) a Redemption or (b) a Liquidation (including a Deemed Liquidation Event) of the Company in which the holders of Series Seed receive less than five times the Original Issue Price per share (the "Cap"). For any other dividends or distributions, participation with Common Stock on an as-converted basis.

> A dividend on Preferred Stock is roughly equivalent to interest on a loan. This paragraph says that investors are entitled to a 5 percent dividend each year on their investment, but that the company's Board decides "when, as, and if" dividend payments are actually made. Since growing companies always need cash, it would be extremely unusual for a Board to declare a dividend payment during the early years. However, "accruing cumulative dividends" means that if the dividends are not paid each year, they continue to accrue until such time as they are.
>
> This paragraph sets out a couple of additional cases where the accrued dividends must be paid: (1) is the highly unusual case in which after seven years (as laid out in a subsequent section) the company is successful but the investors have not been able to get their money out, and therefore require the company to repurchase their stock; and (2) a sale or other winding up of the company ... but only in a case where the investors would otherwise receive less than a 5x return.
>
> Finally, the last sentence says that if the Common Stock (usually held by the Founders) gets a dividend, so does the Preferred Stock held by the investors.

Liquidation Preference:

One times the Original Issue Price plus any accrued and unpaid dividends thereon (subject to the "Cap") plus any other declared but unpaid dividends on each share of Series Seed, balance of proceeds paid to Common. A merger, consolidation, reorganization, sale, or exclusive license of all or substantially all of the assets or similar transaction in one or a series of related transactions will be treated as a liquidation (a "Deemed Liquidation Event").

> This paragraph says that if the company is converted to cash ("liquidated") whether for happy reasons, such as getting acquired for a billion dollars, or sad ones, such as going out of business and selling the furniture, after paying all of its debts (which always get paid before equity), any remaining money first goes to pay back the amount put in by the investors and then goes to pay the accrued dividends. After that, everything and anything that's left goes to the Common Stockholders (typically the Founders and employees).
>
> While this sounds good for investors in the sad case, it means that in the happy case, even if the company is sold for a billion dollars, the only money the investors will get back is their original investment plus the 5 percent dividend. That's the reason for the next section: conversion.

Conversion:

Convertible into one share of Common (subject to proportional adjustments for stock splits, stock dividends, and the like, and Broad-Based Weighted Average antidilution protection) at any time at the option of the holder.

> Here's where investors get their return: while Preferred Stock gets paid off first, it doesn't participate in any upside benefits. On the other hand, Common Stock gets a proportional share of any incoming money (such as from the proceeds of an acquisition), but has to stand in line behind the Preferred. So this paragraph says that investors who hold Preferred Stock can choose at any time to convert it into Common Stock.

The result is that in a bad scenario (the company is going out of business) the investors stay with Preferred, and get the first money out. But in a good scenario (an acquisition at a high price), they will choose instead to convert to Common, and share in the good things.

The "Broad-Based Weighted Average antidilution protection" means that if the company at some point in the future raises money at a lower valuation than that being used for the current round, the current investors will be partially protected. This provision is a middle-of-the-road industry standard, halfway between the Founder-biased "no antidilution" approach and the Investor-biased "full ratchet antidilution" version.

Voting Rights:	Votes together with the Common Stock on all matters on an as-converted basis. Approval of a majority of the Series Seed required to (i) adversely change rights of the Series Seed; (ii) change the authorized number of shares; (iii) authorize a new series of Preferred Stock having rights senior to or on parity with the Series Seed; (iv) create or authorize the creation of any debt security if the Company's aggregate indebtedness would exceed 50 percent of the aggregate proceeds of the Series Seed; (v) redeem or repurchase any shares (other than pursuant to the Company's right of repurchase at original cost); (vi) declare or pay any dividend; (vii) increase in the option pool reserve within two years following the closing; (viii) change the number of directors; or (ix) liquidate or dissolve, including any change of control or Deemed Liquidation Event.

This is where most of the protective provisions for investors are found. It says that even though investors hold Preferred Stock, when it comes to voting we will treat them as if they had converted to Common Stock, so that everyone who owns stock (founders, investors, et al.) gets to vote together on things requiring Shareholder approval. However, in addition to their voting

> alongside every other shareholder, this paragraph provides for a "series vote" on certain issues. That is, even if the Board of Directors and 100 percent of all the other shareholders voted to do something in one of these areas, it wouldn't happen unless a majority of the investors in this round agreed. The subjects requiring a series vote are generally ones that protect the investors from having their rights stripped, or their voting power diluted out of existence, or having the money they just put in go to someone else.

Documentation: Documents will be based on Seed Series Preferred Stock documents published at http:/gust.com/ SeriesSeed which will be generated/drafted by Company counsel.

> A term sheet lays out the general outline of an investment, but the devil is in the details. Once the Term Sheet is signed and the company and investors proceed to a closing, the lawyers then draft dozens of pages of documentation, including an amended Certificate of Incorporation, a Shareholders' Agreement, an Investors' Rights Agreement, etc. The Gust website has a set of standard, model documents that match the provisions of this term sheet and make it very easy for an attorney to use them as the basis for his or her work.
>
> While nothing will be signed and finalized until both the parties and their respective attorneys are satisfied, someone has to take the first step in drafting the documents. This paragraph says that the Company's counsel will do so, based on the Gust standard docs.

Financial Information: All Investors will receive annual financial statements and narrative update reports from management. Investors who have invested at least $25,000 ("**Major Investors**") will receive quarterly financial and narrative update reports from management and inspection rights. A management rights letter will be provided to any Investor that requires such a letter. All communications with Investors shall be conducted through Company's secure investor relations deal room on the

Gust platform, which Company shall be responsible for maintaining with current, complete, and accurate information.

> Because private companies are not required to file any statements with the Securities and Exchange Commission, this section lays out what information the company will be required to provide to its investors so that they are aware of what is happening with their investments. It provides for annual financial and written update reports from the company's management to be sent to all investors. In addition, investors who have put in more than $25,000 are entitled to quarterly reports, and also have the right to visit the company on request and see the corporate books and records (subject, of course, to confidentiality).
>
> A Management rights letter is a particular document required by certain venture funds.
>
> To ensure timely communications with investors, the company is required to keep its information updated and current in its Gust deal room, which will greatly enhance both the company's investor relations, and the investors' portfolio management activities.

Participation Right:

Major Investors will have the right to participate on a pro rata basis in subsequent issuances of equity securities.

> If the company sells additional stock at any time in the future, this says that each investor has the right (but not the obligation) to participate in such future rounds on the same terms as the new investors, at least up to an amount that will enable them to maintain the same percentage ownership after the new investment that they had before.

Redemption Right:

The Series Seed shall be redeemable from funds legally available for distribution at the option of the holders of a majority of the outstanding Series Seed commencing any time after the seventh anniversary of the Closing at a price equal to the Original Purchase Price plus all accrued but unpaid dividends and any other declared and unpaid dividends thereon. Redemption shall occur in three equal annual portions.

> If, after many years, the company ends up as "lifestyle" business, where it is profitable but not likely to ever have an exit, this paragraph gives the investors the right to require the company to buy back their stock for what they paid for it (plus dividends). The repurchase (known as "redemption") would take place over three years, starting at the investor's option any time after the seventh year.

Board of Directors:

Two directors elected by holders of a majority of Common stock, one elected by holders of a majority of Series Seed. Series Seed Director approval required for (i) incurring indebtedness **[exceeding $25,000]** for borrowed money prior to the Company being cash flow positive, (ii) selling, transferring, licensing, pledging, or encumbering technology or intellectual property, other than licenses granted in the ordinary course of business, (iii) entering into any material transaction with any founder, officer, director, or key employee of the Company or any affiliate or family member of any of the foregoing, (iv) hiring, firing, or materially changing the compensation of founders or executive officers, (v) changing the principal business of the Company, or (vi) entering into any Deemed Liquidation Event that would result in the holders of Series Seed Series receiving less than five times their Original Purchase Price.

> The Board of Directors of a company is in charge of making all major decisions, including hiring/firing the CEO. This paragraph establishes a three-person board, with two of the members appointed by the Common stockholders, and one by the investors in this round.

> While this 2:1 ratio means that the directors appointed by the Common (usually the founder(s) themselves) could always outvote the investor, the term sheet equalizes things by setting forth a number of areas in which not only does a majority of the board have to approve, but the director appointed by the investors must also specifically approve. The $25,000 limit on borrowing is rational for smaller deals, but can be increased for larger ones.

Expenses: Company to reimburse Investors a flat fee of $_____ for background check expenses, due diligence, and review of transaction documentation by Investors' counsel. Company shall be responsible for expenses related to Company's Gust investor relations deal room.

> Out-of-pocket expenses related to closing an investment are typically picked up by the company out of the investment proceeds. Given no deviation from this standard term sheet, a moderate flat fee for all of the investors' legal work is eminently reasonable, likely much less than the $20,000 or more when a full-scale NVCA term sheet is used. Including the cost of maintaining the company's investor relations site means that investors are assured of always getting up-to-date information in a form that is immediately usable to them.

Future Rights: The Series Seed will be given the same contractual rights (such as registration rights, information rights, rights of first refusal, and tagalong rights) as the first series of Preferred Stock sold to investors on terms similar to, or consistent with, NVCA or other standard documents customary for venture capital investments by institutional investors.

> This is the magic paragraph that ensures investors are protected with all the provisions included in the NVCA Model Documents, assuming that the company does a follow-on investment round with an institutional investor such as a traditional venture fund. It is what allows us to cut 14 pages worth of detail out of this term sheet, compared to the NVCA one.

Founder
Matters:

Each founder shall have four years vesting beginning as of the Closing, with 25 percent vesting
on the first anniversary of the Closing and the
remainder vesting monthly over the following
36 months. Full acceleration upon "Double Trigger." Each Founder shall have assigned all relevant IP to the Company prior to closing and shall
have entered into a nondisclosure, noncompetition, and nonsolicitation agreement (to the fullest
extent permitted by applicable law), with such
noncompetition and nonsolicitation covenants
to be applicable during the term of his or her
employment by the Company and for one year
after the termination thereof. Founders shall be
subject to an agreement with the Company pursuant to which the Company shall have a right
of first refusal with respect to any proposed transfer of capital stock of the Company at the price
offered.

> This section provides for what is called "reverse vest-
> ing" for the company's founders. Even though they may
> start out owning 100 percent of the company's stock,
> this gives the company the right to repurchase the stock
> owned by the Founder(s) if they leave the company.
> The terms are the standard 'four year vesting/one year
> cliff', which means that if the founder leaves within the
> first year after the investment, the company can reac-
> quire all of his or her stock, and after the one-year
> anniversary, the remaining stock vests monthly over
> the next three years. While some Founders initially
> find this onerous, it is actually *very* much in each of
> the Founders' best interest, because otherwise one
> co-founder (say, out of two) could theoretically walk
> away from the company the day after the closing, and
> retain nearly half of the equity … something that would
> be manifestly unfair to the other founder.
>   The "full acceleration upon Double Trigger" means
> that if the company is acquired before the four years are
> up, and the new owners terminate the Founder, all of
> the remaining stock owned by the Founder immediately
> vests.

> Other provisions of this section include ensuring that the Founder(s) have fully assigned all of their intellectual property so that it is owned by the company, that they have entered into an employment agreement providing for nondisclosure of confidential information, and that if they leave the company they are restricted for a year from either directly competing with the company, or poaching its employees.
>
> Finally, this section says that if Founders want to sell any of their stock, they are required to first offer it to the company.

No Shop/
Confidentiality:

The Company and the founders agree that they will not, for a period of 60 days from the date these terms are accepted, take any action to solicit, initiate, encourage, or assist the submission of any proposal, negotiation, or offer from any person or entity other than the Investors relating to the sale or issuance of any of the capital stock of the Company and shall notify the Investors promptly of any inquiries by any third parties in regards to the foregoing. The Company and the founders will not disclose the terms of this Term Sheet to any person other than officers, members of the Board of Directors, and the Company's accountants and attorneys and other potential Investors acceptable to the Investors, without the written consent of the Investors.

> The idea behind a No Shop provision is that investors do not want to be used as a "straw man" for the purpose of helping the company get a better deal from someone else. So there can be as much discussion as necessary, and as many unsigned drafts of the term sheet exchanged as necessary, but the minute the company signs this term sheet, they are agreeing that for 60 days they won't talk to anyone else about investing, without the investors' approval.

Special Terms:

[Deal specific comments/conditions inserted here. Otherwise "None".]

In order to keep the rest of the term sheet absolutely standard and reduce legal and drafting costs, there should be absolutely NO modifications within the text of the other sections of the term sheet. This "Special Terms" section is the one place that anything unusual or specific to this particular investment should go, although the more special terms or modifications there are, the longer it will take to negotiate, and the more the legal fees will cost. Remember that every page in the Term Sheet ultimately translates into ten or more pages of the actual deal documentation, and every new or special provision added requires that the lawyers on both sides write, read, and negotiate something non-standard. As a rule of thumb, every time the documents need to go back and forth between the lawyers, it adds approximately $5,000 to the overall legal costs for the transaction.

COMPANY: [_____, INC.]   FOR THE INVESTORS:

Name: _____   Name: _____

Title: _____   Title: _____

Date: _____   Date: _____

Since parts of the Term Sheet are legally binding, it should be signed by some-one legally able to bind both parties. This would normally be the CEO of the company, and a Lead Investor who is firmly committed to investing in the company on these terms.

This sample term sheet was developed by Gust with the legal support of Lori Smith, Esq. of White and Williams, and extensive comments from the members of the New York Angels Term Sheet Committee including Larry Richenstein, Jeffrey Seltzer, and Mark Schneider. Annotations and commentary copyright © 2013 by David S. Rose.

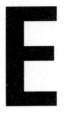

Gust Revenue-Backed Note Term Sheet

Issuer: [insert company name] (the "Company")[1]

Amount of financing: [include Min/Max—$0—$1 million][2,3] (the "Financing")

Closing Date: The Offering will only close if the Minimum Investment Amount is committed by [insert date—see footnote 3]

Type of Security: Unsecured Revenue Backed Promissory Note ("Note")

Investment Amount: $[_____][4] ("Original Principal Amount")

Maturity Date: 5 years from issuance

Interest Rate: 5% per annum calculated based on a 360-day year, compounding annually

Repayment: The note shall require payments quarterly within 30 days after the end of each fiscal quarter of the Company in an amount equal to (a) 5 percent of the Gross Revenue of the Company as reported on the Company's regularly prepared financial statements until the Original Principal Amount plus any interest accrued to date is repaid in full, and thereafter in an amount equal to (b) 2.5 percent of the Gross Revenue of the Company until receipt by the Investor of five (5) times the Original Principal Amount, plus all accrued and unpaid interest thereon (the "Obligation Amount"). Any balance of the Obligation Amount outstanding on the Maturity Date shall become immediately due and payable.

Prepayment: Permitted at any time at the option of the Company, in whole or in part, provided however that the Note shall not be deemed satisfied and repaid in full unless and until the Investor has received 100 percent of the Obligation Amount. Any prepayment must be pro rata among all Notes issued in this Financing.

Use of Proceeds: [insert intended use][5]

Amendment: The Notes may not be amended once issued.

Information Rights: The Company shall provide each Investor with all information required by the JOBS Act of 2012 and the relevant rules issued by the SEC. The Company will (i) file with the SEC annual reports as required by the SEC; (ii) mail each Investor a copy of such annual reports; (iii) make the contents of such annual report available to each Investor electronically through both (a) [insert name of Funding Portal] and

(b) Gust.com, and optionally otherwise make such reports available as permitted by the SEC and applicable laws, rules, and regulations. In addition the Company will provide each Investor with a quarterly narrative report from the CEO with an update on the Company's operations and financial condition through one or more of the above means. No other information rights will be provided unless required by law.

Restrictions on Transfer: Notes issued in the Financing will be subject to a one-year transfer restriction pursuant to the JOBS Act during which time such securities may only be transferred (a) to the Issuer, (b) pursuant to a registered offering, (c) to an Accredited Investor, (d) to certain family members, or in connection with the death or divorce of the Investor or similar circumstances at the discretion of the SEC. Transfers will also be subject to other limitations as the SEC may establish. In connection with any transfer, Investor must notify the Company at least ten (10) days prior to the effective date of such transfer, provide proof that the Transfer is permitted hereunder, and provide the name and address of the Transferee. The Company shall have the absolute right in its sole discretion to refuse to transfer ownership of the Note on its books, and such transfer shall be null and void absent evidence satisfactory to the Company that such transfer is in compliance with all applicable laws.

Events of Default: The sole events of default shall be (i) nonpayment of any principal and interest when due hereunder; (ii) bankruptcy, insolvency, or otherwise seeking the protection of any creditors' rights statute, or (iii) dissolution, liquidation, or complete cessation of business of the Company.

[1]Use of this term sheet is limited to U.S. private companies. The exemption applicable to this offering is not available to foreign companies, issuers already reporting pursuant to Section 13 or 15(d) of the Securities Act, investment companies, and other companies that the SEC determines should be ineligible to use this exemption.

[2]$1 million limitation applies to the aggregate amount of all securities sold by the Issuer, whether of the same or a different class, over the preceding 12 months (including the securities sold in the offering under the crowdfunding exemption. "Issuer" includes all entities controlled by or under common control with the Issuer.

[3]The JOBS Act requires that the offering include a target offering amount, the deadline to reach such target amount, and regular funding progress reports relating to the issuer's progress in meeting the target offering amount. [Note: It appears that prior to close there will need to be a mechanism to allow crowdfunding investors to rescind their investment once all final terms are set and all required disclosures have been made.]

[4]The amount sold to each investor is limited based on the investor's annual income and net worth. For an investor with an annual income or net worth of less than $100,000, the investor's maximum aggregate annual investment in securities issued under the crowdfunding exemption over a 12-month period is capped at the greater of $2,000 or 5 percent of such investor's annual income or net worth. For investors with an annual income or net worth of greater than $100,000, such investments are capped at the lesser of $100,000 or 10 percent of such investor's annual income or net worth.

[5]JOBs Act requires a description of the intended use of proceeds. Note that JOBS Act will also require disclosure of business plan and other information but for purposes of term sheet we have assumed that the funding portal or broker dealer will have a process in place for collecting and disseminating such information.

DISCLAIMER: THE NOTES ISSUED PURSUANT TO THE FINANCING ARE NOT THE EQUIVALENT OF PURCHASING A SHARE OF CAPITAL STOCK IN THE COMPANY. THEY DO NOT REPRESENT ANY PERCENTAGE INTEREST IN THE PROFITS OR LOSSES OF THE COMPANY NOR DO THEY PARTICIPATE IN THE PROCEEDS OF ANY SALE EXCEPT TO THE EXTENT OF THE OBLIGATION AMOUNT. THE NOTES WILL NOT INCREASE IN VALUE AS A RESULT OF THE FUTURE OPERATIONS OF THE COMPANY OR ANY TRANSACTION IN WHICH THE COMPANY MAY ENGAGE, INCLUDING ANY SALE OF THE COMPANY OR ITS ASSETS OR ANY PUBLIC OR PRIVATE OFFERING OF SECURITIES. THE

COMPANY WILL HAVE NO OBLIGATION TO PREPAY THE NOTES ON THE HAPPENING OF ANY EVENT, INCLUDING ANY SALE OF THE COMPANY OR ITS ASSETS OR ANY PUBLIC OR PRIVATE OFFERING.

THE NOTES PROVIDE SOLELY FOR A FIXED MAXIMUM PAYMENT EQUAL TO THE OBLIGATION AMOUNT. YOU WILL NOT BE ENTITLED TO ANY AMOUNTS IN EXCESS OF THE OBLIGATION AMOUNT AND ONCE THE OBLIGATION AMOUNT IS RECEIVED THE COMPANY SHALL HAVE NO FURTHER OBLIGATION TO YOU AS AN INVESTOR, CREDITOR, OR OTHERWISE.

THE NOTES DO NOT PROVIDE YOU WITH ANY VOTING RIGHTS AS A SHAREHOLDER OF THE COMPANY NOR DO THEY PROVIDE YOU WITH ANY RIGHT TO PARTICIPATE IN ANY FUTURE OFFERING OF SECURITIES OF THE COMPANY (INCLUDING ANY FUTURE OFFERING OF NOTES OR OTHER DEBT SECURITIES).

INVESTMENT IN THE NOTES IS OF HIGH RISK. INVESTOR UNDERSTANDS AND ACKNOWLEDGES THAT THE COMPANY HAS A LIMITED FINANCIAL AND OPERATING HISTORY AND THAT AN INVESTMENT IN THE COMPANY IS HIGHLY SPECULATIVE. THERE CAN BE NO ASSURANCES THAT THE COMPANY WILL GENERATE ANY REVENUES OR SUFFICIENT GROSS REVENUES TO MAKE THE PAYMENTS DUE ON THE NOTES. IN THE EVENT THAT THE COMPANY DOES NOT GENERATE SUFFICIENT GROSS REVENUES TO PAY THIS NOTE BY THE MATURITY DATE, THERE IS A HIGH RISK THAT YOU WILL NOT RECEIVE PAYMENT OF ANY AMOUNTS THAT REMAIN DUE. YOU UNDERSTAND THAT YOU MAY LOSE YOUR ENTIRE INVESTMENT IN THE NOTE.

THE NOTES ARE UNSECURED. THE OBLIGATIONS ARE NOT SECURED BY ANY ASSETS OF THE COMPANY. THE COMPANY MAY INCUR ADDITIONAL INDEBTEDNESS TO FUND ITS OPERATIONS THAT MAY BE EITHER UNSECURED OR SECURED BY THE ASSETS OF THE COMPANY AND WHICH MAY GIVE THE CREDITORS

WITH RESPECT TO SUCH INDEBTEDNESS PRIORITY OVER THE RIGHTS OF THE HOLDERS OF THE NOTES IN THE EVENT OF ANY BANKRUPTCY, INSOLVENCY, DISSOLUTION, OR OTHER PROCEEDING INVOLVING CREDITORS RIGHTS. SUCH OTHER INDEBTEDNESS MAY ALSO GIVE SUCH OTHER CREDITORS RIGHTS THAT ARE MORE FAVORABLE OR SENIOR TO THE HOLDERS OF THE NOTES.

IT IS LIKELY THAT THE COMPANY MAY NEED TO RAISE ADDITIONAL FUNDS IN THE FUTURE TO GENERATE THE GROSS REVENUES NECESSARY TO PAY THE OBLIGATION AMOUNT. THERE CAN BE NO ASSURANCES THAT SUCH AMOUNTS CAN BE RAISED OR THAT THE TERMS ON WHICH SUCH ADDITIONAL FUNDS ARE RAISED WILL NOT HAVE AN ADVERSE IMPACT ON THE ABILITY OF THE COMPANY TO PAY THE OBLIGATION AMOUNT.

AS NOTED ABOVE, THE NOTES ARE ILLIQUID. THERE IS NO PUBLIC MARKET FOR THE NOTES AND THERE IS NOT LIKELY TO BE A PUBLIC MARKET FOR THE NOTES. THE COMPANY HAS NO OBLIGATION TO CREATE OR FACILITATE A MARKET FOR THE NOTES. YOU SHOULD UNDERSTAND THAT YOU MAY NEED TO HOLD THE NOTES INDEFINITELY. YOU SHOULD NOT INVEST IN THE NOTES UNLESS YOU CAN AFFORD TO HOLD THE NOTES INDEFINITELY AND BEAR THE TOTAL LOSS OF YOUR INVESTMENT.

EXCEPT FOR THE INFORMATION REQUIRED TO BE MADE AVAILABLE PURSUANT TO THE JOBS ACT, THERE IS NO PUBLIC INFORMATION AVAILABLE ABOUT THE COMPANY AND THE COMPANY HAS NO PRESENT PLANS TO MAKE SUCH INFORMATION AVAILABLE.

F

International Angel Investor Federations

ACA, Angel Capital Association (U.S.),
http://www.angelcapitalassociation.org/

AEBAN, Asociacion Española Business Angels,
http://www.aeban.es/

AANZ, Angel Association New Zealand,
http://www.angelassociation.co.nz/

APBA, Associação Portuguesa de Business Angels, Portugal,
http://www.apba.pt

AAAI, Australian Association of Angel Investors,
http://aaai.net.au/

AAIA, Austrian Angel Investors Association,
http://www.aaia.at

BAE, The European Confederation for Angel Investing,
http://www.businessangelseurope.com/

EBAN, European Trade Association for Business Angels, Seed
Funds and Early Stage Market Players,
http://www.eban.org/

EstBAN, Estonian Business Angels Network,
http://estban.ee/

FiBAN, Finnish Business Angel Network,
https://www.fiban.org/

FNABA, National Federation of Business Angels, Portugal,
http://www.fnaba.org/

France Angels,
http://www.franceangels.org/

HBAN, Halo Business Angel Network, Ireland,
http://www.hban.org/

LINC, The Scottish Angel Capital Association,
http://www.lincscot.co.uk/

NACO, National Angel Capital Organization, Canada,
http://www.angelinvestor.ca/

NBAA, National Business-Angels Association, Russia,
http://rusangels.ru/

NorBAN, Norwegian Business Angel Network,
http://www.norban.no/

TBAA, Business Angels Association Turkey,
http://melekyatirimcilardernegi.org/

WBAA, World Business Angel Association,
http://wbaa.biz/

G

Major Regional Angel Groups

North America

New York Angels, http://newyorkangels.com/index.html

GoldenSeeds, http://www.goldenseeds.com/

Ohio Tech Angels, http://www.ohiotechangels.com/

Tech Coast Angels, http://www.techcoastangels.com/about-us

Hyde Park Angel Network, http://www.hydeparkangels.com/

Pasadena Angels, http://pasadenaangels.com/

Capital Angel Network (Canada), http://www.capitalangels.ca/

Venture Alberta, http://www.vaangels.com

Investors' Circle, http://investorscircle.net

Keiretsu Forum, http://www.keiretsuforum.com/

Atlanta Technology Angels, http://www.angelatlanta.com

TiE Angels, http://www.tiesv.org/

Rain Source Capital, http://www.rainsourcecapital.com/

Boston Harbor Angels, http://www.bostonharborangels.com

Eastern NY Angels, http://easternnyangels.com/

Launchpad Venture Group, http://www.launchpadventuregroup.com

Robin Hood Ventures, http://www.robinhoodventures.com/

Central Texas Angel Network, http://www.centraltexasangelnetwork
.com

StarVest, http://www.starvestpartners.com/

Band of Angels, http://www.bandangels.com/

Space Angels, http://spaceangels.com

Life Science Angels, http://lifescienceangels.com

Alliance of Angels, www.allianceofangels.com

Europe

Paris Business Angels, www.parisbusinessangels.com

Be Angels, www.beangels.eu

Go-Beyond, www.go-beyond.biz

Arts & Metiers Business Angels, www.am-businessangels.org

Grenoble Angels, www.grenobleangels.grenobleecobiz.biz

IT Angels, www.itangels.fr

Savoie Angels France, www.savoie-angels.com

Galata Business Angels, www.galatabusinessangels.com

Saint Petersburg Business Angels, www.soba.spb.ru

Angels Ontime, www.angelsontime.com

Tech Angels, www.techangels.ro

Club Invest 77, www.business-angels-77.fr

Capitole Angels, www.capitole-angels.com

Synergence, www.synergence.fr

ClearlySo Angels, www.clearlyso.com/investors/CSA.html

Keiretsu Forum London, www.keiretsuforum.com/global-chapters/london/

Invent Network, www.inventnetwork.co.uk/

Cambridge Angels, cambridgeangels.weebly.com/

ESADE BAN, www.esadeban.com/en

Inveready, www.inveready.com/

First Tuesday Business Angel Network, www.firsttuesday.es/

Southern Hemisphere

Anjos do Brasil, www.anjosdobrasil.net/

Gavea Angels, www.gaveaangels.org.br

ChileGlobal Angels, www.chileglobalangels.cl

Melbourne Angels, www.melbourneangels.net

Sydney Angels, www.sydneyangels.net.au

Ice Angels, www.iceangels.co.nz

Angel HQ, www.angelhq.co.nz

Angel Investing Blogs and Resources

The Gust Blog on Angel Investing
   http://www.gust.com/blog

Angel Resource Institute Resource Center
   http://www.angelresourceinstitute.org/resource-center.aspx

Angel Capital Association—Angel Investing Resources
   http://www.angelcapitalassociation.org/resources/angel-group-
   overview/

Angel Capital Association—Angel Insights Blog
   http://www.angelcapitalassociation.org/blog/

The Frank Peters Show—A Podcast on Angel Investing
   http://thefrankpetersshow.com/

Bill Payne's Angel Investing Thoughts
   http://billpayne.com/category/angel-investors-2

Angel Blog—Basil Peters on Early Exits for Angels and Other Best Practices
http://www.angelblog.net/index.html

Berkonomics—Dave Berkus on Angel Investing
http://berkonomics.com/

Quora Questions & Answers on Angel Investing
http://www.quora.com/Angel-Investing

A2A: Analyst To Angel—Adam Quinton
http://www.analysttoangel.com

Bloomberg BusinessWeek on Angel Investing
http://go.bloomberg.com/tech-deals/angel-investing/

David Teten on Angel Investing
http://teten.com/blog/category/investing/angel/

Dan Rosen on Investing and the Future of Technology
http://blog.drosenassoc.com

Angel Investing News from George McQuilken
http://angelinvestingnews.blogspot.com/

ScratchPaper Blog on Angel Investing by Christopher Mirabile
http://scratchpaperblog.com/category/angel-investing/

SeedInvest's Blog on Angel Investing
http://blog.seedinvest.com

Seed Funding Blogs and Resources

Fred Wilson (Union Square Ventures)
http://Avc.com

Brad Feld (Foundry Group)
http://feld.com

Charlie O'Donnell (Brooklyn Bridge Ventures)
http://www.thisisgoingtobebig.com

Mark Suster's Both Sides of the Table (Upfront Ventures)
http://BothSidesOfTheTable.com

Jeff Bussgang's Seeing Both Sides (Flybridge Capital)
http://bostonvcblog.typepad.com/vc/

Bill Carleton (Counselor @ Law) on Angel Investing
http://www.wac6.com/wac6/archives.html

Chris Dixon (Andreesen Horowitz)
http://cdixon.org

Rob Go (Nextview Ventures)
http://robgo.org

First Round Review (First Round Capital)
http://firstround.com/review

Paul Graham's Essays
http://paulgraham.com/articles.html

Bill Gurley's Above the Crowd (Benchmark Capital)
http://abovethecrowd.com/archives/

Glossary

ACA Angel Capital Association, the national federation of professional angel groups and angel investors in the United States.

accelerator A for-profit type of business incubator that typically accepts startup teams into a three-month program and provides basic living expenses, office space, and intense mentorship in exchange for equity in the startup.

Accredited investor Defined by the SEC as an individual with at least $1 million in assets not including the value of the primary residence, or at least $200,000 in income for the past two years (or $300,000 together with a spouse).

acqui-hire One company's acquisition of another for the primary purpose of hiring its employees, rather than for the intrinsic value of the business itself.

angel group A formal or informal organization of individual Accredited investors who pool their deal flow, resources, expertise, and capital in order to make angel investments.

angel investor An Accredited investor who invests his or her personal capital in early stage, potentially high-growth companies.

angel round A round of investment into a startup company from angel investors not previously affiliated with the founder. Typically the first money invested in a company after the founder's own money, and the founder's friends and family.

AngelList A prominent website based in Silicon Valley bringing together startup companies and angel investors.

BHAG Big Hairy Audacious Goal, the giant sweeping vision of a startup founder to change the world.

Black Swan An unpredictable event typically with extreme consequences.

board of directors A group of people elected by a company's shareholders (often according to the terms of a negotiated Shareholders Agreement) that makes decisions on major company issues, including hiring/firing the Chief Executive Officer.

bootstrapping Funding a company only by reinvesting initial profits; from "pulling yourself up by your own bootstraps."

bridge A temporary loan used to cover a company's operating expenses until a future financing.

burn rate The monthly negative cash flow from a pre-profitable startup.

business angel networks In Europe, synonymous with angel groups. In North America, a collection of individual angel groups operating under a common brand and leadership that typically syndicate deal flow and investments.

Business Model Canvas A strategic management template for developing or documenting business models through a visual chart with elements describing a firm's value proposition, infrastructure, customers, and finances.

business plan competition A program historically run by a university or other not-for-profit organization to encourage students to develop plans for new businesses. Increasingly a showcase competition for existing startups seeking financing from angels and other investors.

cap The maximum company valuation at which a convertible note will convert into a company's stock.

carried interest A percentage of the profits realized from a venture capital fund's investments that are retained by the fund's General Partners as the incentive compensation component for their investment activities.

co-invest When more than one investor joins in making an investment on similar terms.

Common stock A U.S. term for a form of equity ownership of a company, equivalent to the terms "voting share" or "ordinary share" used in other parts of the world. In a liquidity event or a bankruptcy, Common stock holders receive all of the net value of a company after paying the fixed amounts due to bondholders, creditors, and Preferred stock holders. Common stock usually carries with it the right to vote on certain matters, such as electing the board of directors.

convertible debt A type of loan (also known as **note**) which provides that the amount of money loaned may (or must, under certain conditions) be converted by the investor into shares of stock in the company at a particular price.

convertible Preferred stock Preferred stock in a company that is convertible at the option of the holder into Common stock at a predetermined valuation. This provides the priority and security of holding Preferred stock, as well as the potential value appreciation of Common stock.

corporate venture An investment from one corporation in another, typically at an early stage for strategic reasons.

cram down When a new funding round is done at a lower valuation than the previous one, meaning the original investors (or Founders) end up with a much smaller percentage ownership.

crowdfunding A joint effort by many individuals (collectively referred to as the "crowd") to support a cause, project, or company. **Donation**-based crowdfunding bears no expectation of returns. In **Reward**-based crowdfunding, contributors are promised rewards (such as the ability to purchase a product) in exchange for their contributions. **Equity**-based crowd funding gives funders the ability to purchase equity interests in a company.

dead pool Where companies that die go.

deal flow The stream of new investment opportunities available to a particular investor or investment organization.

deal lead The investor or investment organization taking primary responsibility for organizing an investment round in a company. The deal lead typically finds the company, negotiates the terms of the investment, invests the largest amount, and serves as the primary liaison between the company and the other investors.

debt Borrowed money that needs to be paid back. The entrepreneur rents the money for a specific period of time and promises to pay interest on the money for as long as the loan is outstanding.

demo day The "graduation" day for a class of companies in an accelerator or other business program at which each company has 5 to 15 minutes to present its investment opportunity to potential angel and other investors in attendance.

dilution When a company sells additional shares of stock, thereby decreasing the percentage ownership of existing shareholders. Note that if the valuation of the new sale is at a high enough level, the value of stock held by existing investors may increase, even though the percentage ownership may decrease.

discounted convertible note A loan that converts into the same equity security being purchased in a future investment round, but at a discounted price representing a risk premium for the early investment.

double bottom line In Impact Investing, the goal of measuring a company by its positive societal impact in addition to its financial returns.

down-round When the valuation of a company at the time of an investment round is lower than its valuation at the conclusion of a previous round.

drip feed When investors fund a startup a little bit at a time instead of in a lump sum.

drive-by deal An investment by a venture fund looking for a quick exit through a short-term sale; different from the current "early exit" approach by angel groups, which is a strategic focus.

dry powder Money held in reserve by a venture fund or angel investor in order to be able to make additional investments in a company.

due diligence The careful investigation into a company prior to making an investment to insure that all facts are known.

early exits An approach to angel investing popularized by author Basil Peters, in which the goal of an investment is the sale of the company within a few years without requiring additional large investments from VCs, thereby providing high relative returns without requiring companies to be home runs.

entrepreneur A person who organizes and operates a business or businesses, taking on greater than normal financial risks to do so. Entrepreneurs are the founders of startups and are the people angel investors support.

equity seed round When an entrepreneur first sells a part of his or her business—and therefore a proportional part of the good things (like profits) and the not-so-good things (like losses)—to an investor. Equity investments, unlike loans, do not need to be paid back.

escrow When a third party holds value during a transaction, releasing it only when a specified condition has been fulfilled.

exit When an angel's investment in a company is either acquired for cash, sold during a public offering, or rendered worthless because the company fails.

finder An intermediary engaged by a company to attempt to find investors, in exchange for a percentage of the transaction. Serious angel investors typically do not deal with companies through intermediaries.

flat-round When the valuation of a company at the time of an investment round is the same as its valuation at the conclusion of a previous round.

follow-on investment An additional investment made in a company by one of its existing investors.

founders stock or (founder's equity) The Common stock owned by one or more of a company's founders, typically received when the company was incorporated and not purchased for cash.

Friends & Family round An investment in a company that often follows the founder's own investment, from people who are investing primarily because of their relationship with the founder rather than their knowledge of the business.

funding platform Any online website used to facilitate investments in private companies. As a defined term, a specific type of platform defined by the JOBS Act of 2012 that will allow non-Accredited investors to invest in private offerings.

general partner The manager(s) of a venture capital fund, who are compensated with a Carried Interest on investments made by the fund.

general solicitation When a private company publicly seeks investors in connection with an equity offering. Previously prohibited by U.S. securities law, now permissible under certain conditions according to the JOBS Act of 2012.

grant Money provided by a government agency or other organization that does not need to be repaid and does not purchase equity.

Gust The international online platform for collaboration and investments among angel investors, entrepreneurs, and others in the early-stage economy.

home run When a company has an exit that returns 20 or more times investors' initial capital.

illiquid An investment that cannot be readily sold or transferred into cash. Unlike public stocks for which there is a ready market, angel investments are typically held for 5 to 10 years.

impact investing Financial investments that also aim to have a benefit for society.

incubator Programs or shared office centers designed to support the successful development of companies by offering cost effective resources and support.

initial public offering (IPO) The first public sale of the stock of a formerly privately held company. After a lockup period, investors are typically able to sell their shares on the public stock market, as they are no longer illiquid.

internal rate of return (IRR) The annualized rate of return from an investment, not incorporating other factors such as interest rates or inflation.

investment round A set of one or more investments made in a particular company by one or more investors on essentially similar terms at essentially the same time.

J-curve The appearance of a graph showing the typical value progression of early stage investment portfolios. Values often drop soon after the initial investment during the startup and early stage period, but rebound significantly in later years after companies reach profitability.

JOBS Act of 2012 A law signed by President Obama on April 5, 2012 significantly changing the laws surrounding investments in private companies. Title I made it easier for larger companies to remain private and easier to go public. Title II allowed private companies to generally solicit for equity investments, provided that it only took funding from Accredited investors. Title III authorized limited, structured crowdfunding platforms, through which non-Accredited investors could invest in early stage companies.

law of large numbers A theorem that suggests that the average of results obtained from a large number of trials should be close to the expected value, assuring stable long-term results for the averages of random events. When applied to angel investing, it suggests that large portfolios of investments, made consistently over time, will return significantly positive returns.

lead investor See **deal lead**.

limited partner A passive investor in a venture capital fund, typically an institutional investor such as a university endowment, an insurance company, or a pension fund.

LinkedIn The leading business-oriented social networking website.

liquidation waterfall The sequence in which all parties, including investors, employees, creditors, and others, receive payouts in the event of a company's liquidation through acquisition or bankruptcy.

liquidity event When investors have the ability to convert some or all of their equity interest in a company into cash. Typically as the consequence of an acquisition, this can also happen if a company is very successful and new investors are willing to buy out the interest of early investors.

lock up A period of time (typically after an IPO, or an acquisition of a startup by a public company) during which certain shareholders are not allowed to sell their stock; often 90 or 180 days, but could be a year.

mafia In the context of angel funding and startups, a colloquial term used to describe the loose association of people previously involved with a highly successful technology company, such as Google, Facebook, Paypal, or LinkedIn, as founders, early employees, or investors.

Main Street business A colloquial term used to describe traditional small, local retail, and service companies. They typically serve local markets, provide jobs, and benefit the local economy, but are not aimed at high-growth industries or eventual acquisition by larger companies. As such, they are not usually funded by angel investors.

major investor   As used in investment term sheets, any investor who puts in more than a defined amount into a given round and is therefore entitled to specific information and/or voting rights.

management fee   Typically 2 or 3 percent of the committed capital in a venture capital fund, paid annually to the General Partner to cover operating expenses of the fund.

meetup   A website enabling people with similar interests to coordinate in-person meetings online. There are many thousands of local Meetups related to technology, entrepreneurship, and startup businesses. The New York Tech Meetup has over 38,000 members and is the largest on the platform.

micro-VC   The correct term for organizations often referred to as *super angels*. Structured similar to a traditional venture fund, a micro-VC is typically much smaller in size, with fewer partners, and invests less money but at an earlier stage.

negative control provisions   Terms agreed to as part of an investment round that protect investors from major adverse actions (such as dissolving the company, or selling it to someone for $1), but do not provide the right to affirmatively control the company.

NVCA Model Documents   A standard set of investment documents for a Series A equity investment round developed by a group of most of the major venture law firms for the National Venture Capital Association.

pay to play   A term in VC financings that requires investors to participate in future down-valuation financings of the company, or else suffer punitive consequences (such as getting their Preferred stock converted into Common stock). One reason why investors keep some dry powder on hand.

peer-to-peer lending   A relatively new type of online financing solution through which individuals lend money to other individuals or small businesses.

pitch   A presentation, typically supported by slides developed in PowerPoint or Keynote, in which a startup company's founder describes his or her company and seeks an investment from angels or venture capitalists.

portfolio The collection of all of the companies invested in by an angel or VC.

post-money valuation The value of a company immediately after it has received an equity investment, including both the company's pre-money valuation and the amount it received from the investment.

pre-money valuation The value of a company immediately prior to receiving an investment, used to determine what percentage of a company's ownership will be purchased in exchange for a specified investment amount.

preferred stock A type of equity ownership of a company that has both a fixed value and priority in liquidation sequence.

private companies Companies that are not publicly traded on the stock market.

private equity An asset class consisting of investments in late stage, profitable private companies.

Private Placement Memorandum An extensive document required when securities are being offered to investors other than Accredited or Qualified purchasers, detailing potential risks and other information about the company.

proprietary deal flow When an investor has an opportunity to review a deal before other potential investors.

public companies Companies that are freely traded on the public stock exchanges such as NASDAQ and the New York Stock Exchange.

qualified purchaser An individual with more than $5 million in investments.

Quora A leading question-and-answer website where many industry experts in early stage investing answer questions.

representations and warranties A list of material statements or facts that are included in the investment documentation and to which the entrepreneur unequivocally commits.

reverse vesting When founders of a company agree that they will give back part of their stock holdings if they leave the company before a specified date (typically four years). This is usually required by investors, and a good thing for founders themselves in the case of multiple founders.

return on investment (ROI) The ratio between the amount of money returned to the investor when a company exits and the amount of the initial investment. Serious angels attempt to target 20x or 30x returns on their invested capital in risky startups.

runway How long a startup can survive before it goes broke; that is, the amount of cash in the bank divided by the burn rate.

SAFE Simple Agreement for Future Equity, a new form of funding for early stage companies developed by YCombinator to solve a number of issues with traditional convertible note funding.

SBIR Small Business Innovation Research grant program from the U.S. government.

SEC The United States Securities and Exchange Commission, charged with regulating all sales of corporate securities.

seed fund A venture capital fund specializing in very-early-stage startups.

seed round The first investments made into a company by someone other than the founder. The term comes from planting a seed for the first time.

serial entrepreneur An entrepreneur who has previously founded and run one or more ventures.

Series A Traditionally the first professional outside money that is invested by a venture capital fund in exchange for ownership in a company, generally in the range of single-digit millions of dollars.

Series A crunch A putative problem that has, or may occur if more companies get early stage funding from angels and seed funds than are eventually able to obtain later stage funding from venture capital funds.

Series B, C, D ... Investment rounds from venture capital funds subsequent to the first Series A round.

series seed Used generically to refer to the first equity round from serious seed or angel investors in a company, following its Friends & Family round but prior to a Series A.

shareholders agreement An agreement signed during a financing transaction by all of a company's shareholders in which they agree in advance to various provisions. These will typically include indicating which parties are entitled to designate members of the board of directors, and thus control the company.

Sherpa In the startup world, an advisor who helps guide and support a young company.

sniff test A colloquial expression referring to a quick assessment of a situation to see whether it appears legitimate.

social proof An investment approach leaning heavily on the identity of other, well-known people who are supporting the company.

social venture A company established to create societal benefit through entrepreneurial methods.

soft landing A face-saving acquisition of an unsuccessful startup, usually for little or no compensation.

spray and pray Investing in lots of companies in the hopes that one of them will hit it big.

strategic investor A corporate investor funding an early stage company primarily for reasons related to the investing company's interest.

STTR The Small Business Technology Transfer program, from the U.S. government; intended to assist educational institutions in transferring new technology to the private sector.

success fee A percentage commission paid to an intermediary or other individual as an incentive on the closing of a large financing transaction.

super angel A misnomer describing microVCs. True super angels are active angels who make many significant investments, find and negotiate investments, and can bring other investors along with them.

tag along/drag along Provisions in a Shareholders Agreement that permit investors under certain defined circumstances to sell their shares if you sell yours (tag), or force you to sell your shares if they sell theirs (drag).

term sheet A summary of the major terms of an investment round that is agreed upon by all parties prior to beginning extensive legal documentation for the round.

The Golden Rule The investor with the gold makes the rules. (The same meaning as "those who bring the money drive the bus"; i.e., forget whatever any previous contracts say, if you need money and only one source is willing to supply it, you'll take the money on their terms, period.)

up-round When the valuation of a company at the time of an investment round is higher than its valuation at the conclusion of a previous round.

Valley of Death The period between the initial funding and the end of the Runway. If you get through here, you should be okay. If not ....

venture capital fund An investment fund that puts money behind high-growth companies.

venture debt A type of debt financing provided to venture-backed companies from specialized banks or non-bank lenders.

vulture capitalist A VC whose operating method is to deliberately take advantage of an entrepreneur's troubles.

walking dead A company that isn't bankrupt, but will never succeed, and thus can't be sold or otherwise exited.

waterfall The order in which investors (and everyone else) get their money out on an exit. Almost always this is "last in, first out."

Ycombinator The original, and still leading, business accelerator program.

zombie fund a VC firm that can't raise a new fund, and thus can't make new investments.

Acknowledgments

THIS BOOK IS my attempt to codify and explain current best practices in professional angel investing. As such, virtually none of it is original to me, and I have simply served as the interlocutor who brings together the hard lessons learned over long careers in angel investing by much better investors than I will ever be.

Among those who have educated me, either explicitly, by example, by their writings, or by their legacies, are several people who are no longer with us. They include the late Hans Severeins, founder of Band of Angels and arguably the professional angel investing industry; Luis Villalobos, founder of Tech Coast Angels and one of the inspirations for the founding of the Angel Capital Association; Lionel Pincus, Managing Partner of Warburg Pincus and my first venture investor; and my great-uncle, David Rose, proto-angel and innovation catalyst.

Many more angels who are still active in the field have contributed to my financial education, and I continue to learn at their feet. Chief among them is Bill Payne, former Entrepreneur in Residence at the Kauffman Foundation, co-founder of several angel groups, and the author of *The Definitive Guide to Raising Money from Angels*. These days, Bill travels the world as the leading trainer of angels, through his work with the not-for-profit Angel Resource Institute, and he continues to generate new and advanced courses for angel investors in the *Power of Angel Investing* series. Other significant figures in the pantheon of angel educators to whom I owe much are Basil Peters, Canadian angel investor and author of *Early Exits*; Dave Berkus, former chairman of

Tech Coast Angels and author of the blog and book series *Berkonomics*; John Huston, chairman of Ohio Tech Angels and former chairman of the Angel Capital Association; John May, another former chairman of the Angel Capital Association and founding co-chair of the World Business Angel Association; and Tom McKaskill, Australia's leading angel educator.

It has been my privilege to work, co-invest or become friends over the past decade with many smart, thoughtful and successful investors who have done much to professionalize the heretofore wild and crazy world of early-stage investing. On the venture side have been Henry Kressel, Habib Kairouz, Ed Sim, Jack Rivkin and John Koo, all of whom invested in my first venture-backed company; industry legends including Reid Hoffman (legendary as an entrepreneur, venture capitalist, *and* angel investor, who graciously agreed to write the Foreword to this book), David Hornik, Alan Patricof, Mark Suster, Fred Wilson, Ann Winbland, and the entire team at First Round Capital: Josh Kopelman, Howard L. Morgan, Chris Fralic, Rob Hayes, Phin Barnes, Kent Goldman and Bill Trenchard. Among my fellow early stage investors from whom I learn every day are Angelo Abdela, Mark Allison, Tom Blum, Jeff Bussgang, Bob Chaworth-Musters, Esther Dyson, Joe Ferrara, Avi Fogel, David Freschman, Gideon Gartner, Parker Gilbert, Phyllis Haberman, Brad Higgins, Linda Holliday, Patrick Hoogendijk, John Katzman, Richard Katzman, Charly Kleissner, Lisa Kleissner, Scott Kurnit, Lawrence Lenihan, Bill Lohse, David Marrus, Dave McClure, Dan McKinney, Heidi Messer, Stephen Messer, Peter Nager, Nicholas Negroponte, Stephanie Newby, Charlie O'Donnell, Alessandro Piol, Larry Richenstein, Mark Schneider, Jeffrey Seltzer, Paul Sethi, Jim Silver, Jeff Silverman, Sim Simeonov, John Suhler, David Teten, Yossi Vardi, Ellen Weber, Jon Whelan and Tom Wisniewski.

New York Angels, to which many of us belong and where most of these principles were first put to the test, has been the most active angel group in the world for two years in a row and continues to go from strength to strength under the leadership of chairman Brian Cohen (co-author of *What Every Angel Investor Wants You to Know*) and the administration of program director Vanessa Pestritto.

On the international front, I have found that angel investing is remarkably universal in its practices, and some of the smartest and most successful investors I know are based outside the United States. They include Dusan Stojanovic (European Angel of the Year), Philipe Glunz (founder of France Angels), Peter Jungen (New York Angels' longest distance member), Brigitte Baumman (former chair of EBAN), Paulo Andrez (current chair of EBAN), and many others.

As angel investing emerges to take its place as a subject worthy of serious study, there is a small but growing band of pioneering academics who are beginning to quantify this hard-to-examine world. Chief among them, and the sources for most of the statistics quoted in this book, are Jeffrey Sohl of the University of New Hampshire's Center for Venture Research, Robert Wiltbank of Willamette University and Scott Shane of Case Western Reserve.

My late grandmother used to say that "you can't have a good party without good guests," and that applies equally to angel investors and the entrepreneurs in whom we invest. I have had the pleasure of working with over 100 passionate, driven, high-integrity founders, and have learned from every interaction. While space doesn't permit me to list all of them, I do want to thank those whose stories I tell in this book: Alison and Ron Malloy of Design2Launch; David Steinberger, John Roberts, and Peter Jaffe of Comixology; Tom Bennet, Marcus Engene, and Dana Tower of Pond5; Adam Potash of Mind's Eye Innovation; Ray Steeb of FASTTAC; Jilliene Helman and Justin Hughes of Realty Mogul; Peter Diamandis of ZeroG/Space Adventures; Ryan Rzepecki of Social Bicycles; and Alexa von Tobel of LearnVest.

This book arose from a surprisingly unlikely place: the online website Quora.com, which is the leading question and answer platform for smart people (my description). As part of my goal of "scaled mentoring," I have answered literally thousands of questions there over the years on the subject of angel investing and startups, which are what caught the attention of Richard Narramore, my editor at John Wiley & Sons. It was his idea to turn that outpouring of verbiage into a book and Marc Bodnick of Quora (who also has a secret life as one of the country's leading venture capitalists) arranged for a data dump roughly the length of *War and Peace*. It then fell to my developmental editor, the deft, tireless, and fast-working Karl Weber, to take a first pass at editing that into the book you have in your hands. My agent, Susan Ginsburg, educated me on the intricacies of the publishing world, and Ed Davad designed the nifty cover (as the result of a crowdsourcing competition on 99designs.com!)

Many people were kind enough to read early drafts of the manuscript and provide helpful comments, including Barbara (*Shark-Tank*) Corcoran, Tim (*Business Plan Pro*) Berry, David (*Finish Rich*) Bach, Brian Cohen, David Freschman, John Huston, David Marrus, Bill Payne, Jeff Seltzer, Larry Richenstein, and U.S. Senator Chuck Schumer.

Two groups of very special people have contributed to this book in ways large and small. My colleagues at Gust comprise the most extraordinary team I have ever worked with, and they get up every morning focused on improving and professionalizing the world of angel investing. I am honored to have an extraordinary board of directors in Howard L. Morgan, co-founder of First Round Capital; Bob Rice, Managing Partner of Tangent Capital and Bloomberg Television's Alternative Assets Editor (and author of *The Alternative Answer*); and Richard Zenker, of Overbrook Management. Together, they keep me on a straight and narrow path and provide deep insights into the private equity industry. The extraordinary management team at Gust, Ilana Grossman, Ryan Nash, Jess Compagnola, and Lisa Balter Saacks, has the terrifying job of actually implementing all the crazy ideas I come up with, and they have been preceded in years past by Ryan Janssen, Andrei Godoroja, Mark LaRosa, Tom Pace, Kosta Kostadinovich, and others, all of whose collective impact can be seen in the platform as it exists today.

Finally, I owe a greater debt to my family—nuclear and extended—than can ever be repaid. I can say without exaggeration that I am the underachiever among a group of extraordinary people. My father, Daniel Rose, has always been my role model as a thinker, a doer, an entrepreneur, and a mensch. My mother, Joanna Semel Rose, widely regarded as the single smartest person in New York City, taught me to write in my younger days, and then rose to the challenge half a century later and painstakingly copyedited this manuscript. While I take full responsibility for all remaining errors, without her ministrations I would have come across to you as a complete illiterate. My siblings, Joseph, Emily, and Gideon, have managed to mostly suppress their snickers during my decades-long entrepreneurial career and provided significant help in myriad ways at myriad points where it really counted. My three children—the prime focus of my life—have had the dubious privilege of putting up with decades of my entrepreneuring, investing, and pontificating. One has served as my primary entrepreneurial pupil and protégé, the second keeps me honest on Quora, and without the third I would never have actually finished writing this book.

Most of all, I am grateful to my wife, who has put up with me for over 30 years, and is an enabler for someone who is as different from her as two people could possibly be. She would have preferred to read a book consisting of only stories from my investing career; but never fear, one will eventually be forthcoming!

New York
February, 2014

Index

271